# Readings in Middle School Curriculum

# Readings in Middle School Curriculum:
# A Continuing Conversation

Tom Dickinson, Editor

NATIONAL MIDDLE SCHOOL ASSOCIATION

## *nmsa* ®
## NATIONAL MIDDLE SCHOOL ASSOCIATION

Tom Dickinson teaches in the Department of Curriculum, Instruction, and Media Technology, School of Education, Indiana State University, Terre Haute. A former middle level teacher, he served with distinction as Editor of the *Middle School Journal* from 1990 to 1993 and continues his active involvement with NMSA. The Association is grateful to him for his leadership in securing and organizing the articles which comprise this important volume.

Special recognition is due April Tibbles, Managing Editor, and Cassandra Bonner, Production Assistant, for their valuable work in organizing and producing the special *Middle School Journal* curriculum issues in which the bulk of these articles originally appeared.

Appreciation is also expressed to Ed Brazee, Sue Carol Thompson, and Larry Holt who assisted in the selection of the articles included. Finally, a word of thanks goes to Mary Mitchell for her conscientious work in preparing the manuscript for printing and to Barbara Brannon for the cover design.

ISBN: 1-56090-078-4

*to S.C. Dickinson, Jr.*
*who taught me the curriculum of life*

# Table of Contents

# Foreword

## Curriculum—To run a course

*Tom Dickinson*

> W hat is **currere**? ...**Currere** is to run. It is
> active. And it is not. The track around which
> I run may be inalterably forced, but the rate at
> which I run, the quality of my running, my sensual-intellectual-
> emotional experience of moving bodily through space and time: all
> these are my creations; they are my responsibilities.
>
> [They] may tell me what course to run, but whether the
> course is instructive or not, interesting or not, pleasurable or
> not, liberative or not, ultimately and immediately is my respon-
> sibility, and that of my fellow runners.
>
> The thesis of our dialectic is: I don't know, and I must study,
> and search. I must be open to my experience, open to others', and
> be willing to abandon what I think in the face of what I see.
>
> —William F. Piner, *Toward a Poor Curriculum*

Throughout its history the modern middle school has been running an unusual curriculum course, characterized more by movement away and around curriculum rather than through it. This avoidance has, thankfully, come to an end, and the credit is due in large part to the authors on the following pages. What you will find here is a rich blend of historical perspective, revolutionary thinking, but above all, a call to engage in "a continuing conversation" about the form and substance of middle level learning.

This form and substance has been sorely missing from our schools. Overly focused on organizational agendas, the middle school has been a ship without a compass, rudder, or final destination. We have, in essence, not been running at all, but wandering without responsibility.

Readers should be aware of the "dangerous visions" that the authors in this volume hold out for examination. While John Lounsbury is the only member of what might be termed the middle school's "big three" curriculum experts (Alexander, Lounsbury, and Vars) present here, there is a new "big three" composed perhaps of Arnold, Beane, and Stevenson who are running ahead, showing us potential directions, continuing the conversation on multiple levels.

What is dangerous about these visions and the conversation is that readers are invited in to run with the authors, to help find directions for themselves, to confront the novelty of searching with students as equal partners. The course that this volume sets out is one of accepting responsibility rather than relying on authority, of confrontations with the "what" and the "how" of middle school curriculum.

All of us are fellow runners on this course. We have much to say to each other.

### Reference

Piner, W.F. (1976). Preface. In W.F. Piner & M.R. Grumet, *Toward a Poor Curriculum* (pp. vii-viii). Dubuque, IA: Kendall/Hunt.

# Introduction

## Curriculum change—The time is now

*Sue Swaim*

As society moves toward a global economy and our social
and family structures continue to evolve, today's education challenges are obviously becoming more difficult to
address. Indeed, these difficulties have become the centerpiece of the
educational political arena as society tries to address the needs of
educating our children. The extent of the national debate on education
is so widespread that major changes seem certain to occur. Indeed, the
prevailing limited and traditional views of teaching and learning must
be questioned and the curriculum and instructional practices used in
the past re-examined and realistically assessed. We no longer have an
option to "tinker" with school restructuring. Simply doing better what
we are currently doing will neither meet our children's needs nor
answer the challenge of adequately helping to prepare them for the 21st
century. The time to engage in a national curriculum conversation
coupled with the expectation to implement significant curriculum
change is now.

We have a professional responsibility to move forward in implementing a change process which not only deals with organization and
management issues but struggles with the very heart and soul of
learning and teaching—the curriculum. The curriculum has and will
continue to be the most difficult part of the change. A wide array of
reasons exist to support the difficulties encountered in developing new
curriculum. Unfortunately many of these "reasons" have also become
effective, if only temporary, barriers to change. Certainly changing
what we teach, how we teach it, and how we assess what we think we've
taught is difficult and risky business. There will be trial and error
"moments of discovery." There will be increased stress as teachers,

students, and parents move from their current comfort zones and status quo expectations towards new ways of thinking and learning. In spite of the fact this change is difficult and risky, the fact remains there is a greater risk in not changing our education system now.

In order to be effective at this...to truly move beyond the seemingly apparent barriers of change...I believe we must first engage in what Lounsbury refers to as *unlearning*. He describes unlearning in the following way.

> To learn best one has to escape from those deep channels of familiarity in order to stand above them and consider the many possibilities that do exist. Learning often calls for unlearning as a necessary first step. Only when teachers and students can recognize that few practices are necessarily so, are set in stone, or were handed down from Mount Olympus, can the full range of possibilities be considered. Learning will often be shortchanged if some unlearning doesn't go on.
>
> We are all victims of invalid assumptions, which often act like blinders on our minds. The line of least resistance always leads to a lower level. The higher way, the better way, is usually the more difficult way. To follow it one has to put aside a lot of quick and easy assumptions and be able, mentally, to start from scratch (pp. 33-34).

For me, the most important and most difficult challenge of unlearning is the ability to put aside quick and easy assumptions and to be able to mentally start from scratch. Tradition, teacher training, curriculum guides, community expectations, personal comfort zones, fear of taking risks, and assumed reactions are only a few of the things that get in the way. The ability to look at the big picture, to ask questions and to expect multiple right answers, to give up old assumptions, to anticipate the needs of the future rather than follow the habits of the past become important in unlearning. Risk-taking must be understood, expected and supported if unlearning is to occur. Although, as educators, we strive to minimize the risks of change through anticipating the outcomes and building in safeguards, we must learn that "mistakes" can be powerful learning tools which should be valued rather than feared.

While a continually increasing number of schools have moved to implement interdisciplinary teams, teacher advisor programs, broad exploratory experiences, skill development programs, and other recommended characteristics the basic questions of what we teach and how we teach remain for the most part, unanswered and little challenged. However, these basic questions represent the true challenge which faces education today. How we choose to answer these questions will ultimately determine the success or failure of American education.

How we choose to answer these questions will ultimately help determine the ability of our children to become healthy, productive, and ethical citizens.

Our initial steps toward restructuring schools will in the end become some of our easiest steps since the heart of the issue—curriculum change—is just now being undertaken. As difficult and as important as the management and organizational changes have been, the curriculum, instruction, and assessment changes which must be addressed now will demand new energies, visions, and commitments by all of us. Middle level education over the past thirty years has been a leader and a risk taker in promoting and implementing change in our schools. We have earned the right to be proud of our leadership and progress in this area. But, we must also accept the responsibility that our work is far from being complete and far from being implemented in too many schools which serve young adolescents.

It would be a sad commentary on middle level education to look back on this time ten or fifty years from now to find educational analysts claiming the middle school movement never reached its full potential due to middle level educators who were not aggressive enough in their attempts to develop relevant learning environments, relevant curriculum, appropriate instructional strategies and assessment practices for the young adolescent learner. How sad it would be to have historians record this time in history as one which held great promise but fell short of it due to the political pressures applied in a time of change which caused people to make decisions about schools and schooling that were not child-centered and were developmentally inappropriate for young adolescents.

The *unlearning* curriculum development process must become the priority of the decade of the 90s. The time has come to hold our current curriculum, instruction, and assessment practices and priorities up to the light of day. Those things which are right, which are based upon what we know about teaching and learning will withstand the rigorous debate and examination and appropriately continue. Those things which cannot tolerate the light of day should be discontinued to make room for new practices and priorities of education for the 21st century. The need to mentally start from scratch has arrived. The need to engage in a national curriculum conversation is apparent. The need to implement significant curriculum change is now.

### Reference

Lounsbury, J.H. (1984). *Middle School Education: As I See It.* Columbus, OH: National Middle School Association.

*Sue Swaim is Interim Executive Director of the National Middle School Association.*

# Early Discussions

# Could the middle school be unique?

*Ronald Maertens*

T aking a cue from the ideas and issues presented as "Food for Thought" in the first issue of the *Middle School News-letter,* I would like to discuss various aspects of the question: What, if anything, could make the middle school unique? In discussing this question, I also plan to examine two related questions: What barriers exist to prevent this uniqueness from developing effectively, and what could be done to foster this uniqueness? Of course, the assumption behind my first question is that many middle schools are *not* unique, and in fact have no distinguishing characteristics to differentiate them from any other organizational structure in education.

Regarding the question of what could make the middle school unique, I would like to propose two major factors which not only could but should distinguish the middle school from other educational structures: (1) the curriculum that is provided for the pupils, and (2) the way the teachers interact with the pupils, or in other words, the way they teach middle school pupils. Middle school pupils need a curriculum and personal interactions which are different from the curriculum and interaction found in the school levels preceding and following the middle school experience.

What kinds of programs are found in many middle schools? Although Glatthorn (1970) notes that "one of the advantages of the middle school organization is that it creates a setting for new and

Originally published in *The Midwest Middle School Journal,*
Vol. I, No. 2, December 1970.

imaginative programs..." (p. 100), in practice the curriculum in most middle schools is little different from traditional elementary or junior high school curricula. If practice is weak, ideas regarding the middle school curriculum are just as deficient. For example, Glatthorn observes that *The Emergent Middle School* by Alexander, Williams, Compton, Hines, and Prescott (1968) has many virtues and that it presents "cogent arguments for a new kind of program for young people in transition" (p. 99), but that its major weakness is its discussion of the middle school curriculum. He claims "their discussion of curriculum falls seriously short of the goals they have presented for others" (p. 100). I would add that their mention of any new kinds of interaction falls even farther short of adequate teaching goals for middle schools. However, to be fair to the authors, whenever discussion begins concerning a unique curriculum for, and a special kind of teacher interaction with, middle school pupils, barriers to their effective development are encountered. Moreover, I believe the staff of the middle school should be ones who develop the program and teaching behaviors for their own pupils, and not expect outside experts to do the job for them.

## Barriers to achieving uniqueness

When a middle school staff begins working on a unique curriculum and a special kind of interaction for their pupils, major problems arise if the middle school curriculum and teaching are viewed as autonomous rather than as different, or if what constitutes continuity for a K-12 curriculum is misinterpreted. Although the curriculum and teaching should be different for the middle school pupil, they should not be considered completely independent of what is found in preceding or subsequent school levels. To do so might not only confuse the pupil, but actually disrupt or interrupt his learning habits and patterns, rather than building on and adding to them. The rationale for a middle school includes providing a smoother transition from one school level to another, not making this transition more difficult. Therefore, curriculum scope and sequence should be related to, and be consistent with, that of other school levels. On the other hand, misinterpreting continuity as providing the *same* curriculum and interaction as other school levels provide is also a barrier to the effective development of the middle school's uniqueness.

Another barrier to the effective development of the middle school's curriculum and teaching uniqueness is to confuse organizational changes with real curriculum and teaching changes. How many school systems have been surprised when their reshuffling of grade levels into a middle school structure failed to make any difference! Grasping for a solution to this puzzling outcome, they then resort to introducing innovational practices, such as team teaching, flexible scheduling, closed circuit TV, etc., again with little or no improvement resulting from their efforts. Only when curriculum and teaching changes result from such organizational strategies, or better yet, precede these practices, will a difference appear. Although organizational and innovational practices may facilitate implementing the curriculum, what is needed is clarification and development of the curriculum first. Then if certain techniques appear to be helpful in carrying out the curriculum, they may be introduced as teaching aids, not as the heart of the program.

A third kind of problem may arise when teachers from a different organizational structure bring their "old" curriculum and teaching behaviors with them to a middle school structure. For example, many former elementary school teachers seem to use mothering, baby-talk, and "talking down" kinds of behaviors with middle school pupils, whereas former high school teachers employ the cold, cognitively oriented approach which is so characteristic of many secondary schools. Middle school pupils have left their childhood behind, but are not yet young adults. They need special kinds of relationships with their teachers, as well as with their peers. The problem of teachers interacting appropriately with pupils is exemplified by Kean's (1957) study of the classroom language used by second and fifth grade teachers. Although pupils use more words, more communication units, and more words in communication units in each successive year in the first seven years of schooling, Kean found that teachers used the same amount of language, the same vocabulary, and the same kinds of sentence patterns in interacting with pupils three grade levels apart in school.

## *Fostering the uniqueness*

In spite of the curriculum and teaching problems discussed above, what could be done to foster uniqueness in the middle school? *Priorities* and *balance* are key terms to understand how the curriculum and interaction could be different for middle school pupils. What is emphasized as the most important experiences and interactions to provide in a middle school and what a balanced day of such experiences and interactions looks like for a middle school pupil should be quite different from the emphasis and balance found at other school levels. What is needed is to involve the entire staff in a rethinking of the curriculum priorities and balance for the middle school pupil and in a rethinking of the kinds of interactions that middle school pupils need.

A term currently receiving emphasis in educational literature, *personalization*, also has implications for both a unique curriculum and a unique way of interacting with the middle school pupil. Broudy (1969) says personalized instruction "includes the notion of the personal relationship between the teacher and the pupil, or at least it seems to mean that instruction shall take into account the personality claims of both the teacher and the pupil," and lists as examples: "joint inquiry, discussion, probing, self-examination, processes quite different from imparting knowledge and developing skill" (p. 15).

Regarding personalization Wilhelms (1970) asks, "How much chance have we provided a learner in our school to dig down into the imminent questions of values, of the significance of life, of the possibilities inherent in his humanity? How much help do we ever offer him to see the great options he has as to how to spend himself?" (p. 369) To personalize curriculum and teaching, the middle school teacher will have to familiarize himself with the thought patterns of pupils, including their attitudes, values, beliefs, and interests. Only then will the staff of the middle school be able to help pupils achieve the identity they are seeking so desperately. Perhaps middle school teachers could begin by interacting with pupils regarding questions such as: "What kind of person am I *now*? What kind *will* I become if present habits and trends persist? What kind of person would I *like* to become? What can be done *now* about tendencies and preferences that conflict?" (Metcalf & Hunt, 1970, p. 361)

In regard to curriculum, perhaps some of the new priorities being proposed, such as Berman's (1968) process skills of perceiving, communicating, decision-making, valuing, etc., will provide the means whereby middle school pupils can develop personal meaning from their learning experiences. Assisting middle school pupils with such process skills would probably demand and even foster a unique kind of teacher-pupil interaction which would be quite different from any teaching style that presently exists in our schools. Perhaps "Such a school would *passionately*...seek always to know and accept the child as he is and to help him to know *himself* and accept what he knows about himself," and "make all of its resources available to him to find out what he wants to become and assist him in his becoming" (Weir, 1970, p. 401-402). I could see such a middle school justifying its unique existence.

## References

Alexander, W. M., Williams, E. I., Compton, M., Hines, V. A., & Prescott, D., (1968). *The emergent middle school*. New York: Holt, Rinehart and Winston.

Berman, L.M. (1968). *New priorities in the curriculum*. Columbus, OH: Merrill.

Broudy, H.S. (1969). A philosophy of the ideal school. In G. Kinney (Ed.), *The ideal school* (p. 15). Wilmette, IL: The Kagg Press.

Glatthorn, A.A. (1970). Review of *The emergent middle school*. *Educational Leadership, 28* (1), 99-100.

Kean, J.M. (1957). *A comparison of the classroom language of second and fifth-grade teachers*. (Cooperative Research Project S-331). United States Office of Education and Bureau of Educational Research, College of Education, Kent State University.

Metcalf L.E., & Hunt, M.P. (1970). Relevance and the curriculum. *Phi Delta Kappan, 51,* 361.

Weir, E.C. (1970). The stone on the mountain. *Phi Delta Kappan, 51,* 401-402.

Wilhelms, F.T. (1970). Priorities in change efforts. *Phi Delta Kappan, 51,* 369.

*At the time of this writing,* **Ronald Maertens** *was on the faculty of the University of Toledo, Toledo, Ohio.*

# A successful curriculum change
*Donald H. Eichhorn*

C urriculum change is a fundamental element in the continued development of Upper St. Clair, Pennsylvania, middle schools. While organizational development is important to the successful implementation of curriculum, it is the curriculum which ultimately will improve instruction for the transescent learner. Basic to curriculum change has been an awareness that curricular change should emerge from the goals of transescent education. The following goals have been identified for the middle school.

## Value goal

First, the emerging adolescent school should contribute to the development of values. Students in the years 10 to 14 are at a stage in which value orientation is undergoing a transition from a family-adult base to a peer orientation. Youngsters are searching for deeper understandings of relations with peers, family, adults, and society. The school has a rich opportunity to provide experiences which will enhance growth in value patterns.

In this respect, the climate of the school is indeed a vital aspect. There has been a tendency to equate learning with fear, repression, and joylessness. The values inherent in such an approach are suspect both in areas relating to an individual's mental health as well as those relating to society in general.

Originally published in the *Midwest Middle School Journal*,
Vol. III, No. 3, June, 1972.

## *Learning goal*

A second goal for the school for the emerging adolescent involves the learning program. This is a crucial age for budding scholars. With the rapidity and diverseness of maturation, emerging adolescents are vulnerable as students. Sometimes promising students have encountered learning problems at this level which are far removed from mental ability. Conversely, student characteristics such as determination, enthusiasm, and curiosity provide unlimited potential for learning. A school by its philosophy of how learning takes place can facilitate or retard student growth.

There are a number of aspects of the instructional program which should be considered in developing such a philosophy. The following list is indicative but not exhaustive.

### 1. Individual attention

As students leave elementary school, the range of learning rates and competencies magnify. It is essential to develop techniques and curriculum which insure maximum attention to the learning patterns within the dynamics of the individual learner. This does not imply that individualized attention should be equated only with a self study approach. The emphasis should be placed on monitoring student performance, and measures should be taken to insure maximum opportunity for development either in an individual or group context. Early adolescents are at a stage in their development in which they need opportunities to assume responsibility which will lead to self direction. Inherent in this approach is acceptance of consequences of choices as youngsters begin to see the relationship between choice and responsibility.

### 2. Performance basis

Students should be expected to achieve realistic performance standards. These standards should be established, however, not as group standards, but as personal standards. Through this approach, it is hoped that students will gain a critical understanding of their abilities and realize a sense of achievement in relation to these competencies. This line of reasoning suggests that every student be expected to achieve learning mastery in relation to his personal standards.

### 3. Learning skills and processes versus acquisition of content

Cognitively, the young adolescent is in transition between the concrete operations level of the elementary school and the formal operations stage of the high school. It is vital that emphasis be placed on higher cognitive processes such as hypothesizing, generalizing, synthesizing, and evaluating, as well as on the lower processes such as recalling, recognizing, repeating, and copying. Application of this emphasis again mandates consideration of the individual.

The argument that content is unimportant is not valid. Transescent youngsters should gain considerable content knowledge. This acquisition, however, will not mean a set body of knowledge acquired by all students, but rather a wide range of content knowledge gained as an outgrowth of effort in skills and processes. For example, one student may achieve content knowledge related to the religions in Japan while another may learn a great deal about Japan's government. In both cases, however, the students will have acquired skills in gathering, analyzing and evaluating data.

### 4. Social or interaction skills and processes

In effect, social or interaction skills are skills necessary to function effectively in group situations. Group interaction is essential at this age. Such skills as identification, discrimination, clarification, challenge, debate, and compromise are skills to which young adolescents need exposure. While such skills are closely related to the learning skills of self study, they are employed in a different context in group interaction.

Similar to the thought expressed previously regarding content, considerable content learning may take place through the acquisition of social skills. This is a natural forum for analyzing problems relating to growth and development or the humanities. For example, science has provided our society with a highly cherished technology. A natural problem for group interaction would be to analyze the positive aspects of this technology while debating solutions to its negative aspects such as air pollution.

*Personal development goal*

A third goal of early adolescent education revolves around personal development. Possibly no aspect of emerging adolescent education is given more philosophic support than personal development. It is usually cited as a part of the rationale supporting a program. Research has clearly demonstrated the validity and necessity for inclusion of personal development in an educational program for this age. Unfortunately in actual practice, few early adolescent schools give more than superficial treatment to this goal despite exhortations to the contrary. To be effective, personal development instruction must be an integral part of the early adolescent's daily program.

Maturity, or the lack of it, is an important concern for emerging adolescents. This concern is reflected in all aspects of a youngster's school life and influences his intellectual, social, and emotional progress. Emotional development is crucial at this stage. As students move away from dependence on the family, social relationships become increasingly more vital in their lives.

Thus, there is a need to develop a well-defined program in the area of peer relations. This program should have at least two dimensions. First, learning activities should be arranged to insure maximum interaction with peers and adults. For example, a well-conceived student activity program is needed as part of the curriculum. The concept of "extra curricular" implies that these activity areas are external to program. The opposite approach is needed. Secondly, there is a need to include guidance programs which enable students to study, analyze, question, and discuss their personal growth and development with regard to relationships with family, friends, and adults. The typical health program falls far short of meeting this need. In most cases, this instruction is best achieved through informal discussions with trusted adults and peers. Emerging adolescents need the reassurance which comes from understanding the growth process. This understanding assists students in meeting the challenges of learning.

These few goals which have been stated are not all-encompassing, but hopefully they will set the tone for subsequent program statements. They have become the basis for the curriculum at Boyce and Fort Couch middle schools in the Upper St. Clair School District. The curriculum model for these schools is represented in Figure 1.

There are three curricular components. Each component is intended to provide students with fundamental skills, concepts, and understandings which they need at this stage of their development. These components will now be described in some detail.

There are two areas involved in the analytical component which may be characterized by the terms logical, sequential, and cognitive. The intent of this facet of the curriculum is to provide for each student's needs in the vital cognitive areas. Essentially these areas are extensions of the skills and concepts begun in the elementary school. However, it should be noted that there are certain significant differences from the philosophy of the traditional subjects carrying the same labels. For example, the physical-geographic dimension usually associated with cultural studies is included in the science and mathematics components of the curriculum. The traditional "language arts" concept is altered with the major stress in the analytical component being on the nature and structure of language. Only minor emphasis is placed on the utility aspects of language in the analytical component. These aspects are emphasized in the creative expression facet of the Expressive Arts component.

**Figure 1—Curriculum Model**

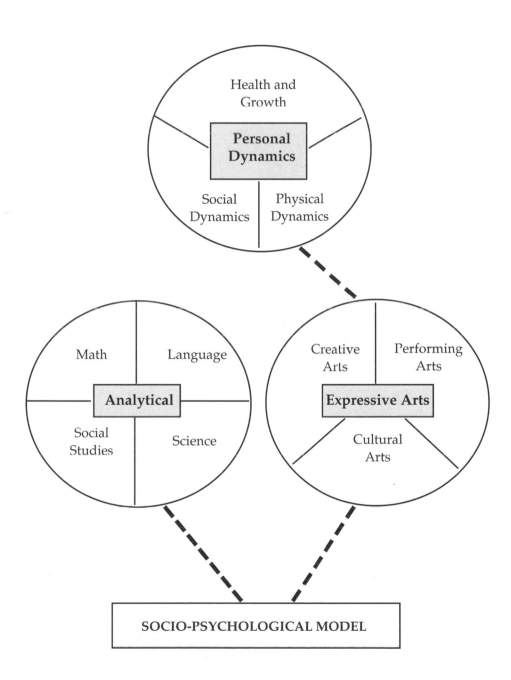

Content has been developed in each of these cognitive areas from Level K (4th level) to Level J (10th level). This means that content material has been developed from the stage of concrete operations to the stage of formal operations or from the concrete to the theoretical.

The current time block for the analytical component has been scheduled as two separate time blocks. Block I has been scheduled for approximately 600 minutes and is devoted to the study of mathematics, physical geography, and language (grammar, writing, reading, listening, speech, etc.). These subjects are felt to be similar in that their basic structure lends itself well to a continuous progress program. Block II has also been scheduled for approximately 600 minutes. This approach is an integrated study of Man and His World. This study is developed around a thematic format and will involve the Science and Cultural Studies teachers.

The second curriculum component is Personal Dynamics. There is considerable evidence that transescent youngsters have a deep need to understand their personal development as it relates to peers and to adults. The primary thrust of this curriculum component is to meet this need through a restructuring of curriculum into Health and Growth, Social Dynamics, and Physical Dynamics. Activities in these areas of the curriculum have been designed to help youngsters adjust to growth changes and to provide practical opportunities for boys and girls to interact in a peer-to-peer social context.

Health and Growth is taught to all students at the middle school on a continuing basis. The main objective is to help students better understand themselves in terms of physical-social-emotional development. Some of the units taught are:

| | |
|---|---|
| School orientation | Personality |
| Understanding Yourself | Growing Into Manhood |
| Home and Family Living | Drugs, Alcohol, and Tobacco |
| Facing, Solving Everyday Problems | Growing Into Womanhood |
| Ethical Standards and Values | High School Ahead |

The third curriculum component is the Expressive Arts. While closely related to Personal Dynamics, this component differs in its emphasis. The intended result is improved divergent mental development. Creative accomplishment, long neglected in traditional curriculum, provides the transescent with unique opportunities. The individuality found in creative expression can play a vital role as the youngster strives for independence. Former segments of the curriculum such as practical arts, fine arts, composition, literature, and the performing arts have been restructured to meet this need.

Expressive Arts is that component of the middle school program which groups art, creative expression, home economics, industrial arts, and music together for the purpose of studying the media of the arts collectively and individually. The objectives of the Expressive Arts curriculum are to enable the students to explore the media of expressive arts, to apply acquired skills to everyday life, to demonstrate the relationship of the media to society, to evaluate their accomplishments in the media, to adapt to their degree of physical maturity through working in the media, to establish security bases outside their family while working with others in the media of expressive arts, to advance their level of divergent mental growth through working in expressive arts, and to gain experience in a democratic environment when working in expressive arts.

Self expression encourages the student to express his creative ideas through drama, speech, and creative writing. Areas explored include poetry writing, basic acting techniques, group discussions, panel discussions, narrative writing, radio and TV production, short story writing, advanced acting technique, and debate.

Music deals with the development of the students' aesthetic potential through explanation and identification of the art. Some of the units included are music reading skills, listening, choral reading skills, music of other cultures, music theory, and a survey of music history.

Home Economics is that part of the expressive arts curriculum in which students experience and gain understandings in food habits, nutritional needs, meal planning, the basics of food preparation, clothing selection and construction, family and peer relationships, and personal appearance and grooming.

As a part of industrial arts, students learn to utilize common tools and materials in the exploration of technical processes and concepts. Units included are general shop safety, reading technical drawings and sketches, metal and wood techniques, graphic arts techniques, mechanical drawing and construction.

The revised Upper St. Clair Middle School curriculum program has been in existence for three years. It is significant that during these years favorable reactions by parents, students, and faculty have been received. Also, there have been achievement gains recorded for students. It is our belief, based upon solid evidence that the innovative curriculum program devised over the past five years has led to improved instruction, a positive student attitude, and support by parents.

**Donald H. Eichhorn** *is retired as Superintendent of Schools, Lewisburg, Pennsylvania.*

# The case for core in the middle school

*James A. Beane*

T he past few years have seen a tremendous increase in the number of school districts moving from junior high school organization to middle schools. During the 1960s many such cases were founded on 4-4-4 integration plans or relief of over-crowding in elementary schools (Gatewood, 1973). Even then, how-ever, leaders in the middle school movement were pointing out that the change was more than just a grade-level reorganization. A growing body of research (Eichhorn, 1973) has clearly substantiated the down-ward trend of pubescent achievement age, and the logical grade levels for the school in the middle now appear to be 5-8 or 6-8 rather than 7-9. But the middle school promised more than that. Many saw in it the possibility for developing programs to meet the needs of transescent learners to replace the traditional "junior" (version) of the high school. In many instances, new programs were developed, but very few have reconsidered one of the patterns which had enjoyed success in the old junior high school movement—core curriculum.

The middle school has been defined in a number of places, and a summary of those definitions would support the notion that it is a school unit which houses emerging adolescents within a district and which has a program designed to deal with the needs, problems, interests, and concerns of that age group. The latter include not only those unique to individual learners but those common to all emerging adolescents such as:

Originally published in the *Middle School Journal*,
Vol. VI, No. 2, pp. 33-34, Summer 1975.

1.  The need to develop a positive sense of self;
2.  The need to accept and get along with others, especially age-mates;
3.  The need to understand pubescent development and accept one's own physical self;
4.  The need to extend intellectual development and the mastery of basic skills;
5.  The need to examine value systems and social issues; and
6.  The need to develop independence in thinking and action.

A middle school program designed to accomplish those purposes would certainly not be characterized by a single curricular pattern. Rather, it would include several provisions or patterns to account for the various specific needs. Such provisions would include generally:

1.  A portion of the program devoted to personal and social problems with regard for and transcending subject areas;
2.  A portion of the program set aside to deal with special intellectual needs or interests, including skill development and subject areas;
3.  A portion of the program in which youngsters could explore and experiment with such areas as home economics, industrial arts, music, drama, and physical education; and
4.  A portion of the program for opportunities to investigate and explore immediate interests or talents through clubs or activity groups.

The focus of interest here is with the first of those provisions. Many middle schools have developed excellent activity programs, exploratory programs, and innovative subject programs. Yet the middle school movement has not committed itself to the idea of directly confronting the social and personal needs of youth and major societal issues through a specially designed program provision. Some would claim that this provision is made through interdisciplinary team teaching, but all too often such teams merely slice up their block of time and carry on as usual with only informal or incidental efforts at correlation.

Alberty (1953) defined six conceptions of core programs. It is his Type V program which should be of particular concern to middle schools. In this design the core program is based upon pre-planned units which focus on youth needs and social problems. Within the unit, organization is characterized by a number of elements (VanTil, Vars, & Lounsbury, 1967):

1.  Use of resource units;
2.  Teacher, teacher-student, and student planning;

3. Units structured around centers of experience and student interests;
4. Problem-centered teaching;
5. Use of large and small groups and individual work;
6. Functional teaching of basic skills;
7. Teacher counseling of students in general problems; and
8. Use of a block of time.

One conclusion seems quite apparent. The purposes of the middle school, the needs of emerging adolescence, and core curriculum are entirely compatible. Certainly core makes a direct attack on the problem of meeting emerging adolescent needs as described above. Self-concept and getting along with others are needs which may be met through cooperative planning, problem-solving, and group work as well as teacher counseling. Extension of basic skills is provided for in their functional use of problem-solving. Independence is developed through individual work, problem-solving, and student planning. Most importantly, experience units provide directly for dealing with values, social issues, and personal concerns. Furthermore, core programs provide a transition from the self-contained classroom of the elementary school to the high school. Indeed, core programs "provide a major opportunity to develop a curriculum based upon...the social realities of our times, the personal-social needs of young adolescents, and democratic values" (VanTil, Vars, & Lounsbury, 1967, p. 227).

Some years ago Alberty (1960) summarized research on core curriculum by noting that it appears superior to conventional, subject-centered programs "in the area of attitudes and values...in providing for more effective guidance of students; for individual differences among students; and for more effective use of community resources in the classroom" (p. 340). This again points to the need to reconsider what core curriculum really was intended to be. Some veterans might disregard renewal with offhand references to past failures. Educational leaders, including professional teachers, must reexamine core theory and research to separate instances of proper use from misinterpretation in implementation (Vars, 1972).

Middle school personnel must carefully think through their own purposes and renew their efforts to represent more than just a change in grade levels, stationary letterhead, and signs in front of the school.

Those who feel that interdisciplinary teaming is serving the purpose of core must carefully examine such programs and compare them to the theory of core. Such patterns may actually get in the way of really achieving some middle school objectives (Vars, 1966).

Middle schools cannot wait for teacher education to supply core teachers. The press for core preparation must come through in-service education with the hope that colleges and universities will soon take the hint.

In the face of technology and specialization, middle schools must carefully study their emerging adolescent populations to demonstrate that there are problems and needs which are broader than those accounted for in subject-centered programs (Vars, 1969).

The purposes of the middle school are varied and thus call for variety and balance in the program designed for emerging adolescence. Certainly every middle school ought to be able to account for the four provisions described earlier. However, in order to develop balance and account for personal and social problems there is need for a reconsideration of core curriculum. In light of the above discussion, there is a strong case for core in the middle school. Conceivably we might meet Wilhelms' (1971) challenge to "go directly at helping each youngster in his personal becoming, no matter what happens in the process to some of our cherished subject matter or patterns of action."

### References

Alberty, H. (1953). Meeting the common needs of youth. In *Adapting the secondary school to the youth, 52nd yearbook of the N.S.S.E.* Chicago: University of Chicago.

Alberty, H. (1960). Core programs. In *Encyclopedia of Educational Research* . New York: Macmillan.

Eichhorn, D.H. (1973). The Boyce medical study. *The emerging adolescent learner in the middle grades*, multi-media package. Springfield, MA: Educational Leadership Institute.

Gatewood, T. (1973). What research says about the middle school. *Educational Leadership, 31*, 222.

Van Til, W., Vars, G.F., & Lounsbury, J.H. (1967). *Modern education for the junior high school years*. Indianapolis, IN: Bobbs-Merrill.

Vars, G.F. (1966). Can team teaching save the core curriculum? *Phi Delta Kappan, 47*, 258-262.

Vars, G.F. (1969). *Common learnings: Core and interdisciplinary team approaches*. Scranton, PA: Intext.

Vars, G.F. (1972). Curriculum in secondary schools and colleges. In *A new look at progressive education*. Washington, DC: Association for Supervision and Curriculum Development.

Wilhelms, F.T. (1971). *And they of the middle years?* Paper presented at the Association for Supervision and Curriculum Development Annual Conference, St. Louis.

*James A. Beane is on the faculty of National-Louis University and is headquartered in Madison, Wisconsin.*

# A responsive curriculum for emerging adolescents

*John Arnold*

T hough not a fan of rock music, I am convinced that some of it contains messages which middle school educators might well heed. Consider the lyrics of "The Logical Song" from the album, *Breakfast in America*, by Supertramp:

> When I was young, it seemed that life was so
>     wonderful, a miracle, oh it was beautiful,
>     magical.
> And all the birds in the trees, well they'd be
>     singing so happily, joyfully, playfully
>     watching me.
> But then they send me away to teach me how to
>     be sensible, logical, responsible, practical.
> And they showed me a world where I could be
>     so dependable, clinical, intellectual, cynical.
>
> There are times when all the world's asleep,
>     the questions run too deep for such a simple
>     man.
> Won't you please, please tell me what we've
>     learned?

Originally published in the *Middle School Journal*,
Vol. XVI, No. 3, pp. 3, 14-18, May 1985.

I know it sounds absurd,
    but please tell me who I am.

Now watch what you say or they'll be calling
    you a radical, liberal, fanatical, criminal.
Won't you sign up your name, we'd like to feel
    you're acceptable, respectable, presentable, a
    vegetable!

At night, when all the world's asleep,
    the questions run so deep for such a simple
    man.
Won't you please, please tell me what we've
    learned?
I know it sounds absurd,
    but please tell me who I am.

Certainly not all emerging adolescents share these sentiments, but the lyrics do express the pain and bewilderment that many youths experience in trying to cope with society. Unfortunately, the curriculum of our schools is sometimes part of the problem instead of part of the solution.

If we genuinely want to develop a curriculum responsive to early adolescent concerns, band-aid measures such as adding a mini-course here or a social event there will not do the job. Nor will extending the school day or year, or increasing time on task. Even structural changes that establish interdisciplinary teams, block schedules and advisor/advisee systems, while usually quite helpful, will not *in themselves* accomplish the task. A responsive curriculum must positively affect the day to day interactions in classrooms, reflecting a deep-seated commitment to meet the needs, interests, and abilities of emerging adolescents. Five key principles of such a curriculum will be explored in this article.

## Understanding self and world

First, a responsive curriculum must help students make sense of themselves and of their world. Young adolescents desperately want to understand themselves—their bodies and their emotions. *What is sex all about? Are my breasts large enough? Will they be? How can anyone like me when I wear braces? What's going to happen if I don't start growing soon? Am I really OK?*

They also want to understand their peers and their parents. They really want to know how to make friends. They want to understand power relationships and what to do when they can't have their own way. They want to know how to be themselves and still be part of a group without losing their souls in the process.

They're also concerned about their competence. Paraphrasing Wells (Arnold, 1979), an adolescent starts to realize, "If I'm going to be a Jacques Cousteau, I've got to know something—I can't just have a Jacques Cousteau doll like I did when I was younger or read Jacques Cousteau comic books. Maybe I'll have to learn those old multiplication tables...Maybe I'll really have to know something about oceanography" (pp. 237-238). The painful awareness begins to dawn that what we do, not what we say or fantasize, is most important.

In seeking to understand the world they live in, young adolescents are jolted from the beliefs that Mom and Dad have everything under control, that the President knows best, that teachers always have the right answers. They start to ask a lot of embarrassing "how come" questions that adults don't like to deal with much: *How come you smoke if it gives you cancer? How come we have two cars, a big house, and take vacations in the Bahamas when people are starving in the world? How come you tell us to be honest while you cheat on your income tax? How come our country pollutes the air and endangers our future? How come it talks about peace but builds and sells horrible weapon systems?*

One of the most blasphemous things we can ever say in middle school education, and unfortunately it is said often, is that boys and girls this age are not interested in anything intellectual. Indeed, many may not be interested in the ten principal products of Peru, or how to diagram a sentence, but that does not mean that they lack intellectual interests. Academic and intellectual are not synonymous terms, and it is a grave mistake to consider them so. I know a group of 30 middle schoolers who met weekly at night with their principal and social studies teacher the entire year, studying utopian political philosophy. All voluntarily decided to write papers presenting their ideal political system.

Young adolescents are asking some of the most profound questions human beings can ever ask: *Who am I? What can I be? What should I be? What should I do?* To respond to them effectively, we must forge a curriculum that frequently deals with their own questions—not just the questions of Professor Jones, the teacher, or the textbook. We also need curricular content that deals with issues such as adolescence itself, adolescence in other cultures, sex and sex roles, rules and authority, competition and cooperation, and conflict resolution.

Moral concerns must be consciously and sensitively explored in dealing with these topics. Young adolescents are long on idealism and short on experience. Hence they find it hard to understand why injustices, once identified, cannot be immediately rectified. It is crucial that we help them confront the human complexities and moral ambiguities of our time without destroying their idealism.

## *Developmental appropriateness*

The second principle of a responsive curriculum is that methods and materials must be geared to students' level of development and understanding. Far too many classrooms exist where students reading on a fourth grade level are asked to read eighth grade level textbooks, or students who don't understand ratios are asked to manipulate fractions and decimals. An enormous problem is that many of the textbooks and other materials used in middle and junior high schools falsely assume that students have attained Piaget's stage of formal operations, and are thus able to think deductively, to deal with a number of variables simultaneously, and to perform a host of other abstract tasks. Only a small percentage can actually think at this level consistently. Most young adolescents are in transition from concrete to formal operational thought, which means that their capacity for abstraction is limited and fluctuating. Failure to comprehend the implications of this situation may well be the biggest problem in middle school education. The problem is fueled by the little publicized fact that less than one percent of all commercial curriculum materials have been systematically field tested with students and revised on the basis of the information obtained (Komoski, 1971).

Gearing curriculum to students' levels means neither placing them in rigid ability groups nor using "individualized" techniques which require them to work in isolation on stack after stack of sequenced ditto sheets. Several years ago a teacher in the process of establishing learning centers in her classroom told me her students demanded, *Where are the sheets?* She replied, *What do you mean, where are the sheets? The **work** sheets*, they responded. *These centers are play stuff. Where are the sheets?* When I told this story to my daughter, Suzy, age eleven at the time and the philosopher in the family, she replied, "Sure. I understand. That's the way school is—you do the sheets."

Gearing curriculum to students' levels does mean, as implied above, acknowledging both the concrete and formal operational aspects of their thought. This necessitates having a rich variety of materials in classrooms for students to manipulate so they can build, measure, compare, contrast, and create. It is sad that a paucity of middle school classrooms provide such materials. We see many such environments in elementary schools, but the higher the grade level, the more barren classrooms seem to become.

A rich environment needs to be accompanied by procedures which provide a variety of options, choices, and structures, letting students find their own levels, as it were. This requires much observation and talking with students to find out what they do and do not understand. At times they must be "stretched" to take on more complex tasks; at other times they must be urged to cut back. This self-leveling strategy is in contrast to the oft-advocated diagnostic/prescriptive approach, whose effectiveness seems limited to highly sequential, rule-bound material. Besides the fact that diagnostic/prescriptive techniques often use cut-and-dried procedures that become boring, it is far more difficult to diagnose and prescribe accurately than advocates acknowledge. A student may be at one level for certain activities and at a different level for others. Few prescribed programs are sensitive to these nuances.

Another aspect of "leveling" curriculum involves providing varying degrees of structure. To some students we can say, *Here are some materials; go to it. I'll check with you in half an hour*, and they do fine. Others need a great deal of guidance. I have no problems whatever in saying to a student, *You sit down and do A, B, C and D, and don't you get out of your seat until you've done them.* But, the crucial point is that we must eventually go beyond this and help the student to become more independent. When a student *can* do A, B, C and D as told, then it's important to say, *That's fine, wonderful. Now I want you to choose between X and Y.* Eventually, we want to lead students to the point where they can design their own options. Unfortunately, we don't have many "weaning" strategies for adolescents. Yet the implicit curriculum for anyone working with adolescents ought to be, *How can I help this boy/girl become increasingly more independent?*

## Knowledge vs. information

Thirdly, a responsive curriculum must emphasize knowledge, not simply information and isolated skills. James (1974) reminds us that information is a commodity, "out there." Knowledge, on the other hand, is an internal process, involving thinking, feeling, and at times doing. It leads us to think about our feelings, to be aware of feelings which accompany our thoughts, and to integrate the two in our actions. Knowledge arises through a question and answer process. It cannot develop effectively where students are given answers to questions they have never asked.

An important way to foster knowledge is to engage students in the disciplines, not just in subject matter. Perhaps an analogy will clarify the distinction. If I obtain some glass, grind it, polish it, and study the refraction of light waves through it, I am involved in the discipline of optometry. I am doing what the people in this field do. If I write a book about my efforts, however, and give the book to someone to read, then they are involved in subject matter.

Illsley (Arnold, 1979, pp. 63-65) points out that scientists do not spend their time performing experiments, the answers to which are already known. They're asking genuine questions, observing, and testing hypotheses. Poets do not spend most of their time reading other people's poetry. Historians do not simply read history books others have written. If we really want students to develop knowledge in history, they will have to do what historians actually do, at least some of the time. This means examining original records, interviewing people, developing hunches, and writing history. In science, instead of studying iron filings with a magnet, students might observe a tree for a whole year and very, very carefully record their observations. Then if they cannot put those observations into a form that we as teachers can understand, we need to help them with that structure.

Nowhere is the distortion of knowledge more obvious than in the current passion for identifying basic skills as those items which can be broken down into small units and tested easily. This trend has led us to a curriculum where workbooks, ditto sheets and short answer quizzes dominate. High reading comprehension scores on national standard-ized tests have become the golden calf of education. Though helping students achieve such scores may be of value, it is far less fundamental than getting them actually to read a lot and enjoy the process. To put the issue in perspective, would we rather have a student whose reading comprehension score is in the 99th percentile but who reads very little, or one who scores in the 50th percentile but who reads omnivorously? Most of us will choose the latter student, for this is the one who will learn and develop through reading. Moreover, it is well known that students who in fact do read a lot improve considerably over time in their reading comprehension, speed and vocabulary development.

It is essential that students read real books, articles and newspa-pers, interacting with their teachers and peers about them. Questions such as, *Why do you suppose the main character did what he did? What other options were available to him? How do you evaluate his action?* build interest and motivation. They also promote higher order thinking skills such as inference, analysis, and evaluation, which the National Assessment of Educational Progress has shown to be on the decline. The basic, lower level skills, ironically, have not declined over the past 10 years.

Despite our rhetoric about reading, an astonishing number of teachers and schools do little to encourage "real" reading. Books frequently are not available in classrooms but are confined to libraries where many students seldom venture. The number of books that students read, perhaps the best evaluative criterion of a reading program, is seldom even considered.

The situation relative to writing is equally distorted. Grammar exercises and other short-answer easily measurable tasks too often receive the lion's share of attention at the expense of actual writing. This is not to say that grammar is unimportant, but it alone is not going to produce good writers. In analyzing some 80 studies on the relationship of writing and grammar, Sherwin (1969) concludes that the teaching of grammar does not lead to proficiency in composing. Grammar involves taking things apart; composition involves putting them together.

The neglect of actual writing stems directly from an exaggerated concern for measurement and accountability. Many teachers are convinced that every dot and tittle students write must be marked with a red pencil. However, teachers have to be real masochists to require much writing if they insist on marking every word. There is simply not enough time to grade 100-150 papers in this fashion very often. But there are all kinds of strategies which allow students to write every day, improve, and learn. We can organize classes into writing workshops where they write about a variety of topics. After discussing their papers in small groups, they can then make revisions. We can grade one paper for certain aspects of grammar, another part for different aspects. Parents can also be enlisted in the process. Papers can be written specifically for them, and they can give assessments of the writing.

The end result of the distorted way in which basic skills are taught is that speech, writing, and reading are isolated from one another, and all three are dissociated from students' experience. The remedy is hardly radical: students must be given ample opportunity to read about, write about, and talk about matters of concern to them.

### Concrete and real world experience

The fourth principle of a responsive curriculum relates closely to the third: we have to value concrete and real world experience. James (1974) points out that we live in a society that doesn't have much respect for the concrete. We value the technical and the theoretical over the practical, thoughts over feelings, ideas over action, the general over the particular. But to neglect the concrete and specific is to miss the essence of life. How does it help our teaching to care about "children" but to fail to notice the pain Sally is experiencing from her parents' divorce? What is gained from identifying a Geraniaceae while paying scant attention to the geranium's vivid colors and aroma? Of what good is it to label a situation as "racist" without understanding the people and dynamics involved, or without a willingness to help better it?

The story of Jacob and the angel of the Lord speaks to these situations. The two wrestled all night long, with Jacob demanding, "Tell me your name." The angel refused, knowing that if our interest is only in naming, labeling or generalizing about something, we can dismiss it very easily.

In helping students deal with the concrete and the specific, we must give far more emphasis to the arts. James warns that if we are to survive as a society, we must find a way to overcome "the gap between art and life." She sees the art as guardians of the senses, deepening our perceptions, expanding our horizons, making us more fully human. They involve optimal opportunities for risk-taking so critical for healthy ego development during adolescence. We must find ways to integrate the arts into our daily teaching as catalysts for learning. Too often they are offered once or twice in isolated courses and that's the extent of their influence.

Another important way of emphasizing the concrete and specific is to involve students in the community and the community in the schools. Compulsory education has isolated adolescents from the adult world, and the technical nature of today's society gives them little opportunity to contribute useful work. They simply aren't needed much by society. Goodman (1960) says, "It's hard to feel good about yourself when you don't have anything good to do" (p. 41). Of all the things that create what we call "adolescence," this isolation from the adult world is perhaps most responsible.

We need to develop apprenticeships and Foxfire-type projects; we need work-study programs; we need to involve kids in assistance in day-care centers and homes of the elderly, and a variety of other community-based activities.

In addition to giving young people the opportunity to perform useful services and develop skills, community activities provide role taking opportunities that attach real world feedback and consequences to behavior. This fact was brought home forcefully to me through an apprenticeship program at Sidwell Friends Middle School in Washington, D.C. where I was once principal. Three months of the year, students left school at one o'clock daily to work for several hours with photographers, veterinarians, electricians, plumbers, architects, etc. One day, a 13 year old boy who worked with a veterinarian arrived a half hour late. The veterinarian met him with hands on hips and demanded "Where have you been?" The boy stammered, *I stopped at a store along the way...* The veterinarian interrupted, *Wait a minute—I don't have any time for that sort of thing. I expect you to be here on time, have the animals cleaned and ready for operations, or I don't have any time for you. Do I make myself clear?* The boy replied, *Yes, you do,* and was on time every day thereafter.

After the veterinarian told me this story, I began to ponder the question, "Where do schools provide such 'real' consequences in the regular curriculum?" When a student is late, we generally put a mark in a book or set up some kind of detention. But what does that mean to a thirteen or fourteen year old? Only two areas in conventional school curricula where "real" and meaningful consequences are consistently attached to students' behavior come to mind. Sports is one area. The basketball player who doesn't pass the ball to an open teammate may well be chewed out. This is usually accepted easily, for the feedback is immediate, real, and related to meaningful goals. The player realizes the team is being let down. The other area is in the arts. An art teacher, for example, might say to a student attempting to throw a pot, "Look, if you really want to do this right, you've got to center it and stay with it." Rarely would a student reply, "Don't tell me what to do" because consequences attached to the behavior are perceived as appropriate. Finding ways to attach meaningful consequences to students' behavior should be a critical area of concern in our schools.

### Trusting instincts

The final principle of a responsive curriculum, and the most significant one, is that the teachers involved must be knowledgeable human beings who trust their own judgments and instincts. I have had the opportunity to know a number of truly exceptional teachers over the years. Not one of them relied heavily on teachers' guides, recommended activities, or prescribed materials. They were all good observers and listeners who understood kids; their assessment of daily classroom experiences guided their planning. Some teachers, of course, need more external direction than others, but excellent teaching will never emerge where one's instincts are made subservient to rules and models.

During World War II, many families in London were bombed out of their homes. Teachers took their children in the countryside while parents remained behind to work in the factories. Often teachers would be responsible for up to 50 children, ages 5-18, for 24 hours a day. Under such circumstances, they had to use their instincts. They obviously couldn't lecture, and they had few materials. Children worked on group projects with the older ones helping the younger ones. Teachers had to improvise, using novels, newspapers, sticks, stones, sand, or what was available. Yet effective and substantive education did occur. And from these unlikely beginnings, the British "integrated day," in my estimation the finest educational practice of our times, sprang forth.

In the current craze for accountability and "effective" teaching, it is sad indeed to see many teachers ignoring what they think is best for students, deferring instead to some vast army of experts whose advice supposedly will cure our educational ills. In denying our instincts, we not only undermine the potential for responsive curricula, we lose also a precious gift—our capacity to share our humanity with others.

I began with a song; I would like to close with a letter which poignantly illustrates the power of trusting one's instincts and sharing one's humanity. The letter was written by Brown (1982), at the time a visiting professor at the University of Georgia. He had been quite excited about the opportunity to teach a graduate seminar on moral development to a small group of women. Two of them had been incarcerated in Nazi concentration camps as children; two were nuns; and one was, in Steve's words, "more brilliant than many of the philosophers being studied." Yet the class was a colossal failure for the first six weeks. No one seemed to talk about anything of personal importance. Students complained that the class was irrelevant, that they couldn't relate Kohlberg's moral dilemmas to real-life situations.

One day in class a woman named Rose described taking her young son to the doctor's office where he saw a child with only three fingers on each hand. The little boy whispered, "Mama, why does this child have only three fingers?" Steve posed for discussion the question, "How might one best respond to the child?" A few biological explanations were suggested, but the group could get no more involved with this issue than they had with previous ones.

Steve was very perplexed and depressed, realizing after class that the child must have been concerned about ultimate justice in the world, not genetic aberrations. He sat down and composed a letter that he subsequently read to the class. It brought tears to everyone's eyes, and in that moment, the veil was lifted. People began to talk from their personal experience; Kohlberg's dilemmas became relevant; the curriculum became responsive. Steve describes the class as the best teaching experience of his career. The letter reads as follows:

> *Dear Ourselves,*
>
> *The classroom—our classroom—is a microcosm of the world; the real world, the ideal world, the imperfect and the perfect one.*
>
> *We have explicit agendas and we have hidden agendas—some so hidden that even we who set the wheels in motion are but barely aware of the tips of volcanoes upon which we sit.*
>
> *So much of our lives is taken up in planning and organizing that the precious moment passes us by—unfelt and even worse unwanted—*
>
> *How does Rose answer her child who queries within earshot of a malformed son and his mother why that boy has*

*only three fingers on each hand? Are there no answers? Answers for Rose? For her child? For the malformed child? For the mother? Dear ourselves—we are all malformed! It is not because I have black hair and you have red or brown hair that one of us is malformed and the other not. I am malformed when I cannot hear you cry for help. I am malformed when I seek personal glory over wisdom. I am malformed if I do not relish every moment with the hope that it will last forever; I am malformed when my fear that I cannot answer your question prevents me from exploring it with the confidence that one of us will emerge the wiser; if not me, then you; I am malformed when I cannot tell you that you have a beautiful thought; I am malformed when I hear you only for how I will respond; I am malformed when I separate scholarship from friendship; I am malformed when I hear only words and not our meanings; I am malformed when I organize a course and forget what I had organized it for; I am malformed when I cannot relate Kohlberg to your practical problems. I am malformed if I can **only** relate him to your practical problems.*

*Why are there malformed and grotesque people upon the world—people with three fingers, no feet and one eye? Perhaps to remind us not only that we are all **different**, not only that the most malformed among us might be the best, and that goodness and beauty are not the same, but more importantly to remind us that we are all **malformed**. We are all malformed, but unlike the grotesque monsters, we can do something about some of that deformity. And that something begins **now** and here! Give us the courage to do so.*

### References

Arnold, J. (1979). *Open education in the middle years* . Raleigh, NC: N.C. State University Publications Office.

Brown, S. (1982). Teaching "whys" and wise teaching. *Teaching Philosophy, 5*(2), 128-129.

Goodman, P. (1960). *Growing up absurd.* New York: Vintage.

James, C. (1974). *Beyond customs.* New York: Agathon.

Testimony based on five years of research by Komoski, K. Educational Products and Information Exchange Institute, before Congressional Subcommittee on Education and Labor, May 11,1971.

Sherwin, J. S. (1969). *Four problems in the teaching of English.* London: International Textbook.

**John Arnold** *teaches at North Carolina State University, Raleigh.*

# In search of quality in
# middle school curriculum

*Les Tickle*

M iddle schools in England were established in 1968. Ten years later there were over 1,700 of them, most catering for the age ranges 8-12 years or 9-13 years. All middle schools span the conventional transfer at 11-plus from primary to secondary school and have been characterized as attempting to achieve a smooth transition from general class teaching of primary practice to specialist subject teaching of secondary schools (Meyenn & Tickle, 1980).

The exploration for appropriate curriculum for middle level students has been carried out in an atmosphere of change, originality, and uncertain ideas. At school and local authority levels the fermentation of ideas led to volumes of reports and working papers. At national level the Schools Council, The Department of Education and Science, the Middle Schools Research Group, and the National Foundation for Educational Research were involved in tackling ideas for educational progress at the middle years level.

Middle schools provided an impetus for problem-solving; they brought into consciousness as never before issues such as how we rationalize teaching; the conditions needed for the professional development of teachers; collegial relations required in team teaching; redefinitions of teachers' roles in reconciling class and subject teaching; liaison between schools; cooperative curriculum planning; and teaching methods.

Originally published in the *Middle School Journal*,
Vol. XIX, No. 2, pp. 3, 34-35, February 1988.

The exploration of these and other issues surrounded the central issue in the enterprise—providing appropriate curriculum experiences through which educational excellence could be achieved for the middle years age group. Within that issue, questions about aims and teaching methods have been paramount. In the early days curricular notions of pluralism, integration of subjects, individualized learning, informal teaching methods, and innovation of new practices were central to the search for a new ethos.

There is considerable evidence that the seeds of this educational Utopia barely germinated in classroom practice, that political and educational rhetoric remained just that. The conventional curriculum with fixed subject content, formal class teaching, and selection of pupils at age 11 for different career routes remained firmly intact (Bennett, 1976; Boydell, 1981; Galton, Simon, & Croll, 1981; Ginsburg, Meyenn, Miller, & Ranceford-Hadley, 1977; Hargreaves & Tickle, 1980). What is more, recent educational policy changes have flourished on the rhetoric of control of standards in the "main subjects," to be achieved through a common curriculum within a national framework, more effective use of teachers' subject knowledge, efficient differentiation of pupils' learning experiences, and more overt monitoring of the work of teachers.

There have been two important reports on practices in middle schools issued by Her Majesty's Inspectors of Schools. *9-13 Middle Schools* (DES 1983) and *Education 8-12* (DES 1985). Both recognize serious flaws in the quality of education in these schools. The influence on standards of major variables, such as quality of head-teachers, available resources, use of specialist subject teachers (in 9-13's), and effective pastoral care (8-12's) are recognized.

A major concern is expressed in both reports about the aims of middle school curriculum and the quality of pedagogy. Criticizing the overuse of didactic teaching dominated by listening to the teacher and writing to instruction, *9-13 Middle Schools* demanded a greater diversity of teaching and learning approaches as a means of enhancing motivation to learn and quality of work. Opportunities for extended discussion, collaborative group work, the exercise by pupils of choice, and responsibility and initiative within the curriculum were called for. Observation, description, the application of skills and ideas towards explanation, reasoned argument, and generalization of principles are explicit demands through which to provide all children with opportunities to acquire and develop levels of skills and understanding of ideas more closely related to their capacities than is often the case at present" (DES 1983).

*Education 8-12* calls for attention to skills and capabilities which require understanding, and the means of developing these through opportunities for children to pose questions, offer explanations, predict, experiment, collect data, consider evidence, and establish conclusions. The fostering of initiative, responsibility, and independence are seen as key aims (DES 1985).

Ironically the connection between the informal teaching methods implied by these aims and the need for a wide range of varied resources is recognized. However it is overridden by the usual HMI rejoinder that as with other HMI reports "no assumption can be made about government commitment to the provision of additional resources as a result of the survey" (DES 1985, p.vi.). Even so, Her Majesty's Inspectorate, like others concerned with middle schools, keep alive a notion of curriculum with Bruner (1960, 1966) at the centre, in which the most general aim of education is to cultivate excellence—for example, helping each student achieve his or her optimum intellectual development. Long-term autonomous learning through an effective educational process is the goal.

As Bruner put it: "The first object of any learning act is that it should serve us in the future. Learning should not only take us somewhere, it should allow us later to go further more easily" (1960, p.17).

Ability then would be judged in terms of the application of understanding in new situations and the further acquisition of knowledge. It is precisely those elements of the educational process which include question posing, testing of hypotheses, and search for possible solutions in conditions of cooperation and ambiguity where risk and failure as well as success are allowed which curriculum developers have consistently urged. These are central to the rationale on which the curriculum of many middle schools was constructed, and which H.M.I. from beneath the weight of educational rhetoric and economic constraint now demand. So we have to ask, what is it to be effective in achieving quality in educational activities? What is the pursuit of excellence? And how is it possible to become effective?

## Teacher effectiveness and learning for understanding

Teacher effectiveness studies are centered on classroom activity and the instructional function of teaching. (Berliner & Rosenshine, 1977; Dunkin & Biddle, 1974; Bennett, 1976; Galton, Simon, & Croll, 1981). They tend to ignore other dimensions of teaching-pastoral care, counseling, curriculum decision making, evaluation, and teacher self-appraisal. Teachers are engaged in these other activities and they make up part of the task of effective teaching, but I will leave these other dimensions aside in this article.

It has been shown that closed instructional techniques leading to higher test performance depend on external control over the learners, while open enquiry approaches lead to increased independence, curiosity, and creativity which call for fostering of an internal personal control sense in students (Peterson, 1979). Elliott (1980) has pointed out the inadequacy of the objectives paradigm in judging teaching performance because it assumes that teaching causes learning—for example, that teachers are instruments performing technical acts (methods) on passive pupils in order to produce preconceived results (outcomes).

Such teaching is necessarily power coercive; learning is power dependent; and it presupposes a bias against self-directed, enquiry learning and the development of autonomy. Elliott cites Doyle's (1979) argument that the emphasis on quantifying learning outcomes leads to the neglect of the qualitative dimension of learning (Elliot, 1985, p.2). Yet it is *quality* which is at the heart of excellence. The issue is about *what* is learned and *how* it is learned, not simply about how much. These depend on the kinds of tasks in which pupils engage as well as the social relations of the educational encounter (Bowles & Gintis, 1975; Hargreaves 1982).

Elliott uses Doyle's distinction of three types of learning tasks:

> *Understanding tasks* which require students to apply cognitive operations such as classification, inference, deduction, and analysis to instances not previously encountered, or to comprehend information, perhaps reproducing it in transformed state;
> *Memory tasks* which require students to recognize or recall facts, principles, or solutions with which they are acquainted;
> *Routine problem solving tasks*, such as the four rules of number which require students to learn and apply a standard and reliable formula or principle.

He illustrated how teacher effectiveness research has concentrated on those aspects of pupil performance which are given to being measured, which ignore understanding categories of learning (Elliott, 1985). He points out that Bennett's (1976) finding that formal methods are more effective than informal ones is an inevitable outcome of the concept of teaching competence held by the researcher in common with other teacher effectiveness researchers. It is a concept of formality involving high teacher control over input and output in relatively low risk memory and routine problem solving tasks. Implied is a clear statement about the aims/objectives and methods of teaching which is at variance with those espoused by Her Majesty's Inspectorate's view of good middle schooling which I cited earlier.

To achieve *that* quality we have to recognize that informal methods are designed to encourage collaboration in learning, the exercise of choice, responsibility and initiative, and the development and application of skills and understanding of ideas. Understanding tasks require the use of judgement and risk taking. Informal teaching in a process-oriented curriculum sets out to facilitate such learning by producing conditions in which enquiry can lead to understanding through dialogue. Instrumental memory and routine problem solving tasks are subsumed or subordinated in effectiveness for understanding through enquiry.

## Classroom experience

The elements of risk, ambiguity, uncertainty and dilemma in the understanding tasks for the pupils and in appropriate curriculum methods adopted by the teacher are considerable. My research into the teaching of art and design has illustrated this.

In case study research with art and design teachers, two main strands of curriculum intention, instruction in 'basic' manipulative craft skills and engagement in expressive, aesthetic, or qualitative problem-solving and creativity, evolved into two distinct curricula. One was for pupils deemed less able and one for those more able, despite the intentions of the teachers to develop both strands for all pupils.

The initial concern for pupils to demonstrate specific competencies in craft skills or particular "adult" modes of representational image making which could be visually judged predominated. Pupils who demonstrated such competence were then expected to engage in decision making and qualitative problem solving while those who did not were expected to persist in those tasks which had already brought relative failure. They were denied access to tasks involving enquiry judgement and decision making which provided other pupils with relative autonomy and self determination.

The kinds of tasks involved can be equated with those distinguished by Doyle and cited by Elliott:

1.  specific and measurable craft skills given to didactic instruction;
2.  the application of knowledge of craft processes to produce required solutions;
3.  and the use of cognitive and affective judgement and under standing in determining personal design solutions and identify ing expressive and design problems.

The kinds of teaching methods, the quality of interactions, and distribution and use of time by the teachers differed with regard to the tasks in which the pupils were engaged.

## Realizing quality across the curriculum of middle schools

In *Education 8-12* (DES, 1985) HMI says that those aspects of skills, understanding, and curriculum processes which are common across different subject boundaries are in need of attention in classroom practice. But these aspects also represent more general conflicting images—those which see education as concerned with maximizing personal development, creative potential, and the cultivation of excellence. They come face to face with aspects in which schooling is seen as anti-creative, and stultifying to the individual because of its function to produce a differentially skilled and compliant work force.

Middle schools have consistently had to contend with this fundamental contradiction and conflict. Those concerned with teacher effectiveness and concerns for quality have to take cognizance of these conflicts and the resulting differences in curriculum tasks and associated teaching methods if they aspire to change classroom practice. Reconception of what counts as quality and excellence, and reappraisal of practice into terms in which decision making, ambiguity, uncertainty and risk are legitimated as part of the learning process are prerequisites. That needs to be understood by teachers, built into their learning experiences, and supported by the acceptance of informal teaching methods. Only then will the potential of educational excellence which middle schools promise be realized.

## References

Bennett, N. (1976). *Teaching styles and pupil progress*. Open Books.

Berliner, D.C., & Rosenshine, B. (1977). The acquisition of knowledge in the classroom. In R. Anderson & W. Montague (Eds.)., *Schooling and the acquisition of knowledge.* Hillside, NJ: Lawrence Erlbaum.

Bowles, S., & Ginlis, H. (1975). *Schooling in capitalist America*. London: Routledge and Kegan Paul.

Boydell, D. (1981). Classroom organizalion 1970-7. In B. Simon & J. Willcocks (Eds.). *Research and practice in the primary classroom*. London: Routledge and Kegan Paul.

Bruner, J. (1960). *The process of education*. Boston: Harvard University Press.

Bruner, J. (1966). *Towards a theory of instruction*. Boston: Harvard University Press.

Department of Education and Science. (1983). *9-13 Middle schools: An illustrative survey*. London: Her Majesty's Stationery Office.

Department of Education and Science. (1985). *Education 8-12 in combined and middle schools*. London: Her Majesty's Stationery Office.

Doyle, W. (1979). *The tasks of learning*. Paper presented at the annual meeting of the American Educational Research Association, San Francisco, California.

Dunkin, M.J., & Biddle, B.J. (1974). *The study of teaching*. New York: Holt, Rinehart and Winston.

Elliott, J. (1980). Implications of classroom research for professional development. In E. Hoyle & J. Megarry (Eds.). *Professional development of teachers, world year book of education 1980*. Kogan Page.

Elliott, J. (1985). *Teacher evaluation and teaching as a moral science*. Available from School of Education, University of East Anglia, Norwich, England.

Galton, M., Simon, B., & Croll, P. (1981). *Inside the primary classroom*. London: Routledge and Kegan Paul.

Ginsburg, M.B., Meyenn, R.J., Miller, H. & Ranceford-Hadley, C. (1977). *The role of the middle school teacher*. Aston Educational Monograph Number 7, University of Aston in Birmingham, England.

Hargreaves, A., & Tickle, L. (Eds.). (1980). *Middle schools: Origins, ideology and practice*. London: Harper and Row.

Hargreaves, D. (1982). *The challenge for the comprehensive school*. London: Routledge and Kegan Paul.

Meyenn, R.J., & Tickle, L. (1980). The transition model of middle schools. In A. Hargreaves and L. Tickle (Eds.), *Middle schools: Origins, ideology and practice*. London: Harper and Row.

Peterson, P.L. (1979). Direct instruction: Effective for what and for whom? *Educational Leadership, 37*, 46-48.

*Les Tickle* teaches at the University of East Anglia, Norwich, England.

# Rethinking the middle school curriculum

*James A. Beane*

E fforts to reform middle level education have made considerable progress in the last thirty years, particularly those having to do with developing more widespread awareness of the characteristics of early adolescence and reorganizing institutional features such as school climate. Important as these are, the movement has been seen by many as limited to these kinds of changes and, in fact, many schools presently involved in the initial stages of reorganization simply seek to replicate common structural features of other middle schools—interdisciplinary team organization, block schedules, advisory programs, activities programs, and so on. In this search for improved middle level education a central question in this or any other kind of school reform has been obscured, namely, ***What should be the planned curriculum of the middle school?***

The importance of the curriculum question cannot be overestimated since it opens up the way to several key issues that are only partially addressed by structural reform. For example, if the middle school is to be based upon the characteristics of early adolescence, then the curriculum ought to be redesigned along developmentally appropriate lines rather than simply a slightly revised version of the traditional high school curriculum.

Furthermore, if reform means that the relations among schools, teachers, and young people are to be reconstructed, then the planned curriculum itself, as one of the powerful mediating forces in that

Originally published in the *Middle School Journal*,
Vol. XXI, No. 5, pp. 1-5, May 1990.

relationship, must also change. In other words, being sensitive to early adolescent characteristics is only a part of reform. The *how to teach* question must be accompanied by a *what do we teach and learn* question.

In opening up the question of the middle school curriculum we face what is sure to be a more perilous journey than the one taken to date. The reform movement has probably succeeded partly because it has not been attached to any larger social issues that might conflict with special, dominant interests in the larger society and partly because it has not taken on substantive curriculum change that would touch deep subject loyalties held by educators both inside and outside middle schools.

This is not to say that the curriculum question has been entirely ignored. As early as the 1960s, theorists like Donald Eichhorn (1966), William Alexander and his colleagues (1968), and Theodore Moss (1969) promoted thinking about the curriculum in terms of the characteristics of early adolescence. However, in the final analysis, these and other more recent works ended up modifying the usual subjects rather than offering some uniquely middle school conceptions of the curriculum.

Set against this backdrop are only a handful of alternative views. John Lounsbury and Gordon Vars (1978), building upon earlier attempts to reform the junior high school, proposed a "core" based upon personal-social problems while Chris Stevenson (1987) described a curriculum developed with students using their own life experiences. John Arnold (1985) and Edward Brazee (1989) stopped short of describing an alternative curriculum, but called for serious rethinking and delineated some of the principles that might be used to do so.

Making decisions about what ought to form the basis for the middle school curriculum, or any curriculum for that matter, involves making choices from the array of possible interpretations about what is important. The present state of middle school curriculum represents something of a failure of nerve in this matter. That is, the planned curriculum of a growing number of middle schools consists of a collection of specific programs intended to meet all expectations— interdisciplinary teams to create subject area correlations but still based on subject area identities, exploratory courses to cover aesthetic and technical concerns, advisory programs to address personal-social development of early adolescents, and so on. While such a program helps to maintain an "acceptable" equilibrium among competing interests, it also creates a fragmented program without any coherent or broadly unifying theme. In other words, the middle school curriculum is not really a "curriculum" in the sense of having some clearly identifying purpose or theme that grows out of a widely held definition of what middle level education ought to be about.

That this description seems harsh does not reduce the fact that it is largely an accurate picture of more than a little of what is the middle school curriculum experienced by many early adolescents. Nor can it simply be blamed on teachers and other local educators since they are often caught in the web of competing expectations and regulations. However, such a picture, true as it is, can help us to understand that in the wide array of topics that have been addressed by middle school theory, it is the organizational and climate aspects that have been taken most seriously while the curriculum remains thoroughly problematic.

## A different view

I want to propose that the middle school curriculum ought to be based upon the idea that the primary purpose of the middle school itself should be general education: that is, education that is concerned with the common needs and interests of young people. By this I do not mean simply the momentary interests of early adolescents, although they do enter the picture, but rather the shared interests they have as individuals and as participants in the larger world. Emphasis here is placed on the concept of *common* interests or needs as opposed to those that are specialized along the lines of possible future career or educational predictions made by the school.

Early adolescents are in a stage of dramatic change: certainly they are no longer young children, but neither are they full adolescents who are nearing the end of secondary education and coming increasingly closer to the actuality of their post-secondary plans. Thus, the idea of specialization is neither timely nor appropriate for early adolescents.

Moreover, the specialized and fragmented curriculum form now found in the overwhelming majority of middle schools is based upon the very tenuous assumption that the content found in separate and distinct subject areas reflects the *common and shared interests and needs* of early adolescents. The fact is that the subject area curriculum is more accurately reflective of the interests of scholars and other academic specialists whose influence has relentlessly pervaded the schools for several centuries.

Outside of their limited world, the common and shared interests and needs of people are actually found in the personal and social issues that arise in the course of their lives and which are derived from the related concerns for self-actualization and the common good.

How then, we might ask, has the subject area approach to the curriculum held up for so long? After all, since the early 1940s (Aiken, 1941) we have been getting clear signals that the subject approach does not measure up well with other approaches, even in its claims regarding preparation for further education. Here, I think, we come up against two powerful forces. One is that the subject does not measure up well with other approaches, even in its claims regarding preparation for further education.

Here, I think, we come up against two powerful forces. One is that the subject area approach is what people generally believe is *the* way that the curriculum is supposed to be organized. Second, within the profession itself, the subject approach constitutes the structural constant in the symbiotic relationship among schools, universities, state departments (including certification bureaus), commercial text and testing concerns, and other education elites. Even the widely applauded Carnegie report (1988) suggested that improving health and fitness was desirable so as to improve academic performance. Furthermore, to think that the formation of the subjects and the relationships they undergird did not involve a highly political struggle (Kliebard, 1986; Apple, 1986; Popkewitz, 1987) is to miss the point that the subject approach is, after all, only tenuously defended on educational grounds.

In criticizing curriculum organization around subject areas, I do not want to imply that the content they include, or at least some of it, is not important enough to bring to the attention of early adolescents. Indeed, the concepts and skills involved in various subject areas constitute a good deal of what we know about ourselves and our world as well as the ways of exploring meanings and new understandings and of communicating with each other. Instead, I want to argue that the subject approach is only one way of organizing such content and skills, that the content usually associated with these areas is not necessarily all that is known, and that the subject approach limits access to content and meanings beyond the particular areas themselves.

Nor do I want to denigrate the efforts within many middle schools to break the stranglehold of the separate subject approach through interdisciplinary curriculum units. Yet we must admit that the reasons behind such efforts are not necessarily widely understood, even by some of those actually involved in them and, moreover, the overwhelming number of these cases retain subject area identification in constructing only mild correlations among subject areas. Perhaps what is called *interdisciplinary* curriculum in most of these cases might more accurately be called *multidisciplinary* instruction.

## A middle school curriculum

What, then, might present a more appropriate and defensible curriculum for the middle school? If we return to the concept of the middle school as a general education program, the larger question turns on what we take to be the common, shared interests of young people to be. Here, two sources surface. One is the needs, interests, problems, and concerns that emerge in the lives of early adolescents as a result of developmental characteristics at that stage (Beane & Lipka, 1987) and the interactions they have with the particular environments in which they live; that is, those concerns that are personal and immediate.

The second is needs, interests, problems, and concerns that emerge from the fact that early adolescents are people who do and will live in a larger world in which self and social interests are inextricably intertwined in the fate of the common good; that is, concerns that arise from immediate and distant relationships in the social world.

To clarify this concept, and without pretending to be exhaustive, several examples might be helpful. Personal concerns of early adolescents include such themes as understanding the particular stage they are in and dealing with the changes it involves, developing a sense of personal identity, finding a place in the peer group, dealing with multiple expectations in the home, school, and other settings, developing independence from adult authority figures, responding to the dizzying array of commercial interests that are aimed at them, and exploring topics of personal interest.

Social concerns include such themes as global interdependence, cultural diversity, environmental problems, economic issues, political processes and structures, and the place of technology in various aspects of life. Obviously these social concerns are not necessarily recognized by all early adolescents, but they do represent issues that enter into their lives now and quite likely will do so in the future, regardless of the paths their lives take individually.

An examination of the examples in each type reveals considerable overlap among them. More specifically, concerns in the personal and social areas are often micro or macro representations of each other. Such, for example, is the relationship between self-esteem and collective efficacy, between finding a place in the group and pursuing global interdependence, between earning status in the group and respecting cultural diversity, between physical wellness and environmental improvement, between understanding developmental changes and conceptualizing a society and world in transition, and between developing independence and larger struggles for human rights. Taken this way, themes that are found at the intersections of personal and social concerns, like *transitions, wellness, interdependence,* and *commercialism,* offer a promising possibility for identifying the interests of early adolescents and of the larger world. Thus, they present a justifiable version of what ought to be meant by general education in the middle school.

To fully explore themes such as these, early adolescents need to apply a variety of skills. Among these, of course, are many of the usual skills promoted in middle schools, such as those involved in communications, computation, and researching. However, since a living curriculum calls for more than just *knowing,* other less commonly emphasized skills are also called for: valuing, problem solving, reflective thinking (critical and creative), critical ethics (identifying the morality in problem situations), and social action skills.

Although both kinds of skills are presently promoted in middle schools, they are most often taught in separate parts of the program and in isolation from their use, as if they were ends in themselves. I want to propose that such skills are worthwhile only when they are actually applied to real situations and, further, that they are most likely to be learned when they are so applied. Thus, the skills named here, and others like them, ought to be applied across a curriculum that emerges from the personal-social issues that ought to form the basis for the middle school curriculum.

Skeptics of this and other parts of this proposal may argue that this is impossible since many early adolescents do not have these skills and would have to learn them first, before undertaking projects where they are needed. However, we might hypothesize first, that early adolescents may not have the skills for precisely the reason that they have been taught in isolated parts of the program where they are removed from functional application and second, that because the use of such skills is only connected to subject areas that typically do not engage young people in meaningful ways, some early adolescents may have these skills but simply not demonstrate them.

## Thematic units as major component

Given this view, it is now possible to create a picture of how the middle school curriculum might begin to take shape. The main component would consist of thematic units whose organizing centers are drawn from the intersecting concerns of early adolescents and issues in the larger world. Across the units opportunities would be planned to develop and apply the various skills identified including those usually emphasized in the middle school and those that are called "desirable" but are typically found only on the periphery of the curriculum, if they are present at all. At the same time such concepts as cultural diversity, human dignity, democracy, and the search for explanations would be brought to life in both the content of units and the processes used to carry them out.

We can begin to imagine early adolescents engaged in a unit on *human relationships* studying the peer group structure in the school and community, investigating how societies and cultures are formed, exploring ways of promoting global interdependence, participating in service projects to help elders in the community, and interviewing people about how technology has changed their relationships with others.

We can picture a unit on *environmental problems* in which early adolescents develop a school recycling program, learn about the scientific aspects of pollution, investigate environmental regulations and their relationship to business practices, explore how various countries approach environmental issues, and plot correlations between pollution and health problems in various regions.

We can imagine a unit on *living in the future* where early adolescents develop scenarios on what they consider desirable personal and social futures, recommend ideas for improving their communities, learn about biotechnical developments, investigate work trends, and debate the moral issues of advancing technology. And we can picture a unit on *independence* that involves examining conflicts with authority figures in the community and school, identifying the historic causes of national revolutions, analyzing the commercial media's pressure to conform, and studying movements for human and civil rights.

In each case we can also imagine early adolescents reading, tabulating data from surveys, researching information, thinking about consequences of decisions, formulating hypotheses, listening to the ideas of others, constructing models, artistically displaying ideas, writing reports, and examining ethical issues—in other words, developing and applying a wide array of skills. And we can easily see how such a curriculum creates a sense of unity and coherence among the concepts and skills the school seeks to promote.

Lest my intention be misunderstood here, I am proposing that such a curriculum replace the present collection of academic and "special" subjects that now make up the school program. I mean that this version of general education should become *the* curriculum in the middle school. In this sense I am departing from other proposals that have recommended such general education for a part of a school program (sometimes called *the problems core*), although I am also building from some aspects of those. As such proposals typically include additional study in separate subject areas, they too kindly accede to the special interests of subject specialists and our own history tells us that those other parts eventually wash away the general education program in a bath of academic rhetoric.

Beyond the curriculum I have described, it is possible that the middle school would also offer a school-sponsored activities program, including clubs and intramurals as well as opportunities for participation in such activities as school governance. However, such programs as physical education, advisory, and other specials might more appropriately be integrated into ongoing units.

## The practical arena

Proposals such as the one I am making often disappear almost as quickly as they are made. This is partially due to attempts to envision implementation of a new curriculum within the categories and structures of present practice. This proposal is surely open to such a risk since it is meant to transcend present practice. Thus I will attempt to anticipate reactions with a few ideas about practical matters.

The ideas described above suggest a way of thinking about curriculum rather than defining specific details. Before any action is taken we need to open a dialogue about the middle school curriculum in which a broad spectrum of people are involved: educators inside and outside the middle school, parents and other community representatives, and early adolescents themselves.

The selection of particular themes and curriculum development around them ought to be done by local educators who are in touch with particular early adolescents. While the conception of the curriculum might be common across schools, actual unit themes, sub-topics, and activities might look quite different from school to school depending upon concerns of local early adolescents, available resources, and other factors. Local planning is also necessary if the collaboration between teachers and early adolescents implied by the general themes themselves is to become a reality.

This description of a desirable curriculum also suggests that teachers be repositioned in relation to the themes rather than separate subjects. A small group of teachers might stay with a particular group of early adolescents for all three or four years of the middle level school and work through a series of units with them. Some teachers might work with particular units with different groups of students or some teachers might work individually with units in a self-contained setting. Again, such matters need to be decided locally and would likely be different from school to school.

Of course any "new" curriculum would also require rethinking the institutional features of the school. For example, the one I have proposed clearly implies the use of heterogeneous grouping as it dissolves the already questionable argument for homogeneous grouping based upon academic differences that are created among early adolescents by the subject curriculum itself. Arrangements such as *gifted and talented* and *remedial* classes would be eliminated as variability in activities and materials is developed within thematic units. So too traditional procedures for evaluating and reporting the work of students would need to be reformed as would relations with the community school schedules, allocation of resources, and so on.

Before considering these concerns, however, middle level educators would need to publicly articulate the reasons behind such a curriculum so as to gain widespread understanding of its possibilities. Yet if the middle school movement has really generated the enthusiasm and commitment that its advocates claim, all of this may well be possible. Moreover, I believe that such a curriculum would have more than a few supporters in the community especially since not all parents are thoroughly enamored with the academic push so common in schools; many know that the problems *of* school are deeper than the rhetoric of popular educational reform.

Finally, I want to make clear that I take the curriculum view proposed here to appropriately apply to other levels of education, not just the middle. However, it is at the middle level that perhaps the greatest progress has been made toward substantive reform in recent years and for which persistent claims regarding progress are made. If such claims are valid and if middle level proponents really believe their own rhetoric, then the road ahead should lead them toward an obvious conclusion—genuine reform along the lines that I have proposed.

## References

Aiken, W. (1941). *The story of the eight year study*. New York: Harper and Row.

Alexander, W.M., Williams, E.L., Compton, M., & Prescott, D. (1968). *The emergent middle school*. New York: Holt, Rinehart and Winston.

Apple, M.W. (1986). *Teachers and texts*. New York: Routledge and Kegan Paul.

Arnold, J. (1985). A responsive curriculum for early adolescents. *Middle School Journal, 16*(3), 14-18.

Beane, J.A., & Lipka, R.P. (1987). *When the kids come first: Enhancing self-esteem* Columbus, OH: National Middle School Association.

Brazee, E.N. (1989). The tip of the iceberg or the edge of the glacier. *Mainely Middle. 1* (1), 18-22.

Carnegie Council on Adolescent Development. (1989). *Turning points: Preparing American youth for the 21st century*. New York: Carnegie Corporation.

Eichhorn, D.H. (1966). *The middle school*. New York: The Center for Applied Research in Education.

Lounsbury, J.H., & Vars, G.F. (1978). *A curriculum for the middle school years*. New York: Harper and Row.

Kliebard, H.M. (1986). *The struggle for the American curriculum: 1893-1958*. Boston: Routledge and Kegan Paul.

Popkewitz, T.S. (1987). *The formation of school subjects: The struggle for creating an American institution*. New York: Falmer.

Stevenson, C. (1986). *Teachers as inquirers: Strategies for learning with and about early adolescents*. Columbus, OH: National Middle School Association.

*James A. Beane teaches for National-Louis University and is headquartered in Madison, Wisconsin.*

# Revolutionary Dialogue

*A fresh start for the middle school curriculum*

*Towards a middle level curriculum rich in meaning*

*You've gotta see the game to see the game*

*Gender issues and the middle school curriculum*

*Preparing prospective middle grades teachers
to understand the curriculum*

*Middle level curriculum:
The search for self and social meaning*

*The Cardigan experience—An eighth grade integrated curriculum*

*Curriculum for identity:  A middle level educational obligation*

*Middle level curriculum:  Making sense*

*The core curriculum in the middle school:  Retrospect and prospect*

*What is your dance?*

*Sexuality education in the middle school curriculum*

*Turning the floor over:  Reflections on A MIDDLE SCHOOL CURRICULUM*

# A fresh start for the middle school curriculum

*John H. Lounsbury*

ully and courageously the middle school curriculum needs to be examined. As Beane (1990) pointed out in *The Middle School Curriculum: From Rhetoric to Reality*, the middle school movement, while chalking up victories on other fronts, has all but ignored the curriculum issue itself. The reality is that American education has continued to give homage to a curriculum that was established in the last century under vastly different circumstances and for a markedly different clientele. It is time to take on this demanding but essential task of reformation. We need to make a fresh start.

Nearly every aspect of curriculum will have to be faced and the inherent questions resolved if the reformation is to succeed. My vision concerning some of the kinds of changes needed, set in a context of urgency and challenge, follow.

To make a fresh start in developing the middle school curriculum we will have to employ zero-based curriculum development in the mode of zero-based budgeting. We can no longer achieve success by simply making further adjustments or refinements in the prevailing program. Simply doing better will not suffice.

Unfortunately, the current curriculum is seen by students as a thing apart. What we have been doing only rarely coincides with the issues that young adolescents are concerned about. Life at school and life outside of school are simply too far apart. We need to go back, then, and build up anew from the foundations of democratic values, social realities, and our knowledge of human growth and development. We have to be free to think outside of and beyond the big four subjects, state courses of study, scope and sequence charts, 45 minute periods, and even state certification.

## *The inadequacy of special programs*

Too long we have tried to meet various student and educational needs by instituting special programs. Surely we now know that we cannot solve educational problems in any enduring fashion by additional separate programs. There are some crises that call for stopgap measures, but we are already program poor, trying, for instance, to juggle schedules to accommodate Chapter requirements, or the pull-out program for the so-called gifted and talented, or setting up separate classes to give instruction in study skills, or even creating advisory periods to meet affective needs.

Now educators have embraced the label "at risk" and have been conjuring up alternative or supplementary programs to try to "save" this recently identified category of students. I do not deny that there is a significant portion of our students unable to profit from the available curriculum, that is an all-too-obvious fact, but the assumption underlying this and other special programs is that the regular program is satisfactory for the rest of the kids—and it is not! We do not need "choice" either. We need a common curriculum for our common clients in our common school, a school in which all Americans can be together and work together, where distinctions based on ability, economic status, national origin, race, religion, or anything else do not predetermine who will experience success. That philosophy was captured beautifully by a simple statement on an automobile dragstrip program which read, "Every effort is made to insure that every entry has a reasonable chance." In such a common curriculum, diversity is dealt with by varied activities and responsibilities rather than by separate programs. It is resource-based not textbook-based. We must remember that the real curriculum, the one the pupil experiences, does not and cannot exist prior to and independent of a particular time and setting. As the curriculum becomes relevant and some success for all becomes available the need for everything from in-school suspension to gifted and talented programs will be eliminated.

And are not all young adolescents at risk as they negotiate this major developmental level? Their inevitable vulnerability is intensified when they receive so little help from family and contemporary society. Then when at risk is defined as "those students whose potential is not nurtured by their educational experiences," nearly all young adolescents are included for very few schools do enough with the humanities, with exploratory experiences, with helping individuals understand the developmental changes they are undergoing, or with assisting them in ascertaining their particular aptitudes and interests. Just as the exploratory responsibilities of the middle school cannot be taken care of in courses labelled *exploratory*, neither can the affective education responsibilities of the school be fulfilled in smidgeons of time labelled *advisory*. Affective concerns and exploratory approaches both need to be integrated fully into all ongoing academic and related activities.

While we have made great strides in organizing teams we must not let up in our efforts to bring wholeness to the educational experiences of youth. Where no teams exist they must be instituted. Where they exist, efforts must be extended so that teaming enters into the instructional program itself. To date, this has seldom happened. Even in many teamed situations the schedule still resembles a page in *TV Guide*, a series of unrelated programs appearing in uniform time blocks. Where the number of teachers on a team is too large, as it usually is in the sixth grade, it ought to be reduced in order to lower the number of different pupils a teacher engages each day while increasing the time that teacher and those students are together.

As we pursue the efforts needed to reform the middle school curriculum and continue to activate interdisciplinary teams there is a danger that we must guard against. The recognition that interdisciplinary instruction is the way to go is bringing about considerable teacher planning of interdisciplinary units. This is certainly appropriate, but there are already indications that a significant aspect of effective learning is being bypassed . Care must be taken lest teachers over-plan and leave no more room for student -teacher planning to occur than presently occurs. Middle school students need to be and should be actively involved in helping to decide what to study and how it might be learned. We needs hands-joined experiences as much as hands-on experiences.

The following generalized set of principles, the original source of which, regrettably, I do not know, may lead one to argue over the specific percentages but its overall message is undeniable and should be taken to heart as we initiate efforts to integrate the curriculum and involve students.

> I remember:
> 10% of what I read
> 20% of what I hear
> 30% of what I see
> 50% of what I see and hear
> 70% of what I discuss with others
> 80% of what I experience by doing
> 95% of what I teach to others.

A prescribed and fully preplanned curriculum counters inevitably real and meaningful learning. And force feeding a canned curriculum to young adolescents is not the way to educate effective, responsible American citizens who will live as adults in a world not yet known.

## School as family

A fresh start will call for us to do still more to provide a continuity of caring, to emulate a sense of family, to create a real learning community. An article written by Leonard Sagan that appeared in *The Sciences* published by the New York Academy of Science was brought to my attention. It dealt with the relationship between family and longevity. The last paragraph presented a significant point that related to the need for middle schools to be as family-like as possible. Specifically, it claimed "Good health is as much a social and psychological achievement as a physical one—and the preservation of the family is not so much a moral issue as a medical one. Unless we recognize the medical importance of the family and find ways to stop its deterioration, we may continue to watch our health expenditures rise and our life spans diminish." Too many young people lack a sense of association and engagement with other individuals, particularly adults. We need schools which encourage meaningful relationships, which foster a sense of community.

As more and more kids are growing up without the nurture of a functional family the provision by the school of a family-like atmosphere becomes more important. Providing pastoral care has always been a part of education, though this responsibility has generally been given little public attention, certainly not comparable to the attention given test scores. Now pastoral care has to be more openly acknowledged as an essential function of our schools.

Establishing close rapport with students is not, however, important simply because of its contribution to meeting psychological needs. Teaming is advocated for what it can do to enhance the school's primary responsibility, academic and intellectual development. We must not overlook that point. But at the same time we must remember that underachievement is not the result of deficiencies in the head so much as it is the result of deficiencies in the heart!

The education of young adolescents must, of course, be an integrated venture; physical, social, emotional, and intellectual development are intertwined and interactive. To rank one dimension above the others, to try to separate them out, is to misunderstand the nature of the 10-14 year old.

## The importance of attitudes and values

I believe further that unless America can be brought to a deeper appreciation of the place of values, attitudes, and the affective domain in public education, reform efforts will fall far short of the success so desperately needed in this last decade of the twentieth century. The separation of church and state never was intended to lead to a divorce of information from values. Unfortunately people continue to talk about training, performance on tests, mastery of discrete subjects, and grades, as if these were the beginnings and ends of education.

Education in its fullest sense has to involve heart as well as mind, attitude as well as information, spirit as well as scholarship. That our nation is suffering from moral leukemia is hard to deny. Our easy sophistication and ample affluence has encouraged much inconsequential living that does little to ennoble humankind, but much to advance hedonism. Eisenhower rightly warned us that "A people that values its privileges above its principles soon loses both." And we are dangerously close to that time. Our educational practices have compounded the ethical decline problem by over-emphasizing the knowledge acquisition objective of education and virtually ignoring in any official way the more important behavioral objectives, other than to report on "conduct," defined simply as the absence of overt misbehavior.

When students do not know important or desirable information, it is certainly a cause for concern, but the kind of ignorance that bothers me most is when they do not know that there are better things and better ways of doing things. When they do not have a sufficient sense of personal or social responsibility to act other than in self interest or to try to see and do better things. We need an education that not only helps people think logically but also helps them think higher. The 3 R's are basic, but they do not constitute an education, any more than the silver, crystal, and china of a place setting comprise a fine dinner. Too much of life today plays up the sordid side of humankind.

A statement made by T.S. Eliot comes to mind in that connection, especially in relationship to TV, MTV, and movies. He said, "Those who say they give the public what it wants begin by underestimating public taste and end by debauching it." I am afraid that is exactly what has happened.

As educators we must accept what Archibald MacLeish called the "terrible responsibility of the teacher"—that moral responsibility to decide and to teach, not merely to select and report, to practice as well as preach. We need teachers who are able to hear what words do not say, and who are willing to act accordingly. We need classrooms in which beauty is savored, truth honored, compassion practiced, and fellowship engendered; classrooms where creativity is encouraged, where youngsters are assisted in dreaming of a better life; classrooms that are laboratories of living rather than places in which teachers stand and talk and students sit and listen.

Young people today are bombarded by an array of conflicting value systems. The family's authority has been diminished; so too has the church's and the community's. We cannot immediately alter that. Young adolescents are nevertheless faced now with developing and confirming their own individual ethical and values code, but find sure models few and far between. All of them need to find their individual ethical anchor in order that their place in the world can be confirmed and the future faced confidently. The school must not attempt to dictate a particular set of values, but it must assist young adolescents in exploring their values, attitudes, and standards.

Each of us has a title. For some it is *teacher*, others *counselor*, others *principal*, others *teacher educator* or *supervisor*. But whether we want it or not, know we have it or not, each of us also carries the title, *professor of ethics*. Middle level teaching is inherently and inevitably a moral enterprise. As L. Thomas Hopkins reminded us a half-century ago, "What a teacher really teaches, is himself."

## Narrow concepts of educational goals

The public school system in the United States, however, has rested on what is, partially at least, a false assumption, as I have already alluded to. The policies that guide the educational enterprise, the plans, the programs, the tests, nearly all aspects of organized education reflect this assumption. Schooling, it is widely assumed, is a matter of acquiring knowledge and that, further, knowledge is power. Human behavior, however, is much more driven by attitudes than by knowledge, by feelings rather than facts. And knowledge, unless appropriately internalized and put into action, is of limited value. The "I will" is as important as the I.Q.

There exists presently an unprecedented adolescent health crisis in our country. It is so serious that the National Commission on the Role of the School and the Community in Improving Adolescent Health entitled their report *Code Blue* (1990). That term denotes a life-threatening emergency, one that brings concerted and immediate action by all hands. A significant thing, however, about today's adolescent health problems unlike fifty years ago when the causes were physical factors, diseases, today's "plagues" are rooted in behaviors rather than physical causes. Drinking, smoking, pregnancy, violence, suicide, all result from overt actions by individuals who choose to engage in practices which all too often result in very serious mental and/or physical health problems. Changed behavior could virtually wipe out all the causes of the present adolescent health crisis. In alleviating this crisis educators are more important than doctors.

Do not jump to the conclusion that I really do not care about students acquiring basic knowledge. To do so would be to make a completely false assumption, although I recognize my apparent obsession with behavior and attitudes rather than knowledge *per se* may lead one to such a conclusion. But I believe firmly that to improve learning, we must improve learners. Improved performance on tests is not separate from and does not precede improved behavior; it more nearly follows, although the two are closely related.

There was a time when schooling was taking shape that formal education was primarily, though never completely, a matter of acquisition of information. Other institutions and aspects of life dealt more with behavior and attitudes and the teacher's head was the best and sometimes the only source of information; but those days are gone forever—and have been gone for decades. Public education now, whether we like it or not, has new responsibilities—life building, character forming, personal growth responsibilities—that cannot be effectively carried out in a system and by a curriculum that was designed for transmitting prescribed knowledge. Increasingly, it is becoming obvious that one's ability to learn outweighs in importance any particular discrete bodies of knowledge that one has learned. And as Sir John Lubbock pointed out, "If we succeed in giving the love of learning, the learning is sure to follow." I also like the desirable condition for education that was stated by George Bernard Shaw when he said, "What we want to see is the child in pursuit of knowledge, and not knowledge in pursuit of the child."

The public school as it has operated is essentially conservative, rather elitist, and heavily reliant on extrinsic motivation in which knowledge does pursue the child and which reflects a rather pessimistic view of human nature. Schooling has been seen primarily as a preparation for a future life, rather than as life itself, yet the school day consumes the bulk of most days and is the largest single occupier of a youngster's time save sleep. *The middle school does not exist to prepare students for high school.* It exists to guide, support, and educate youth during life's most critical phase, a significant and demanding task in and of itself. And if it does that successfully the high school will be negotiated successfully.

So long as we measure the success of our educational efforts on the basis of paper and pencil tests, so long as we let the public continue to assume that the essence of education is in the acquisition of information, so long as we do not directly concern our educational efforts with behavior, so long as we cling to conducting instruction in the middle grades by separate subjects, so long as we restrict our instruction to predetermined content, we shall fail to provide the kind of education needed to succeed in today's world.

Essential to a successful fresh start in reforming the middle school curriculum is a clarification of and a consensus on the attributes we want our graduates to possess—our real educational goals. Assumptions about educational goals being held in common by all teachers are misplaced. In fact, individual teacher's goals and various department goals are often in conflict with those of other teachers and other departments or components. Needed is universal acceptance by all constituencies on a few major beliefs and goals, a true mission. The needed shift from cognitive goals measured by test scores to behavioral ones will require a shift in the nature of the teacher's role. The *fountain of wisdom* will have to give way to the *director of learning*. Selecting the proper means to achieve behavioral objectives then can follow; currently we continue to assume the old means—classes, courses, textbooks—as givens.

## The challenge we face

In education, patience is universally recognized as a key virtue. But there comes a time when patience is no longer a virtue. In middle level education, this is such a time. To produce change, someone has said, "rub raw the sores of discontent." If the current extent of the previously mentioned social pathologies have not rubbed the sores on our body politic raw I do not know what it will take. The misguided and timid reform efforts of the past decades have obviously not gotten to the heart of the matter. Restructuring has become the vehicle for reform in current educational lingo. Restructuring is indeed, needed, but it must be the restructuring of attitudes and assumptions not merely the manipulation of the organizational aspects of education.

The winds of change are blowing across American education. Those of us active in middle level education recognize that these fresh breezes are swirling strongly at our level. We cannot ignore them. Before long each one of us, regardless of our particular position, will have to make a number of decisions that will ultimately fashion us as a soft blade of grass easily bent by the wind whichever way it blows, or like a stiff reed resisting the wind but increasingly vulnerable to breaking, or into one of the huffers and puffers that will help to determine the exact direction the winds will ultimately take.

Would that all of us become sufficiently convinced of the direction that middle school curriculum should take and be willing to take the initiative in implementing that curriculum so that we might be, without exception, among the huffers and puffers that will bring to middle level schools the kinds of educational experiences the critical importance of these formative early adolescence years deserve and the youth now in them so desperately need.

"Dare the school build a new social order?" George Counts asked in 1932. It was a proper question then and it is a proper one now. I, for one, believe the school does have a social and political responsibility to work toward change for the better in our larger society. But recognizing the key role that only the middle school can play in building better human beings perhaps the question might be rephrased to ask: "Does our society dare to build a new order of middle level schools?" We who are in education and who are also citizens can work to answer affirmatively both questions.

As educators who count ourselves among those seriously and intellectually active in middle level education, we have an especially rare opportunity to truly make a difference. We can make the needed fresh start. Despite the discouraging lessons clearly evident when reviewing this century's history of curriculum improvement efforts, I do have real hope and genuine optimism about our ability to institute fundamental change in middle level curriculum.

A part of the reason for my optimism, even in the face of historical reality, is that the middle school movement, unlike the curriculum movement of earlier decades, heavily involves classroom teachers. It is *teachers* who are the only real change agents. Those of us above that level may do a fine job dealing with ideas, but we do not implement those ideas with kids. It takes a teacher to do that. And the middle school movement does include hundreds and hundreds of teachers, teachers who do not feel that they are "just teachers" but who know they are professionals of competence, the front line soldiers in the battle to overcome ignorance and apathy. Facilities matter a little, instructional materials have some importance, curriculum organization certainly matters a good deal, as does administrative leadership, but teachers matter most. So often teachers become frustrated and suffer from a low sense of efficacy. They travel the comfortable pathways of their classrooms with little vision to inspire them and urge them to grow. But the middle school movement has been providing a growing number of teachers with that needed vision and the opportunity to be true professionals whose involvement is sought because of its irreplaceable importance.

I cannot help but be optimistic about our movement's ultimate triumph because of a special condition that I believe prevails. Middle school education simply can not fail. It is based exclusively on the realities of human growth and development, and it is completely compatible with the tenets of our democratic way of life.

In a middle school classroom I visited several years ago was a statement that caught my eye. As a collector of quotes I stopped to copy it. The poster read: "On the plains of hesitation lay the bones of those who—on the road to success—stopped to rest. Resting they died."

In 1933, the principals of the 30 schools that had begun their participation in the Eight Year Study met with the directing Committee. The schools had been given complete freedom to experiment with new ways and new curriculum. On that occasion one principal made a statement that we must consider and face now, 60 years later, when site-based management, faculty empowerment, and autonomous teams are being advocated and established. She said, "My teachers and I do not know what to do with this freedom. It challenges and frightens us. I fear that we have come to love our chains" (Aikin, 1942, p. 16).

## References

Aiken,W. (1942). *The story of the eight year study*. New York: Harper.

Beane, J.A. (1990). *The middle school curriculum: From rhetoric to reality.* Columbus, OH: National Middle School Association.

The National Commission on the Role of the School and Community in Improving Adolescent Health. (1990). *Code blue: Uniting for healthier youth.* Alexandria, VA: National Association of State Boards of Education.

*John H. Lounsbury is Publications Editor, National Middle School Association, Georgia College, Milledgeville.*

Editor's Note: This article is adapted from an address given at NMSA's Minneapolis Conference on Curriculum, May 5, 1991.

# Towards a middle level curriculum rich in meaning

*John Arnold*

L et us say it straight-away: far too often, middle level curriculum is boring. Despite all the good things that are happening in the way of teams, advisories, intramurals, flexible schedules, and overall climate in middle level schools, little improvement has occurred in basic curriculum. Too often students sit in desks bleary-eyed, cranking out worksheets or listening to teachers drone on (and on) about topics which have little significance to anyone, much less young adolescents. Or perhaps they are making sugar-cube igloos, pasting examples of grammar usage they have cut from magazines, or doing some other equally stimulating activity.

Help us!

It is ironic that in all the rhetoric about reform in education, virtually nothing is said about the lack of substance and meaning in curriculum. Yet ask virtually any dropout or disenchanted student what is wrong with education, and these factors will be at the top of the list.

My thesis is an obvious but grossly neglected one: if middle level curriculum is genuinely to educate students, it must have content which is rich in meaning. In elaborating this thesis, I will explore reasons why curricular content is so often devoid of substance, examine characteristics of meaning-full curriculum, and suggest guiding questions for developing such a curriculum.

## *Curriculum neglect and impoverishment*

There are numerous reasons for the general lack of curriculum rich in meaning in middle level education. Prominent among them is the fact that curriculum has been largely neglected by the middle school movement. As noted above, most of our attention has been devoted to improving school organization and climate. There are of course notable exceptions where innovative projects, exploratory courses and inter-disciplinary units have been fashioned (Arnold, 1990), but in terms of day-to-day curriculum, little has changed. And working on the day-to-day curriculum is how students spend most of their time in schools.

It is interesting to speculate as to how much of this neglect may stem from the fact that the middle school movement has been led largely by administrators, not people concerned with curriculum. Administrators better understand and have more control over school organization than curriculum; hence the movement's emphasis on the former.

A result of this neglect is that the middle school movement has been substantially cut off from the mainstream of curriculum theory and development. Seldom is a Dewey or Bruner, a McDonald or Freiere referred to in the literature; discussions related to the nature of knowledge, the structure and role of the disciplines, equity, and empowerment are largely non-existent.

The lack of clarity about the crucial relationship between content and process in curriculum development is symptomatic of our isolation from the mainstream. One of the most gifted middle level teachers in this country recently said to me, "I'm a process person. Content really doesn't matter. It's the way kids do things that matters." I in no way wish to deny the importance of methodology in relationship to curriculum and have focused heavily upon it elsewhere (Arnold, 1984; 1985). However, I believe the quotation is fundamentally off-base. Content and process are inextricably bound. I think what the teacher really meant to say was, "I'm such a good teacher that I can get kids turned on to a lot of topics because I have a good sense of what's important and worth knowing in life. I can help students apply important principles to numerous endeavors."

The attempt to separate content and process, or to make one subservient to the other, belies a faulty epistemology. James (1974) tells us that knowledge involves both question (process) and answer (content). One of the major faults of schooling, and perhaps a reason why content tends to be denigrated, is that we are constantly giving students answers to questions that they have not asked. Such practice involves students with information, not knowledge, and breaks the fundamental unity of content and process. Reading provides another example. In and of itself, skill (process) in reading is of no avail if one does not actually read something (content). And what that content is matters. An educated person knows how to learn, but also knows about significant issues and ideas.

The near universal tendency for middle level curriculum to focus upon the traditional disciplines is another critical source of difficulty. Whereas the disciplines may be a useful way to organize certain types of information, it is not at all clear that they provide the best vehicle for teaching young adolescents. Where they are taught in a conventional manner, much time is spent on irrelevant information while topics of vital concern which do not fit neatly into any discipline, as well as connections among ideas, are ignored.

In addressing this issue recently, Beane (1990) argues forcefully for a curriculum organized entirely around broad themes related to adolescent and societal concerns. While this proposal has a great deal to recommend it, I do not believe the disciplines can be entirely abandoned. Much in mathematics, foreign language, and studio art, for example, does not fit easily into a theme approach and will be lost or distorted. An alternative is James' (1972) four-fold curriculum, which includes: (a) interdisciplinary inquiry, in large blocks of time on a regular basis; (b) autonomous studies, where single disciplines are taught, but not necessarily on a daily basis; (c) "orbital," or special interest studies; and (d) remedial and enrichment activities. Surely the role of the disciplines and of interdisciplinary endeavors is worthy of much deliberation.

Most of the problems related to curriculum are not unique to grades 5-8; they exist throughout the K-12 continuum. One such problem is the pervasive influence of textbooks which too often shun controversy for fear of offending and losing sales; tell you more about penguins than you care to know; fail to distinguish important from unimportant ideas; and conceive of learning as the ingestion and regurgitation of facts. Sadly, studies (Goodlad, 1984) show that the content learned in school is almost entirely confined to that contained in textbooks.

Perhaps the most powerful force negatively influencing curriculum is our obsession with measurement. In a perverted attempt to be objective and accountable, we have trivialized curriculum by emphasizing only those things which can be broken down into small units, tested, and marked right or wrong. As a result, in lieu of reading and discussing books, writing meaningful prose, and engaging in inquiry and problem solving, students often are relegated to answering multiple choice questions about short paragraphs they have been assigned, doing grammar exercises, and working on drills.

One of the driving forces behind the testing mania is the profusion of state and local curricular mandates, usually geared to minimal measurable competencies. Where mandates flourish, teacher initiative and control over curriculum tends to decline. However, I think it is fair to point out that these forces are often used as crutches.

Textbooks are not the mandated curriculum in any state; the state course of study is. Thus all material in texts need not be covered. Though state guidelines must be met, these are often stated in terms of skills or concepts, giving considerable leeway with regard to curricular content. Further, highly innovative teaching and good test scores are not mutually exclusive. Where students are challenged to think, they do well on tests. Outstanding teachers have always manipulated external forces in a manner that allows them to teach what they deem important. The pity is that it takes additional energy which could be put to much better use elsewhere.

## Curriculum rich in meaning

While the phrase "curriculum rich in meaning" could be defined in numerous ways and elaborated upon indefinitely, I wish to suggest three major characteristics it embodies.

First, and quite obviously, it deals with material which is genuinely important and worth knowing. True, there will be disagreements over what is important, and this will vary from situation to situation. However, Bloom (1987) pointedly asks that if we have no idea about what is important in life, how can we possibly presume to educate anyone? The argument here is neither for a body of knowledge developed by dead white men which everyone should know, nor for "political correctness." Rather, it is for exploring substantive ideas, in the process examining what people from all walks of life have to say about them. Clearly it is more important to learn about principles of democracy than the state flower and motto; to understand the concept of ratio than to memorize an algorithm for reducing fractions. The great themes in literature such as compassion, death, and destiny, issues of justice, freedom and equality, and the fate of our environment are but a few of the topics that virtually everyone would agree are worth studying. This of course is true only if topics are taught in an appropriate manner, a matter to be discussed later.

Important perspectives on what is important and worth knowing are found in the work of Bruner and Dewey. Bruner (1960) insists that structure must be taught. Structure conveys the way thing are related, a fundamental understanding of the underlying principles of a subject. Structure not only helps explain a subject, it aids in retaining what we have learned, enhances the transfer of learning to other topics, and helps us to have intuitive insights within and across disciplines.

Dewey (1938) reminds us that important ideas and experiences open doors to new learning. Contrary to popular belief, Dewey did not say that "we learn from experience;" he said that we learn from good experiences, that is, those that lead to future growth and development. Some ideas, such as "drugs are cool" or that unbridled greed is a "virtue" are clearly miseducative; they close doors to fruitful growth instead of opening them. The capable teacher for Dewey is the one who knows which experiences and ideas are genuinely educative and who can engage students productively in exploring them.

The power of important ideas that are worth learning is witnessed by the fact that seventh graders scarcely capable of reading have managed to complete and comprehend *The Autobiography of Malcolm X* because of its compelling content. Further, one of the chief findings of Oakes' (1985) study of tracking is that curriculum which has personal significance for students is a key to moving from homogeneous to heterogeneous grouping.

Second, meaningful curriculum deals effectively with values. The emphasis must not be upon brainwashing students with the teacher's views or a particular ideology, nor is it upon espousing the moral relativity found in values clarification approaches. Rather it is to have students reflect upon issues and ideas studied, asking questions such as, *What do I personally think about this issue? Are particular positions relative to it right or wrong? Why ?* In doing such reflecting universal principles of justice such as those described by Kohlberg (1975), Rawls (1971), and others must be drawn upon.

Though many insist that morality is relative to what individuals or cultures believe is right, such a posture is ultimately naive and perilous. To hold this view is to believe that if Hitler thought it right to kill six million Jews, it was right simply because he believed it to be so. While it may be difficult at times to apply ethical principles which lead to clear cut answers, this does not mean such principles do not exist, or that some applications are not more just than others. There is universal support for virtues and principles related to caring about others, to not willfully injuring others, to being honest, to having integrity, and a host of other values. To make everything relative seems a cop-out on personal responsibility and a highly miseducative approach to teaching.

Should anyone doubt our need for moral education, let them peruse Patterson and Kim's (1991) *The Day America Told the Truth,* which shows that 74% of adults say they would steal from those who really do not need it, that 64% would lie when it suits them, and that for $10 million, 25% would abandon their entire family and 7% would murder a stranger.

To those who maintain that teaching values will arouse too much controversy from parents and community groups, it must be asked, "How can we genuinely educate *without* teaching values?" The term moral education is a redundant one in that a chief goal of education has always been moral, that is, to create good people. Moreover, we constantly teach values whether we intend to or not by means of the content we choose or do not choose, the questions we ask, body language and expression, school rules, and other variables. To focus on values does not mean to create a storm about every touchy issue that exists in a community (there is such a thing as enlightened self-interest). Some must be dealt with, yes, but there are also many pro-social values with which the community wants students to be engaged. And because values engage students at such a deep and personal level, they are keys to motivating them to explore important ideas and concepts in curriculum.

Third, for curriculum to be rich in meaning, both its content and methodology must relate substantively to the needs and interests of young adolescents. Unfortunately, developmental responsiveness has become a cliche; it is bandied about but seldom understood or applied to curriculum. Text after text begins with a discussion of young adolescent characteristics, but in the pages dealing with curriculum that follow, there is no connection with these characteristics. Again, a school will have a flowery mission statement about developmental responsiveness, but its practice amounts to little more than a few hands-on activities, an occasional field trip, a dash of Piagetian jargon, and business as usual.

It is for these reasons that developmental responsiveness is approached only after a discussion of important ideas and values in curriculum. Developmental responsiveness is not something that can be substituted for important ideas and values; it must be skillfully interwoven with them for curriculum to be rich in meaning.

As I have written at some length elsewhere (Arnold, 1984; 1985), the content of a truly responsive curriculum must deal with young adolescents' own questions, not just those posed by texts and teachers. Especially, it must help them to make sense of themselves and the world about them. Some of the topics most appropriate to that task include helping students to understand their changing bodies and emotions; sexuality; sex roles; parent and peer relationships; being an individual and part of a group without losing one's soul in the process; the changing aspects of competency; issues of identity—who am I? what can I be? should I be? should I do?; rules and authority; personal values and shades of grey; competition and cooperation; conflict resolution; adolescence in other cultures; and adolescence itself.

Too often curricular efforts ignore societal forces which interact with development. To cite but two examples: adolescents raised in a society where there are few ways to contribute positively to that society find it difficult to feel useful or needed; those bombarded by advertisements portraying adolescents with perfect features can scarcely keep from feeling insecure about their changing bodies. Where curriculum neglects these social forces, teachers understanding of development is distorted and much information potentially rich in meaning to students is lost.

In terms of methodology, developmental responsiveness also involves gearing curriculum to students' levels of understanding. Particularly important here is the recognition that most young adolescents are in transition from concrete to abstract thinking, but are still most at home with concrete thought. This implies that as we attempt to help students make this transition, we need to use lots of manipulative materials, demonstrations, and making/doing activities; engage students in community service experiences; emphasize inquiry and problem finding/solving; offer choices relative to content, method, time, and mode of presentation; and provide varying degrees of structure.

A major difficulty arises where curricular relevance becomes an end in itself. While curriculum should build upon the needs and interests of young adolescents, it must not be confined to them. Teachers must expand these interests, and relate them to other topics; they must stretch and extend students. At the same time, they must build new interests, for as mentioned earlier, education is a matter of opening doors.

As Dewey (1902) said better than anyone in his timeless essay, *The Child and the Curriculum*, education is not a matter of the child versus the curriculum; both the needs of the child and the nature of curriculum must be taken into account. Yet this accommodation is not a simple one. On the one hand the child (and young adolescent) is largely preoccupied with self, is wedded to the concrete, has a short attention span, and seeks immediate gratification. On the other hand the various disciplines, as repositories of the wisdom of the ages, are organized from an adult perspective and extend far beyond students' interests and frames of reference. Where child-centered education dominates, there is risk that students will be "spoilt," lacking in rigor and well-developed skills and interests. Where subject centered education dominates, the risk is that education becomes rigid and irrelevant, producing apathy.

To resolve the dilemma, Dewey tells us two things must happen: (1) On the subject side, the disciplines must be "psychologized" to coincide with students' levels of understanding and frames of reference. (2) On the student side, it must be shown that the disciplines emerged in response to human questioning through using the same sensory apparatus and thought processes that students have or are developing. The basic principles and internal logic of the disciplines must come alive. For example, to understand mapping, students might best begin by seeking to make simple scale maps of their classrooms or school grounds. At the same time, they must be led to understand that the advanced maps in books emerged from explorers engaging in activities similar to, but more complex than these exercises.

Clearly, developmentally responsive teaching is demanding, requiring effective teachers who can think on their feet. While good curriculum materials and ideas are surely preferable to poor ones, none are teacher proof. Meaningful curriculum requires an interactive process between teacher and student in which teachers must be able to observe, assess, prod, see new opportunities, help students make connections, and engage in a host of other complex tasks.

## Questions to guide curriculum development

In working with teachers to develop curriculum which embodies many of the principles set forth above, I often suggest that they use four straight forward questions to guide their thinking. I will briefly illustrate how they might be used in a study of the Great Depression as part of an American history course or a topic for interdisciplinary inquiry.

### (1) What are the really important issues/ideas/concepts/principles involved in the topic?

While chronology, statistics, names of New Deal agencies and the like should not be neglected, neither should they become the chief focus of attention. Issues related to causes of the Depression, to poverty, greed, loss of hope, suffering and courage, the nature and assessment of the New Deal, its accomplishments and legacy, the proper role of government in society, and the leadership and heroism of FDR are but a few of the "big ideas" around which curriculum might be developed.

### (2) What major values/ethical issues are involved?

The entire topic is of course value-laden. In addition to assessing the justice of various decisions, policies and outcomes related to the Depression, value questions must elicit students' personal feelings and beliefs. If poverty, for example, is to be addressed in depth, we need to explore with students questions such as, *What do I personally feel and believe about poverty? Why is my family poor and others well off, or vice versa? How does this affect me? How equitable is the distribution of wealth in our society? How does this compare to other societies? If a particular policy is adopted, who is affected? Who wins and who loses? Is this good or bad? Why? What alternatives are there? What should we do?* Clearly this must be done in a thoughtful manner, with arguments and opinions backed by available facts, with openness to diverse viewpoints, and with particular attention paid to students' level of moral reasoning.

**(3) *How does this topic relate to students' lives here and now, and how can this relation be extended?***

Unless issues related to historical topics can be used to inform the present and guide the future, they are of little concern to anyone but historians. And owing to the immediacy and concreteness of most young adolescents' interests, it is usually wise to begin with the present. Numerous comparisons of students' own living conditions with those of adolescents who lived during the Depression thus need constant comparison, as implied above. Since homelessness has much in common with certain conditions during the Depression and is an issue with which students are familiar, it might serve as a starting point for delving into poverty issues. Similarities and differences between homelessness and the plight of the destitute during the Depression might then be drawn.

**(4) *How can we develop activities that stimulate inquiry, promote first-hand knowledge, and encourage expression, taking into account questions 1-3?***

Developing substantive activities is by far the most important step in this process, for activities are what students actually do. If activities are poor, little learning will occur regardless of the quality of our rationale and objectives. Focusing only on homelessness, some activities which meet the spirit of this question might include interviewing homeless people and/or people who lived through the Depression, presenting findings and interpretations through a videotape or slide show; compiling a book of community resources which deal with the homeless; searching local archives for stories written during the Depression and creating a newspaper; surveying and analyzing attitudes toward poverty among classmates and in the community.

While space considerations limit full elaboration of how these questions might be used in guiding curriculum development, I trust this brief outline conveys some of the flavor and potential of such an approach.

Too often young adolescents perceive that curriculum has nothing to do with them; there is nothing that excites their passions. It is viewed as something done to them, a series of hoops to jump through for extrinsic rewards. We need a vision of curriculum that enables them to see that the world is full of exciting ideas and that education might make them a more vital, interested, and interesting person. We need a curriculum rich in meaning.

# References

Arnold, J. (1984). Progressive education and qualitative reform. *Private School Quarterly,* Summer, 16-21.

Arnold, J. (1985). A responsive curriculum for emerging adolescents. *Middle School Journal,* 16(3), 3,14-18.

Arnold, J. (1990). *Visions of teaching and learning: 80 innovative middle level projects.* Columbus, OH: National Middle School Association.

Beane, J. A. (1990). *A middle school curriculum: From rhetoric to reality.* Columbus, OH: National Middle School Association.

Bloom, A. (1987). *The closing of the American mind.* New York: Simon and Schuster.

Bruner, J. S. (1960). *The process of education.* Cambridge: Harvard University Press.

Dewey, J. (1902). *The child and the curriculum* . Chicago: University of Chicago Press.

Dewey, J. (1938). *Education and experience.* New York: McMillan.

Goodlad, J. (1984). *A place called school.* New York: McGraw-Hill.

James, C. (1972). *Young lives at stake.* New York: Agathon.

James, C. (1974). *Beyond customs: An educator 's journey.* New York: Agathon.

Kohlberg, L. (1975). The cognitive-developmental approach to moral education. *Phi Delta Kappan, 56,* 670-677.

Oakes, J. (1985). *Keeping track: How schools structure inequality.* New Haven: Yale University Press.

Patterson, J., & Kim, P. (1991). *The day America told the truth.* New York: Prentice-Hall.

Rawls, J. (1971). *A theory of justice.* Cambridge: Harvard University Press.

*John Arnold* *teaches at North Carolina State University, Raleigh.*

# You've gotta see the game to see the game
*Chris Stevenson*

*Vignette*

Patty and Erica, seventh graders, use crude but accurate homemade calipers to measure the thickness of leading and trailing edges of the ailerons and elevators on a red and white Piper Cherokee, a four seat airplane housed at their community airport. They have calculated wingspan and maximum rib circumference; now they are sketching and measuring functional components of the wing assembly. Mr. Morris, the Cherokee's owner, demonstrates how his movement of the yoke (control wheel) affects the wing surface which in turn determines how the plane will perform in flight. Soon the girls will take their data and information back to the classroom where they and several classmates who are also studying flight will create a display of air travel in their community, prepare a technical presentation of concepts about flight, and compile a book of related human interest essays and anecdotes.

This work is one part of an interdisciplinary study of transportation. Some of Patty and Erica's classmates are studying the railroad that has existed in their town for 150 years. Although passenger service is no longer available, some local retired railroad workers and the public library's turn-of-the-century newspaper accounts of rail travel illustrate vividly what was historically the primary mode of long distance travel. Still other students are interviewing truck drivers—contract carriers for a local freight line as well as ones who own their rigs and haul independently. The students begin to comprehend the complex of considerations drivers must make in scheduling and coordinating hauls, selecting routes and travel times, conforming to Interstate Commerce Commission regulations, and considering fuel purchases at prices that often vary from one state to another. They find out special considerations involved in trucking perishable or volatile freight, and they learn the safety regulations truckers observe. They come to appreciate at close range that truck drivers must be good geographers.

Additional small groups of students are also developing components of the unit according to their interests: four students are writing a history of bus travel in their state; another group has traced the history of a local taxi industry from its late 19th century beginnings as a livery to its current fleet of cabs and a more recent foray into limousine service; yet another group is producing a catalog of world travels made by community members. The theme is transportation, and the intellectual engagement is concrete, firsthand, and personal.

## Vignette

Jerry and his fourteen advisees are "Chicagoing." That is to say, they are spending two days and an evening in a Polish neighborhood of their great city. Their purpose is to learn as much as possible about the rich personal and ethnic heritage of the people who live there. After stashing sleeping bags and personal gear at St. Michael's Church where they will sleep that night, a contingent of senior citizens welcomes them to the community center next door. Introductions are quickly made, whereupon each student sits down with one or two senior hosts to begin learning about the neighborhood and Polish heritage. Notes from these discussions will be exchanged later with classmates.

After an hour, Jerry reassembles the students for debriefing and to set an itinerary for the afternoon. Kids pass along suggestions made by their hosts, and in short order a plan is made. Working from a city map of the area, a walking tour is laid out that takes in a variety of shops, historic sites, and especially bakeries. For two hours they explore the neighborhood, making connections between what they were told and what they now see, taking photographs, making sketches, copying signs printed in Polish on storefronts for later translation, and writing assorted notes to help recall the details of their tour. Later they will join a community festival for food, music, polka and more conversations with new friends. The students also sense a growing spirit of collaboration and interdependence among themselves. Feelings of connectedness become palpable.

Saturday morning is the time to begin pulling together the experiences and insights that will become a presentation they will make in two weeks to an assembly of classmates and parents back at their suburban middle school. Jerry helps them identify and organize the things they have learned that they want to share while at the same time helping identify questions and issues to be explored further in the hours left in their visit. These assimilation and classification tasks accomplished, the group returns to the community center and streets to gather what they need.

Peter is an eighth grader on a multi-grade team in a small Vermont town. His team's study of the American Civil War includes a home-school project—a study each student selects and works on with his or her parents. Lacking very much interest in the topic, Peter's beginnings are random and vaguely conceived. After some unsuccessful fishing for possibilities, one of his teachers suggests that he look into Vermonters' participation in that war, knowing that local resources are plentiful and easily accessible. She urges him to telephone the local historical society.

Peter's call strikes paydirt—several books, some primary records, and even a few artifacts which recount the exploits of the Vermont Brigade are available. That evening he and his father find ample information in the town library about the Brigade's formation of farm boys, its long encampment in Washington marked by a mysteriously high noncombat mortality rate there, and its subsequent role in the Battle of the Wilderness in May of 1864. Their special attention is drawn to that campaign since records showed the Brigade suffered 10,000 casualties, many of which occurred in a single afternoon in the little heralded Battle of Orange Plank Road. The librarian offers further that two Brigade casualties from that battle lay buried in the town cemetery.

Peter and his dad become caught up in a shared quest for this history. They visit the two fallen soldiers' graves, noting that just a few feet away is also the grave of another—one who died in Viet Nam. The wars of the world begin to be more personal, and the safety of two neighbors in the Persian Gulf War becomes more urgent to them than had previously been the case. Reflecting on his new knowledge and ideas, Peter decides to build a diorama depicting his ancestors' fierce fighting over 125 years ago in a dense thicket along a temporary road to Orange, Virginia.

## Is it what or how the curriculum should be?

"What should the middle level curriculum be?" is a question fraught with contrasting and sometimes clashing points of view. In recent years educators have sustained some uncommonly hostile fire about students' alleged lack of knowledge (Hirsch, 1987; Ravitch & Finn, 1987). There is a good bit of pressure on us to cover more content faster so that our students might show up better against the rest of the world on standard measures.

Colleagues and parents sometimes confront us with the fervent view that the primary task at the middle level should be to get kids ready for high school. High school colleagues blame us for failing to "give kids the basics." Subject matter specialists especially offer compelling arguments for comprehensive investment in their particular areas of expertise. Most middle level educators with whom I have discussed the issue likewise have earnest convictions about what is essential to teach and for youngsters to know. The problem is that there is simply much more worth doing than circumstances permit. We have to conscientiously and responsibly choose what to do and what not to do. And that is no trivial undertaking.

Many middle level experts argue convincingly that curriculum is the most critical question facing the reconceptualization of middle level schooling and sustaining its reform (Lipsitz, 1984; Arnold, 1985; Beane, 1990). In an earnest attempt to successfully resolve what has become popularized among middle level educators as "the curriculum question," often heroic efforts have been made to posit frameworks which are responsive to the developmental nature and capabilities of young adolescents while at the same time perpetuating the integrity of academic disciplines (James, 1974; Lounsbury & Vars, 1978; Vars, 1987; Beane, 1990). Still, the question presses us, "What should the middle level curriculum be?"

The manner in which the question is framed solicits a direct answer, so I will comply. I contend that there is no single framework, no universal design that will be valid and appropriate for the diverse school contexts that exist. There—I said it. I propose further that the question itself is misleading. The real issue is, "How should the middle level curriculum be?"

Having spent most of my adult life working with young adolescents and their teachers, I have seen that our preoccupation with "what" typically diverts us from the essence of authentic learning: *engagement.* By *engagement* I refer to a *personal intellectual investment in learning* that enhances a youngster's scholarly competence and confidence. Arguments over the merit of a particular topic are moot unless youngsters engage learning in a manner like those depicted in the three opening vignettes. Those particular engagements derived from teachers working singly or in teams to create curriculum designs complementary to students' interests, readiness, and approaches to learning. Those designs were also driven by teachers' visions of what authentic learning looks like.

I know of no more visionary and provocative volume of middle level curriculum than the eighty exemplary projects described in

Arnold's recent book, *Visions of Teaching and Learning* (1990). The projects described in that volume also reflect selected teachers' understanding of engagement as I use it here. Furthermore, those descriptions teach us a great deal more about the "how" than about the "what."

There are manifold answers to the "how" question. The three opening vignettes portray students engaged in a variety of firsthand learning experiences—often referred to as "hands-on learning." But what is absolutely crucial to recognize in those vignettes is that they are *minds-on* engagements. Students' activities were germane to their inquiry; nothing was trivial or contrived as "busywork." It is fundamental that we focus on *how* students were learning in order to comprehend "the real curriculum."

It is easy to recognize when young adolescents are engaged in authentic learning. They talk with each other a lot about what they are doing, and that talk is a young adolescent equivalent of the discourse shared by scientists in a laboratory. Young thinkers ache to flex their growing intellectual muscles. Their talk is problem-centered, speculative, reflective, and often though not always analytical. It reflects high interest, genuine bewilderment, and commitment to resolution. And when learning is at its absolute best, we get glimpses of the manchild and womanchild manifesting newfound intellectual empowerment— an emerging, growing awareness of the intrigue of the world and an appreciation of their personal efficacy. Self respect and dignity also derive from new expertise.

Perhaps the most familiar of all rhetoric associated with the middle level education movement is the appeal for schooling "based on the developmental nature and needs of young adolescents." We also know quite well how widely different youngsters are during these middle years. Given such differences and unpredictability about rate and dimensions of developmental change, how do we go about addressing "the how question"?

### Answering the HOWquestion

We must think and function in two distinct roles. First, we must become *students* of *young adolescent development*—experts about the particular students we serve. General knowledge of young adolescent development must be given context and balanced by continually expanding direct knowledge of our immediate students—the very ones we engage every day. I have written elsewhere of strategies by which teachers can use inquiry to learn with and about their young adolescent students (Stevenson, 1986).

Second, we must become *curriculum theorists*. We must be well-informed, imaginative about possibilities, and integrative in our design of original curriculum that will complement our students' disposition to learn and abilities to comprehend. At its simplest, our task is to create matches between students and possibilities, rather than attempting to fit students to an externally defined curriculum. The validity of our theories will be evident in the quality of their exploration and evolving understanding.

Empirical experience has provided some trustworthy principles I keep before me in designing and thus defining, "how the middle level curriculum should be."

1.  **Their interests are primarily existential.**

    *What do you think about reincarnation? I think I used to be a hawk.*

    This assumption has two seemingly contradictory dimensions. First, 13 year olds are primarily concerned about being 13. Adult concerns and priorities may matter momentarily, but these kids are preoccupied with the here and now—what exists in their immediate sphere. Second, 13s also ponder metaphysical matters—musings on the meaning of life. Abstract reveries about *existence* proliferate, whether or not they become articulated. Studies which engage students' immediate concerns generate the ideas and speculations that feed their appetite for larger questions and personal aspirations for the ideal.

2.  **They care deeply about what they know and can do.**

    *I was pretty smart in third grade. I don't know what happened.*

    Thirty years of conversations and interviews with 10 to 14 year olds have convinced me of youngsters' urgent need to be competent and recognized by others as competent. In fact, even the apparently most discouraged children who have told me about themselves evidence hunger for the self-esteem that derives from personal competence. Schooling that ignores this most vital human need is bankrupt, and practices that destroy children's fragile regard for their personal worth are immoral.

3.  **They think and learn like young adolescents.**

    *Mrs. Jones doesn't expect us to do things we can't do.*

    Perhaps our greatest single self-deception is our failure to recognize and understand our students' intellectual readiness. Is it their often rapid physical change and increasingly adult-like appearance that fools us? Most schoolwork seems to be based on assumptions about curricular fit—a consideration detached from students' real intellectual needs and readiness. Too little curriculum deliberately complements their ability to comprehend. I have found these youngsters to be generally literal and gullible—increasingly doubtful yet still trusting adult answers more than we may credit. They also make generally conservative decisions when given choices about what to learn.

4. **Self-esteem derives from hard work, competence, and success.**
   *Look! Look what I did!*
   Compliments, platitudes, stickers, and gold stars may provide encouragement, but young adolescents are remarkably savvy about what is genuinely worthwhile, what really counts. They know better than anyone when they have struggled, sacrificed, persisted— exhibiting the qualities which ultimately bring success if the goals are realistic for them. They also know what "cognitive dissonance" means when they find coherence in the midst of confusion. And it is just such commitment and achievement from which authentic self-esteem derives. They also recognize the diversity among them—gifts or talents as well as deficiencies—that make their struggles inherently unequal.

5. **They learn best with and from other people.**
   *I'll do whatever you want as long as I can work with Joe.*
   Why do some of us appear to assume our job is to break up chums or cliques? My greatest intrigue about various within-class grouping strategies are the academic and interpersonal influences of particular students on their peers, especially when an individual's work ethic becomes increasingly responsible and productive. It appears to be well known that during these years many youngsters shift from recognizing their parents as the primary source of authority to their peers. We should exploit these natural attractions and bonds for constructive use.

6. **They want very much to please and impress selected adults.**
   *Mr. Black should be a teacher. He saved my life.*
   Many young adolescents have shared their perceptions with me that teachers as a class seem different from other adults. They admit the irrationality of the perception, yet the discrimination may for the time being remain entrenched. On the other hand, adults outside the school and even older adolescents are often perceived as being more fully in tune with "the real world." When we fail to create opportunities for our students to engage in working relationships with responsible older people—even ones just two or three years older, we miss an opportunity to build constructive, mutually beneficial, intergenerational partnerships. Guest teachers/tutors from the parent body, high school, and/or community, apprenticeships in the community, formal mentor programs, collaborations with senior citizens, service projects with adult service organizations—all these provide opportunities for relationships that instruct, portend approval, and affirm kids.

7. **They want to help others.**

*A lawyer helped my grandfather, who's in a coma  because*
*he got in a car accident. I think I might become a lawyer, too.*

Although the desire to do what adult society generally acknowledges as "good works" may sometimes appear hidden beneath a camouflage of pretense and bravado, I am convinced that there are few, if any, kids who are indifferent to the needs of others, especially ones whose misfortunes render them particularly vulnerable. "Others" includes animals, the environment, younger children, and needy people in the neighborhood, community, or school— some of whom may even be siblings or other relatives. They also empathize with suffering across the world that is brought home through media. For some youngsters the idea of being helpful in a meaningful way may be only an abstract notion. For others it is a sense of personal destiny, an idea of doing things in adulthood that will improve the lot of humankind. If we are to be at all hopeful about the potential influences of schooling on the future, should we not cultivate the most precious of all our natural resources—the desire of youth to improve the world they are inheriting from us?

## Conclusion

Our dubious if not ignoble tradition of teaching all students the same content at the same time in the same way flies in the face of our knowledge about our young adolescent constituents. That is not to deny that selected learnings may be accomplished best through traditional direct instruction. Specific techniques in mathematics or writing, for example, are certainly accomplished more efficiently and effectively with concentrated direction and evaluation. But to continue the tradition of teacher-focused, textbook-centered instruction in semester-long courses is to ignore the rich opportunity for the authentic explorations portrayed in the vignettes. In order to cultivate the individual interests, talents, and dispositions of young adolescents, we must reconceptualize how the middle level curriculum should be.

My proposition that the answer to "what" is found in "how" is not radical. Viable topics for study abound. As experts about our students and curriculum theorists, our challenge is to take fullest advantage of what we know about who our students are and what they can do in creating curricular opportunities which complement them.  The study of transportation, for example, capitalized upon kids' interests matching them with available resources—"found curriculum," so to speak. The overnight study of a Polish neighborhood likewise grew from the teacher's awareness of his students and available latent resources. And Peter's engagement of the Civil War brought the dimension of parent involvement implored by Carnegie's publication of *Turning Points* (1989).

We all know at least in a general way the kinds of scholarly work that are appropriate for our students: reading for pleasure and understanding, writing that is clear and coherent, problem solving in a variety of modes, and so on. There are at least three certain sources of guidance for choosing topics of study. First, we must capitalize on the already existing interests, ideas, questions, and curiosities of our children. Accessing them is simply a matter of inquiry. Second, no matter where we live, we are surrounded with resources and possibilities: people, the physical environment, local culture and history, the free enterprise system, art and artifacts. Eliot Wigginton (1985) has clearly demonstrated the efficacy of cultivating the resources of this found environment. Third, what may be the most overlooked source of appropriate topics for young adolescents are teachers' passions, regardless of how conventionally "academic" those passions may be—fishing, automobiles, fiction, cooking, the opera. Teachers who are openly passionate about what they are teaching infect the youngsters around them. And being able to share our own passions for learning should be high on our list of professional aspirations and satisfactions. It is the stuff from which our efficacy derives. Units of engagement that rise from these sources embody awesome potential for education that more fully captures young adolescents' scholarly potential. And it makes an enormous difference for us, too.

Casey Stengel is an institution in American culture for his accomplishments as a player and teacher of baseball. He is also revered for leaving us with "Stengel-ese," statements that seem confused or self-contradictory on the surface but which on second thought reveal profound truth. Consider his admonition to his players who were mindlessly going through the motions of throwing and catching and batting—the fundamentals of the game: "You've gotta see the game to see the game."

So it is, I submit, with the middle level curriculum question. In order to comprehend the complexity and awesome potential of educating young adolescents, we have to become "students and strategists of the game." In order to transcend the persisting charge of "mindlessness" by Silberman almost twenty years ago (1973), we must become child development specialists about the students we teach so that the designs we create and teach reflect the viability of our curriculum theories.

# References

Arnold, J. F. (1990). *Visions of teaching and learning: Eighty exemplary middle level projects*. Columbus, OH: National Middle School Association .

Arnold, J. F. (l985). A responsive curriculum for emerging adolescents. *Middle School Journal, 16*(3), 3, 14-18.

Beane, J. A. (1990). *A middle school curriculum: From rhetoric to reality*. Columbus, OH: National Middle School Association.

Carnegie Council on Adolescent Development. (1989). *Turning points: Preparing American youth for the 21st century*. Washington, DC: Carnegie Corporation.

Hirsch, E. D. (1987). *Cultural literacy: What every American needs to know*. Boston: Houghton Mifflin.

James, C. (1974). *Beyond customs: An educator's journey*. New York: Agathon.

Lipsitz, J. (1984). *Successful schools for young adolescents*. New Brunswick, NJ: Transaction.

Lounsbury, J. H., & Vars, G. F. (1978). *A curriculum for the middle school years*. New York: Harper and Row.

Ravitch, D., & Finn, C. E. (1987). *What do our 17 year olds know?* New York: Harper and Row.

Silberman, C. E. (1973). *Crisis in the classroom*. New York: Random House.

Stevenson, C. (1986). *Teacher as inquirers: Strategies for learning with and about early adolescents*. Columbus, OH: National Middle School Association.

Vars, G. F. (1987). *Interdisciplinary teaching in the middle grades: Why and how*. Columbus OH: National Middle School Association.

Wigginton, E. (1985). *Sometimes a shining moment*. New York: Agathon.

***Chris Stevenson*** *teaches at the University of Vermont, Burlington.*

# Gender issues and the middle school curriculum

*Deborah A. Butler*
*Sharon Sperry*

*D*espite the advances made in the last 30 years, our schools are still primarily oriented toward the white male student. Research indicates that schools and teachers (both males and females), are still more responsive to boys, their learning styles, their needs, their futures, than they are to female students.

—"Are schools responding?," 1990

This is the conclusion given in a recent article in answer to the question, "Are schools responding to females?" At a time when middle school educators begin to reconceptualize the curriculum for the middle years, educators cannot afford to shrink from looking closely at the impact of the current curriculum, as well as upon the suggestions for reforming it, with an eye to the effect of curriculum and instruction on the different genders. While educators may feel that legal mandates such as Title IX and the move in the textbook industry to eliminate portraits of bias may have made this a moot issue, a great deal of recent research on the learning environment and curriculum suggest that the issue is still very much alive. Middle school educators, too, should ask the question: "Are our schools, especially their curricula and instruction, responsive to young adolescent females?"

## *The case for gender equity*

The literature describing most school curricula and instruction, including that of the middle grade, abounds with examples of continued gender bias in the schools. For example, Peltz (1990) reminds teachers of the great gap remaining between men's and women's achievements in science, and reviews comprehensively those "environmental pressures," in school and out, which affect girls' attitudes toward science: (a) early experiences; (b) cultural biases; (c) peer pressures; (d) the paramount importance of relationships for girls, especially in problem-solving behaviors; (e) discomfort with risk-taking behavior required in science; and, (f) types of questions asked. Most important for those of us at the middle level, Peltz notes that "attitudes toward science are strongly differentiated by the time a student reaches 11 years of age" (p. 44). He continues: "By age 14 (eighth grade) differences in classroom achievement become significant" (p. 46).

While science and math have been touted as primary harbingers of sexism, they are by no means the only part of the curriculum harboring gender bias. Other subjects, such as English or social studies, may still retain texts and materials that suggest sex-role stereotyping. Certainly the "canon" of American and English literature, works which often pervade the middle school language arts curriculum, has grown only slowly to include works by women, especially women of color. In social studies, particularly history, the story told of one's heritage remains primarily "his story" not "her story." In addition, in many schools, the curriculum remains peppered with a variety of single-sex courses.

Certainly, recent curriculum reformers at the middle level (Beane, 1990; Arnold, 1985; Stevenson, 1986) describe a middle level curriculum in place which may very well enhance the problems encountered by females in middle schools. Many middle level practitioners agree that despite "different instructional procedures, interdisciplinary teaming...advisory programs, efforts to expand school sponsored activities" (Beane, 1990, p. 6) the curriculum continues to be a "subject-centered, largely academic curriculum" (p. 8). Beane pushes this indictment of the current curriculum further when he labels it an entity existing because of "strong historical tradition and the symbiotic relationships among educational elites" (Beane, 1990, p. 33-34). And of course, historically, the educated elites have been the white male population.

Shadow study research (Lounsbury & Johnston, 1985; Lounsbury, Marani, & Compton, 1980; Lounsbury & Clark, 1990) describe the dominance, in many schools, of these traditional departmentalized curricula, with their all-too-often passive teaching modes. If the sepa-

rate disciplines approach still dominates middle level curricular thinking, as these studies all indicate, then those subject area's biases are
likely to infiltrate courses at the middle level, too—at a critical time for
both young adolescent girls and boys of diverse backgrounds.

Clearly, teacher expectation, teaching and learning styles, and
issues of classroom communication confound these curricular biases.
After three years of research on sexist interactions in classrooms, the
Sadkers confirmed that: "Boys still get more attention, encouragement
and airtime than girls do" (Sadker & Sadker, 1985, p. 54). They continue:
"We found that at all grade levels, in all communities, and in all subject
areas, boys dominated classroom communications" (p. 56). This may
not seem to be significant until one recalls the primary principles of
learning which include the finding that student participation in classes
and in discussions encourage more positive attitudes toward school,
which in turn results in more learning (Goodlad, 1984).

The American Association of University Women's recent report on
gender bias in schools ends with a call for an entire restructuring of
schools in every dimension to support gender equity and equity in
general ("Restructuring education," 1990). The report reminds educators that "prevailing patterning of gender-role socialization create what
amounts to different cultures for females and males, and that these
cultures mediate intellectual experiences in ways that create different
learning styles" ("Restructuring education," p. 3). The passive and rote
learning patterns dominating classes as well as the emphasis on individual competition tend to contrast with many females' preferences for
collaborative approaches and relational needs ("Restructuring education," pp. 3-4).

The description of this condition is again echoed in the middle level
shadow study reports: "Our look inside grade 8, however, does show
that there is still far too much 'dead wood'—old routines and practices
that in the late 1990s are no longer appropriate for, or effective with,
early adolescents" (Lounsbury & Clark, 1990, p. 133). If not appropriate
for young adolescents, then certainly not females, given what is now
being found out about not just early adolescent development, the
supposed foundation of the middle school curriculum, but especially
about the special developmental concerns of young adolescent females.

The questions now must arise: *What did past studies of females tell us
about the unique developmental concerns of young adolescent females? What
is being found out about young adolescent female development in the current
research? What data give rise to such a curricular speculation as the one just
given?*

## Female development: The older models of interpretation

The first question above can be answered rather simply: many of the older models of development either did not differentiate girls' development from boys', or interpreted the differences that were seen as deficiencies in females. Not only educators, but the public at large, derive still their ideas from old models like Freud's or Erikson's, or developmentalists who consistently interpreted girls and women as domestic creatures with little interest or inclination for work outside the home. Even Piaget, for example, assuming that the higher levels of cognition were identical to the kinds of thinking done in math and sciences, sealed girls into a divergent, de-valued, subgroup by virtue of their assumed lack of intellectual capacity. Therefore, not only were girls and women not fit psychologically for the rigors of the world beyond the home, they lacked the intellectual skills to master the "language" of that world—analytical thinking (Gilligan, 1987).

The effects of such a powerful psychological definition of female identity and capability which saw women as impaired for work in the world, together with an assumption that good thinking is analytical and identical to thinking in math and science, has had the most damaging effect on the continuation of attitudes of men, and women as well, which have petrified prejudice and made it seem rational, made it seem, in fact, common sense. What the average adult and young person believes has been documented in attitudinal research:

1.  Girls are not as competent as boys;
2.  Girls lack the ability to achieve in math and science;
3.  Because girls cannot succeed in math and science, they cannot succeed in the public world because success in the world depends on being analytical (Broverman, Vogel, Broverman, Clarson, & Rosenkrantz, 1972; Goldberg, 1968; Fidell, 1970).

And the "facts" as they have been documented in this older research (Berkovitz, 1979; Blenenstock & Epstein, 1979) about the performance of girls in school and the work world seem to empirically confirm such assumptions as this: girls do less well than boys in school the further along they go (therefore, they must not by nature be educable). And as we saw earlier, these attitudes as well as the continued relative dearth of achievement by girls in these particular curricular areas continue on into the classrooms of the 1990s. Is it any wonder that schools perpetuate a bias against girls when such attitudes are the stuff of "common sense"? That these attitudes rest on "facts" and theories which need reinterpretation has only been acknowledged in the past 15 years.

## *Female development: What researchers are now discovering*

The difference in school for boys and girls in the middle level years is caused by a difference in the developmental concerns of boys and girls. Once again, we can look at the research on the abilities of girls and boys in math and science for some clues.

Berkovitz (1979) found that at the point when curricular choice is possible in the middle grades years, boys do take more math courses than girls, but the reason does not lie in native ability. School counselors and parents, schooled in and believing in the older paradigms of development tend to steer girls away from math and science. According to Peterson and Wittig (1979), prior to the middle grades, girls do as well at math as boys. Furthermore, when higher level math problems are re-worded to fit a girl's experience, girls show as much capability at mathematical analysis as do boys (Berkovitz, 1979).

Block (1984) explains the difference as one of spatial skill ability being developed more by the play of young boys which girls miss prior to the middle level years, in part due to sex-role stereotyping in the kinds of play parents encourage in boys but not girls. Other researchers have found that this can be remedied, although school situations generally do not emphasize the teaching of spatial skills before middle school which would allow girls to catch up.

The more likely explanation of apparent differences in development and ability between boys and girls, then, is in socialization, not biology. This socialization can account for the perceived differences in abilities between adolescent girls and boys on the part of parents, teachers, and the society at large. Much recent work by researchers on female development (Gilligan, 1982; Gilligan, Lyons, Hanmer, 1990; Hancock, 1989; Belenky, Clinchy, Goldberger, & Tarule, 1986) shows repeatedly that females approach knowledge, events, and experiences from a set of goals very different from those of boys. Boys are socialized to excel in the individuating activities of competition (in sports, in making grades, in argumentation) and, therefore, find personal self-worth in activities the culture associates with the rugged individual. These researchers continue to find that girls locate their identities in the nurturing atmosphere of relationships and their connection as indi-viduals to the needs of the other. So, as Hancock (1989) points out, when women report their experience of the identity crisis, which begins in the early adolescent years, they recall an "authentic, real, and true" self, "present, intact, in the earliest part of...life" (Hancock, 1989, p. 4) which was obscured by the socializing demands first met during the middle school years.

Twelve years old seems to be the watershed. It is at that point, in the middle of the 10-14 year old range, that girls feel the pressure to bury the autonomous self. The value placed on the development of the individual self and the consequent emphasis on detachment, leads the 12 year old girl to a loss of self (Gilligan, Lyons, & Hanmer, 1990). Gilligan's work convinces her that there is the need to view girls' development through the dilemma that "one can only experience self in the context of relationship with others and that one can only experience relationship if one differentiates other from self" (Gilligan, 1987, p. 325). She underscores the fact that in facing the social and educational expectations that to grow up is to grow apart, girls face terrible difficulties in school and out in the early adolescent years (Gilligan, Lyons, & Hanmer, 1990).

To complicate the picture of girls' development further, other researchers (Belenky, Clinchy, Goldberger, & Tarule, 1986) have described, based on their research of women, a very different developmental paradigm of intellectual development that primarily characterizes women's growth. While this research is not yet related specifically to middle level students, the existence of this paradigm certainly raises questions about its relationship to other intellectual models all educators use such as Piaget's.

Thus recent research suggests that, due to differences in the way boys and girls are socialized in our society, different developmental paths as well as different developmental concerns (moral, social, and intellectual) are created by the time of the middle level school years for females and males. The research is becoming a significant part of a body of research on learning styles, cultures, and gender. It is a body of data that suggests that "girls respond differently to the classroom environment than boys" ("Restructuring education," 1990, p. 3), and that educators, especially middle level educators, whose claim is that their very curriculum arises from the nature of young adolescent development, cannot afford to ignore these findings.

## Pedagogical suggestions for gender equity

The middle level curriculum (and instructional practice) is meant to be firmly grounded in the development of the young adolescent. If early adolescence is a slightly different developmental stage for females than males, if gender relates to learning style as well, educators now must ask: *What sort of curriculum, what sorts of instructional approaches, should exist in our middle level schools so that the learning environment is enhanced for our female students as well as our male students?*

General curriculum and instruction suggestions abound in the literature on gender and schooling, but it may be that the suggestions for a gender equitable curriculum and instruction for the middle level specifically may have already taken shape with the suggestions in the middle school literature (Beane, 1990; Arnold, 1985; Stevenson, 1986; Lounsbury & Clark, 1990). A remarkable overlap between general suggestions in the literature for curriculum and instruction and in the mandates for reform offered by these theorists exists as a comparison of some of the major and similar ideas might indicate.

Curricular suggestions run a gamut of ideas. Heading the list is that recent call cited earlier for an "entire restructuring of schools" to support gender equity ("Restructuring education," 1990, p. 3). Such a restructuring to support female education is a major effort, including the "abandonment of tracking," the development of "curricula that reflect a core of common themes providing cultural unity, but which do not entail teaching the same material to every student," "interdisciplinary teaching which tackles real-world problems...combined with hands-on projects," and a "literature, history, and social studies curricula that reflect the pluralistic and multicultural context of American society and show women and minorities as doers, leaders, and decision-makers rather than as helpers or victims" ("Restructuring education," pp. 4-5). Other sources support the move to "unity," suggesting that gender-fair education avoids separate courses that exclude one sex. This includes avoidance of electives, extracurricular programs, and curricular materials which reinforce stereotypical roles (Sadker & Sadker, 1982).

Middle level educators cannot help but hear echoes of the already powerful organizational components recommended for middle level schools in some of these suggestions: interdisciplinary teams and teaching, the use of interdisciplinary units, the call for a curriculum with a problem-centered core (Vars, 1987). These have all long been a hallmark of the middle level concept, as has been the belief in multiple models of grouping students, models which go far beyond the notion of homogeneous grouping. Clearly, the components of the organizational model support the recommendations for gender-fair education to a large extent.

Add to this the call for revisioning the curricular component as a general education (Beane, 1990), and the middle level school may move even closer to accommodating the needs of female development by going beyond the mere mirroring of calls for gender equity and striking at the very heart of female identity. Beane states that a general education is the central purpose of the middle school. By this, one means an education that "focuses on the common needs, problems, interests, and concerns of young people and society" (p. 35). Furthermore, the content of concerns arises out of the issues of young adolescent development (Beane, 1990), including, one assumes, female development, as well as issues of a diverse population of emerging adolescents.

Even more important for females, whose selves are defined now as "self-in-relationship," the content arises from the fact that all humans live their lives in relation to others: we all live in a social world, a truly diverse world. Fully one half of this definition, then, relates to the central ground of female development—self in relation to others. In essence, what is being proposed here is a middle level curriculum which includes ultimately three dimensions: "themes arising from the intersection of personal and social concerns, skills necessary to fully explore those themes, and the enduring concepts of democracy, human dignity, and cultural diversity" (Beane, 1990, p. 45).

Certainly, such a curriculum vision might begin to satisfy the calls from the developmental studies or from gender experts for the acknowledgment of women's places, achievements, their call for a theme orientation to knowledge, skills, and affect, the emphasis on the unity of those, not their separation. The further and supportive suggestions for curricular reform by Stevenson (1986) which suggest the use of real inquiries (real questions in Beane's terminology) into young adolescent concerns offer the chance for young girls to reflect on the self as their own unique changes and way of being begin to emerge. Thus, concerns posed by one's differences in intellectual, moral, or social development could be addressed openly.

In the general literature suggesting the pathway to gender equitable education, appropriate instructional approaches and environmental factors relating to curricular goals often include suggestions highlighting collaborative forms of learning rather than competitive forms. For example, Peltz (1990), in suggesting antidotes for the sexism in science instruction, advocated the use of cooperative learning strategies, a coaching technique of instruction, equity strategies, the encouragement of risk-taking behaviors in classroom activities, and the very conscious avoidance by teachers of sexist interactions and communications. Again, one is struck by the echo of many previous exhortations for the middle level teacher's approach to the classroom, but one may also be struck by the overlap with the emphasis in the recent reform literature on the use of collaboration dealing with almost every form of middle level education. Again, Beane advocates collaboration not only for instructional practice in classrooms, but for the entire development process for the curriculum, a collaboration including adults in the school, students, and parents (Beane, 1990).

Still other literature defining gender-fair instruction encourages the use of interactive forms of teaching, and increased individualization, including the use of multiple standards for student growth ("Restructuring education," 1990). These are yet more suggestions which call up earlier middle school teaching rhetoric. Furthermore, after delineating a possible intellectual development paradigm for women,

Belenky, Clinchy, Goldberger, and Tarule (1986) termed the kind of teaching many women responded to best as "connected teaching," a form of teaching in which the instructor fosters student thought, encourages risk-taking, focuses on student knowledge, not a body of objective knowledge, poses problems for mutual reflection, and encourages an environment of safety where one can use one's own knowledge. These kinds of classes and teachers are open, encouraging of dialogue, collaboration, and involvement. They can enhance female development. It, too, is a description that could be pulled not only from past literature on necessary teaching characteristics for middle level instruction, but it also echoes the teaching characteristics suggested as ideal by the recent middle level shadow studies, and these recent curriculum reform suggestions.

What is being speculated about here are two possibilities: (a) that perhaps it is the traditional curriculum itself as an underlying structure (separate disciplines), which is the "hidden curriculum" undergirding content and instructional strategy which promotes unseen those overt signs of sexism. That individual, separate discipline approach is metaphorically and inherently "male." It may be the deep structure of sexism to the surface structure of sex bias in content, strategy, and resources. And it is harmful to males often as well as the females (Sadker & Sadker, 1982); and, (b) that current middle school curriculum reform may indeed provide the alternative paradigm for curriculum development that destroys, by nature of its very structure, the deeply embedded sexism that current curricula and instruction often wittingly promote. Finally, what is being suggested here, too, is that middle level educators consciously make the issues of female early adolescence and pedagogy a part of the continuing "curriculum conversation."

## References

Are schools responding to females? (1990). *NASSP Bulletin*, 74 (530), 94.

Arnold, J. (1985). A responsive curriculum for emerging adolescents. *Middle School Journal, 16*(3), 3,14-18.

Beane, J. A.(1990). *A middle school curriculum: From rhetoric to reality.* Columbus, OH: National Middle School Association.

Belenky, M. F., Clinchy, B. M., Goldberger, N. R., & Tarule, J. M. (1986). *Women's ways of knowing: The development of self, voice, and mind.* New York: Basic Books.

Berkovitz, I. H. (1979). Effects of secondary school experiences on adolescent female development. In M. Sugar (Ed.), *Female adolescent development.* New York: Brunner/Mazel.

Blenenstock, A., & Epstein, N. B. (1979). Current adaptive challenges facing young females. In M. Sugar (Ed.), *Female adolescent development*. New York: Brunner/Mazel.

Block, J. H. (1984). *Sex role identity and ego development*. San Francisco, CA: Jossey-Bass.

Broverman, I. K., Vogel, S. R., Broverman, D. M., Clarkson, F. E., & Rosenkrantz, P. S. (1972). Sex role stereotypes: A current appraisal. *Journal of Social Issues, 28*, 59-78.

Fidell, L. S. (1970). Empirical verification of sex discrimination in hiring practices in psychology. *American Psychologist, 25*, 1094-1097.

Gilligan, C. (1982). *In a different voice*. Cambridge, MA: Harvard.

Gilligan, C. (1987). Adolescent development reconsidered. In C.E. Irwin, Jr., (Ed.), *Adolescent social behavior and health* . San Francisco, CA: Jossey-Bass.

Gilligan, C., Lyons, N. P.,& Hanmer, T. J.(1990). *Making connections: The relational worlds of adolescent girls at Emma Willard School*. Cambridge, MA: Harvard.

Goldberg, P. (1968). Are women prejudiced against women? *Transaction, 5*, 28-30.

Goodlad, J. (1984). *A place called school*. New York: McGraw-Hill.

Hancock, E. (1989). *The girl within*. New York: Random House.

Lounsbury, J. H., & Clark, D. C. (1990). *Inside grade eight: From apathy to excitement*. Reston, VA: National Association of Secondary School Principals.

Lounsbury, J. H., & Johnston, J. H. (1985). *How fares the ninth grade?* Reston, VA: National Association of Secondary School Principals.

Lounsbury, J. H., Marani, J., & Compton, M. (1980). *The middle school in profile: A day in the seventh grade*. Columbus, OH: National Middle School Association.

Peltz, W. H. (1990). Can girls + science - stereotypes = success? *Science Teacher, 57*, 44-49.

Petersen, A. C., & Wittig, M. A. (1979). Differential cognitive development in adolescent girls. In M. Sugar (Ed.), *Female adolescent development*. New York: Brunner/Mazel.

Restructuring education: Getting girls into America's goals. (1990). *Outlook, 84*, 1-6

Sadker, M. P., & Sadker, D. M. (1982). *Sex equity hand book for schools*. New York: Longman.

Sadker, M. P., & Sadker, D. M. (1985). Sexism in the schoolroom of the 80s. *Psychology Today, 88*, 54-57.

Stevenson, C. (1986). *Teachers as inquirers: Strategies for learning with and about early adolescents*. Columbus, OH: National Middle School Association.

Vars, G.F. (1987). *Interdisciplinary teaching in the middle grades: Why and how.* Columbus, OH: National Middle School Association.

**Deborah A. Butler** *teaches at Wabash College, Crawfordsville, Indiana.* **Sharon Sperry** *is a doctoral student at Indiana University, Bloomington, Indiana.*

# Preparing prospective middle grades teachers to understand the curriculum

*Thomas O. Erb*

H ow can prospective middle school teachers come to understand and appreciate the scope and characteristics of middle grades curriculum? The answer to this question is of major significance. Although the middle school movement of the past quarter century has been reasonably successful in raising awareness of the developmental needs of young adolescents, in advancing the cause of improving school climate, and most significantly in restructuring schools to include interdisciplinary teams and advisory programs, this movement has been far less successful in reforming the curriculum of the middle grades to meet the needs of learners. Lipsitz (1984) concluded in *Successful Schools for Young Adolescents* that "translating philosophy into curriculum is the most difficult feat for schools to accomplish" (p. 188). She went further to point out that the definition of academics was very narrow, being limited for the most part to the transmission of facts accompanied by the relative lack of inquiry. This notion was reinforced by Lounsbury and Clark (1990) who quote one of their middle grades data analysts:

> ...data manipulation, problem solving, and
> higher order decision making are getting short shift
> in the very schools that are preparing students for
> the changing and uncertain world of the 21st
> century. We still seem to be teaching as though
> passing on the accumulated wisdom of the past is
> the best preparation for living in the future (p. 127).

Beane (1990a) reached the conclusion that organizational and climate changes have far outstripped curricular changes in the redesign of middle grades schools. Clearly the element of schooling most resistant to change in the era of middle grades reform is that of curriculum.

The preparation of new middle grades teachers to understand their roles in the development and execution of middle grades curriculum must be part of the solution to this lingering problem. However, some critics have dismissed pre-service teacher education as not a viable player in this reform effort: "waiting for teacher education to change before undertaking change in the middle school curriculum would most likely mean that we would grow old just talking" (Beane, 1990b, p. 59). However, the pre-service middle grades classroom would seem just as likely a place to begin the transformation of middle school curricula as the interdisciplinary teams that exist in the field. Indeed, providing pre-service teachers viable models of interdisciplinary curriculum from the field is a challenging task since so little of it is going on in actual classrooms. If we are to be successful in bringing about the curricular reforms that will serve the needs of today's 10 to 14 year olds, both teachers who are currently serving on interdisciplinary teams and teacher candidates who will be taking their places on those teams in a year or two must understand the scope of middle grades curricula beyond the confines of their specific certification areas.

Admittedly, the task is not easy. Unlike studying teaching methods which can readily be demonstrated, the study of the curriculum is more abstract. Not only is the study of curriculum a more abstract study than that of instruction, it transcends students' interests in a particular subject area. While the expectation of teaching English or math, reinforced by the completion of a major or minor in that area, tends to focus pre-service students on a specific subject, the study of the curriculum demands that one look at the big picture and how all of the parts fit together. Yet many pre-service candidates are already overwhelmed by the task of learning to teach "their subject" to young adolescents. Added to this problem is the fact that a good middle school curriculum is not just a collection of isolated subjects with some extra-curricular activities thrown in for the talented. However, middle grades teacher candidates have experienced this configuration of curriculum in the high schools from which they have only recently graduated. Consequently, the image of curriculum that pre-service teachers carry in their heads has to be transformed, not reinforced. Finally, the paucity of examples of interdisciplinary curriculum that could be used as positive field experiences for pre-service teachers makes the task of teaching middle grades curriculum to neophytes a most challenging one.

*What to teach about the curriculum*

Yet, if teacher education is to contribute to breaking the inertia of curricular tradition, then programs must expose pre-service teachers to the characteristics of curricular organization that are unique to the middle grades. Before beginning the *how* of teaching about middle grades curriculum, teacher educators must determine what to teach about the peculiarities of middle grades curriculum. One source that remains among the most thoughtful discussions of curriculum was written by Lounsbury and Vars (1978) who divided the middle school curriculum into three related components: the core, the continuous progress, and the variable. Subsequently, Arnold (1985) advanced five principles which characterize what he called a responsive curriculum for emerging adolescents. First, the curriculum must help students make sense of themselves and of their world. Second, methods and materials must be geared to the developmental levels of the students. Third, knowledge—consisting of thinking, feeling, and doing—must be emphasized over simple information and isolated skills. Fourth, the curriculum must focus on concrete and real world experiences. Fifth, the curriculum must be taught by teachers who are knowledgeable human beings who trust their own judgments and instincts enough to rise above rules and models (p. 3,14-18).

Recently, Beane (1990a, 1990b) has challenged all middle grades educators to reorganize the middle grades curriculum around a problem-centered, as opposed to a subject-centered, approach. He has suggested that the curriculum be organized around the themes that emerge at the intersection of the concerns of young adolescents and the social issues facing contemporary society. Skills and subject matter would be called forth to serve the inquiry into these emerging themes. Cutting across all curricular themes would be the concepts of democracy, human dignity, and cultural diversity. Students preparing to become middle grades teachers need to become familiar with the meaning and application of a half dozen curriculum concepts. The curriculum must be *diverse* and *balanced*. Young adolescents themselves are diverse and changing on several developmental dimensions at once. The curriculum that serves them must be no less diverse. This balance among diverse components calls for teachers to comprehend the notion of *basic core*, general education, or common curriculum. Much of what is taught to young adolescents represents a common education required of all participants in our society. There are certain basics that all students must be exposed to and master. The curriculum must at the same time be one of *exploration*. Some experiences should focus on exposure rather than mastery. In addition, not all students need necessarily have all of the same exploratory experiences. There should be plenty of opportunity for students to make choices regarding the pursuit of their interests and talents. Activities, clubs, and mini-courses are not extracurricular but part of the balanced curriculum provided for all students. Athletics, clubs, and other special interest activities are included in the middle grades program because they have something to teach young adolescents. Consequently, they are not extra but are an example of the last concept that must be mastered by pre-service teachers: *integration.* The curriculum should not be organized around basic and exploratory classes but around the notion that the common core, exploration, and special interests should be integrated into every aspect of the middle grades program. Students should be learning basic skills, exploring new possibilities, and pursuing personal interests equally in English, band class, model train club, and all of the other offerings of the school.

## Other considerations before beginning a study of curriculum

Overcoming the parochial perspectives of pre-service subject specialists requires these students to be given an opportunity to engage in interdisciplinary curricular planning. Providing such an opportunity to learn about middle school curriculum by planning some of it has the copacetic side effect of modeling good middle grades instructional strategies for pre-service teachers. The method of teaching about middle school curriculum that is about to be described engages the students in a group investigation type of cooperative learning that balances teacher structure with student decision making. It provides hands-on experiences with an otherwise abstract notion, that of curriculum. The outcomes are student products or curriculum units that have applicability in the real world, unlike traditional tests. The method of teaching about middle school curriculum should be at the same time an appropriate model of middle grades instruction.

The method of teaching about the middle school curriculum should be a cooperative, hands-on experience for another reason. Not only must middle grades teachers know about the curriculum of the middle school, they must also play a major role in creating that curriculum. The importance of engaging teachers in their own curriculum planning is a fairly pervasive theme that has emerged in the last decade in the face of school reform efforts that often run counter to promoting teacher involvement. Though state and school board mandates and textbook series will continue to exist, it is the teachers in a local setting who must fashion the curriculum to the particular learners for whom they are responsible. In addition to Beane's (1990a) most recent plea to involve teachers in local planning to create the themes that would organize the curriculum, Arnold (1985) emphasized the importance of teachers trusting their own judgments and instincts. Compton (1984) also used the word *trust* to describe teachers planning the specifics of a school program, and Erb (1988) argued that collaborative planning by teachers at the local level was crucial to meeting the needs of particular learners. Good middle grades curriculum is not something that can be handed down in its entirety by higher authority. In the final analysis it must be fashioned locally by teachers who collectively are responsible for the education of a specific set of youngsters.

Curriculum planning at the local level will be undertaken by teachers with different academic backgrounds and personalities who nevertheless are responsible for delivering the curriculum to a diverse set of learners. Therefore, a pre-service curricular experience must allow students to take advantage of these diverse academic backgrounds. This can be accomplished by having students share personal knowledge of their academic majors to cooperatively identify themes that have the potential to integrate knowledge from their various subject areas and, at the same time, be motivating to young adolescents. A number of authors have provided guidance for engaging in interdisciplinary planning (George & Lawrence, 1982; Erb & Doda, 1989; Jacobs, 1989; Caine & Caine, 1991).

Regardless of which approach is selected to structure an interdisciplinary planning experience for pre-service students, several prior experiences are required. It should go without saying that curriculum planners for young adolescents must have a thorough grounding in young adolescent development. Before the curriculum planning can proceed, pre-service teachers must master the essentials of early adolescent social, emotional, cognitive, moral, and physical development. Secondly, since curriculum does not rest on the nature of the learner alone, potential curriculum planners must be required to study, and reflect on, some major societal trends that should have an impact on effective curriculum planning. Pre-service students must grapple with the meaning of such societal changes as: the changing nature of family structure, both nuclear and extended; the profound changes that are occurring in communications technology; the changes in human demographics characterizing a world of nearly 6,000,000,000 people; changes in humans' relationships to the biosphere; changes in social equity issues; and changes in other public policy issues such as pro-life/ pro-choice, obscenity, racism, drugs, and tax equity. Finally, we must assume that the potential curriculum planners have a sufficient passion for, and knowledge of, some area of human inquiry such as those associated with the liberal arts disciplines.

## *Learning middle grades curriculum by planning it*

The pre-service teacher educator is responsible for structuring curriculum development activities that will call upon the students to analyze and integrate these background experiences into a unique curriculum plan. The pre-service teacher educator needs to select curriculum planning teams that are composed of three to five students with different academic backgrounds. For help in getting started, these team planners can be given one of the available personality character- istics inventories in order to assist them in understanding their own decision making preferences and to help them appreciate how each team member can contribute to effective group decision making.

The teacher needs to structure a curriculum development activity such as requiring the teams to develop two-week interdisciplinary units that fully integrate the background disciplines that the students bring to class. There are several concerns that need to be addressed early in this planning process. Students need to be helped to avoid the "potpourri" problem (Jacobs, 1989) which results when teachers choose a theme that provides for only a loose sampling of learning activities from the various subjects. To avoid this problem that often plagues attempts at integrating the curriculum, Erb and Doda (1989) suggest that an interdisciplinary unit be planned backwards starting with the culminating activities that students will be expected to carry out. To be effective, these culminating activities must possess several characteris- tics. They must require students to produce products and/or perfor- mances that demonstrate what they have learned. These activities must also require students to integrate knowledge and skills from the various academic areas that form the basis for the unit. It is not sufficient to have students take tests in the separate subject areas to end the unit. Nor is it acceptable to merely have the unit end in a "fun" activity as some reward for finishing the unit. The final activities must hold students accountable for their learning and be of sufficient breadth to require skills and knowledge from all areas that contribute to the unit.

The theme chosen to integrate the study must be significant, of interest to young adolescents, and sufficiently broad to include all academic areas relevant to the inquiry. An extrapolation from Beane (1990b) can provide a very useful exercise for identifying a theme with these characteristics. On a sheet of paper have the students create a grid. Along the left side of the grid have the pre-service curriculum team members brainstorm the concerns of young adolescents, an excellent application of their own earlier study of the characteristics of young adolescent learners. Across the top of the grid have the curriculum planners brainstorm societal issues, an application of their prior study of societal changes. On the grid wherever a young adolescent concern intersects a societal issue, there is a potential theme around which to structure two weeks of inquiry, or any other length for that matter.

With themes selected and culminating activities designed, prospective teachers can proceed to discuss connections to the theme by using a webbing strategy (Levy, 1980; Jacobs, 1989). At this point they bring their respective academic backgrounds into the planning of curriculum. By placing the theme at the center of a piece of paper the curriculum planners brainstorm potential links between the disciplines they represent and the theme. Any ideas are acceptable at this point: concepts, activities, questions, subtopics, names of people, and resources are all allowable.

It is now time for the planners to provide further focus for their developing unit. Through the use of either guiding questions (Jacobs, 1989) or unifying objectives (Erb & Doda, 1989), the pre-service teachers need to limit the scope of the curriculum plan that they are creating. Whether they are planning for two weeks, a full semester, or only for a day, they must make the unit of study manageable for the time to be allotted to the inquiry.

Taking a lead from the requirements for carrying out the culminating activities, curriculum planners now must plan the experiences that students will need in order to acquire the skills and knowledge to successfully complete the unit of inquiry. Planners will need to consider and make decisions about several matters at this point. How will students be grouped and regrouped for various activities? How will the varieties of student abilities, interests, and levels of development be provided for in the unit? How will students be held accountable for their learning? Will there be day-to-day provisions for checking accountability in addition to the accountability associated with the culminating activities? How will activities be sequenced? How will facilities and materials be used and/or shared? Answering these questions will require a combination of individual decision making and collaborative group decision making.

The pre-service students' cooperative planning activity needs to culminate in a product and/or academic performance of its own. In addition to writing down the results of the various steps in the curriculum planning process such as theme selection, description of culminating activities, sequencing of a variety of student activities, and methods of evaluation and accountability, the pre-service teachers should have the opportunity to share the fruits of their labors with some audience. This audience could include fellow pre-service teachers, the teacher education faculty, practicing middle grades teachers and/or young adolescent learners. In any case the curriculum planning activity deserves some type of real audience to react to the curriculum plan developed by pre-service teachers.

Only by collaborating to develop a curriculum unit for use with young adolescents in a changing society can pre-service teachers begin to understand the meaning of the middle grades curriculum concepts discussed earlier in this article. As pre-service teachers receive feedback from a live audience, they are forced to reflect on how they dealt with diversity, balance, basic core concepts, exploration, and integration in the curricular planning they did. In addition, by providing a cooperative learning experience by which prospective teachers can learn about middle grades curriculum, the middle grades teacher educator can integrate the study of curriculum with the modeling of sound middle grades instructional strategies. The teacher educator thereby takes another step closer to "practicing what she or he preaches" regarding the preparation of middle grades teachers.

## References

Arnold, J. (1985). A responsive curriculum for emerging adolescents. *Middle School Journal*, 16(3), 3,14-18.

Beane, J.A. (1990a). Rethinking the middle school curriculum. *Middle School Journal*, 21(5),1-5.

Beane, J.A. (1990b). *A middle school curriculum: From rhetoric to reality.* Columbus, OH: National Middle School Association.

Caine, R.N., & Caine, G. (1991). *Making connections: Teaching and the human brain.* Alexandria, VA: Association for Supervision and Curriculum Development.

Compton, M.F. (1984). Balance in the middle school curriculum. In J.H. Lounsbury (Ed.), *Perspectives: Middle school education, 1964-1984* (pp ). Columbus, OH: National Middle School Association.

Erb, T.O. (1988). Focusing back on the child by liberating the teacher. *The Early Adolescence Magazine,* 2(3),10-18.

Erb, T. O., & Doda, N. M. (1989). *Team organization: Promise—practices and possibilities.* Washington, DC: National Education Association.

George, P., & Lawrence, G. (1982). *Handbook for middle school teaching.* Glenview, IL: Scott, Foresman.

Jacobs, H.H. (1989). The interdisciplinary concept model: A step-by-step approach for developing integrated units of study. In H.H. Jacobs (Ed.), *Interdisciplinary curriculum: Design and implementation* (pp). Alexandria,VA: Association for Supervision and Curriculum Development.

Levy, P.S. (1980). Webbing: A format for planning integrated curricula. *Middle School Journal*, 11(3), 26-27.

Lipsitz, J. (1984). *Successful schools for young adolescents.* New Brunswick, NJ: Transaction.

Lounsbury, J.H., & Clark, D.C. (1990). *Inside eighth grade: From apathy to excitement.* Reston, VA: National Association of Secondary School Principals.

Lounsbury, J.H., & Vars, G.F. (1978). *A curriculum for the middle school years.* New York: Harper and Row.

**Thomas O. Erb** *teaches at the University of Kansas, Lawrence.*

# Middle level curriculum:
# The search for self and social meaning
*Middle Level Curriculum Project*

What meaning does the word curriculum have for educators? For parents? For community members? For the students who are the consumer of *it*? Participants in The Middle Level Curriculum Project have been exploring the question, "What should the middle level curriculum be?" We assert that the time has come for stating curriculum beliefs which have authentic, practical applications in all middle level schools across the country.

In this article, we present both a rationale and a framework for designing a middle level curriculum, one which can and will meet young adolescents and their teachers where they are at any moment in their development. It will extend their world to encompass what lies beyond the school walls. It is a curriculum of and for the young adolescent, and it is a curriculum which embraces and addresses the social meanings sought by them and all members of the school community.

Our definition of curriculum differs from the common notion that describes it as a defined set of texts and materials that are arranged around a subject or topic. Rather, we define middle level curriculum as that which encompasses the dynamic interaction of all experiences during the young adolescent's school day. This includes the instructional strategies, organizational arrangements, integrated curricular content, and cultural environment experienced by the young adolescent. This curriculum is not imposed on the student by the institution.

Instead, young adolescents and members of the school community (students, teachers, parents, and community members) create curriculum in the process of seeking answers to questions and concerns in their search for self and social meanings.

We know that when people are asked to think about curriculum possibilities, apprehensions result. Inevitably, questions arise that interfere with imagining anything other than what is presently in place. Such questions include the following:

> *But we've just finished writing our curriculum...you mean*
> *you want us to throw it out?*
> *But will our students be able to pass the standardized tests if*
> *we change the curriculum?*
> *But what if our students are already doing well?*
> *But what about state mandates?*
> *But what will happen to the K-12 sequence if we change*
> *middle level curriculum?*
> *But will the school board allow such a curriculum change?*

While these may be valid questions in the present educational structure, we set them aside because we believe that the present curriculum of most middle schools—the one that leads to such questions—is not appropriate for young adolescents. The present curriculum results in isolated and fragmented content, alienated and passive students, underdeveloped social skills, and low-level intellectual development. Evaluation of that curriculum often is characterized by inauthentic or inappropriate assessment.

The Middle Level Curriculum Project identified and addressed a different set of questions. We believe these questions help us to focus on a middle level curriculum that is both valuable and appropriate:

> *Who are young adolescents?*
> *What questions do they have about themselves and their*
> *world?*
> *What questions does the world pose for them?*
> *In what kind of future world might they live?*
> *How can adults help all students learn?*
> *What activities should young adolescents engage in at school?*
> *How do we design a curriculum that is good both for young*
> *adolescents as well as for the adults who share their*
> *world?*
> *In the school experience, how do we utilize all ways of know-*
> *ing and all areas of human experience?*

Questions like these must guide responsible curriculum decisions. Such decisions not only involve what is to be learned but also how it is learned since the process creates content, not only in the classrooms but throughout the entire school community. A responsive curriculum is living and evolving and should be viewed within the framework of all experiences provided by the educational community.

## *What stereotypes inhibit curriculum development?*

Young adolescents live in a complex world. One aspect of that world is early adolescence itself, that time in life when the physical, intellectual, emotional, and social changes of puberty affect the way in which young adolescents perceive themselves and their experiences. While this is a challenging stage of development, young adolescents have not been helped by the stereotypic "storm and stress" views. These views have been promoted by the mass media, psychiatric case studies, and unwittingly, by educators who draw chuckles by labeling young adolescents with such terms as "hormones with feet" and "range of the strange."

In addition to ridding ourselves of stereotypes, we must recognize societal forces which affect specific developmental processes. For example, in terms of *physical development* a culture dominated by images of girls with long hair, shapely, slender bodies and perfect features, and of macho boys with bulging biceps and clear complexions, heightens greatly the adolescent concern about growth and appearance. In terms of *intellectual development*, healthy relationships and self-esteem are difficult in a society where support systems are decaying and where meaningful roles for the young have all but disappeared. Peer groups inevitably take on undue importance in a society which systematically isolates youth from the adult world. In terms of *moral development*, consider the effect of our society's obsession with violence, glorification of greed, promotion of early sexual experimentation, and leadership lacking in integrity and the replacement of heroes with celebrities.

When such stereotypes and the inattention to societal forces enter our middle level schools they are highly destructive, for they induce self-fulfilling prophecies. If adults expect young adolescents to behave in negative, antisocial ways, they virtually guarantee that behavior. Moreover, stereotypes and neglect to study society influences provide us with excuses to maintain the status quo. If educators say that young adolescents are developmentally destined to act in bizarre ways, they are reduced to simply coping. Our strategies then become ways to help our students (and ourselves) adjust to an ineffective and inefficient educational system.

These narrow conceptions demean early adolescence. They deny that this is a time of heightened intellectual activity when the capacity to think systematically and hypothetically, to reflect critically, and to see shades of grey while developing personal values begins to emerge. None of the prevalent stereotypes about early adolescence hold up to scrutiny.

## What should be included in a curriculum context?

A middle level curriculum confronts and addresses the stereotypes. It provides a more accurate, positive, and empathic view of young adolescents and their potential. This view must be translated into a curriculum that is genuinely responsive to their needs, interests, and abilities, assisting them in making sense of themselves and the world about them. In particular, we seek their empowerment by helping them understand their own development and the forces in society which are either enhancing or distorting it.

The complex world of the young adolescent is comprised of a variety of cultures, families, communities, and societies that result in global citizenship. Some of these systems are immediate to young adolescents. Others are distant or invisible to them. However, whether immediate or distant, perceived or not, all young adolescents are part of a larger world, and the middle level curriculum must take in that larger world.

Because of this, middle level educational practices should demonstrate the value of human diversity, wherein all members of the school community are treated with equity, justice, dignity, and respect. Oppression has no place in schools or society. Race, gender, sexual orientation, class, creed, language, nationalism, regionalism, ability, or age must not restrict access to the richest and fullest experiences within the school community.

We also believe that diversity must be celebrated. Middle level curriculum must illustrate a sense of community between and among all people. From such a sense of community grows appreciation, respect, and concern for others. The curriculum must foster a sense of belonging and a willingness to strive for collective goals. As learners work together to pose and pursue questions about themselves and their world, they develop skills for active and responsible participation in the world community.

All young adolescents have unique needs which can and must be addressed through a common curriculum. In a practical sense, then, neither the young adolescents themselves nor the curriculum content can be divided or tracked into ability groups or levels. Independent and small group learning within the whole group context, as well as cooperative and flexible grouping, meet the unique needs of individual young adolescents. The hallmark of these or any other method is that community is preserved while uniqueness is celebrated.

## What are the sources of middle level curriculum?

The search for self and social meaning poses questions that arise from all aspects of our complex world. Some questions occur to many young adolescents because of the developmental stage they are in:

> *Who am I?*
> *Why and how am I changing?*
> *How can I find a place in my peer group?*

Other questions occur to young adolescents as they look out toward their world:

> *How do I fit in the larger world?*
> *Why can't people get along?*
> *Why are there such extremes of wealth and poverty in my*
> *community?*

Still other questions may not occur to some young adolescents, depending upon their circumstances, but nonetheless are posed to them by the world in which they

> *How can we live in harmony with those different from us?*
> *What are the human issues created by advancing technology?*
> *What are the long-term hazards of environmental pollution?*
> *What do shifts in political systems in other countries mean for*
> *our future?*

A middle level curriculum that serves self and social meanings thus grows out of questions from three primary sources:

**Questions young adolescents have about themselves;**

**Questions young adolescents have about the world around them;**

**Questions that are posed to them by the world in which they live, but which they might not be aware of.**

These questions give meaning, method, context, and power to a curriculum. They serve to provide ends and means to determining content and processes for learning. A middle level curriculum that is meaningful, powerful, and coherent begins with and works toward answers to these significant self and social questions.

Some educators would presume that they know the questions and concerns of young adolescents. However, to design an educational experience which is truly responsive to the young adolescent, The Middle Level Curriculum Project developed the following items to serve as a framework for curriculum themes. This eleven item survey, which expands the three original questions, was designed to elicit student responses. All students are asked to complete the following sentence starters:

> I am...
> I wish I knew why...
> I wish I knew how...
> I wish I knew more about...
> I wish I knew when...
> What are the things you daydream about?
> What are the things you worry about?
> Ten years from now, what do you see yourself doing?
> I like classes that...
> I don't like classes that...

Reading the responses reveals the breadth and depth of student experiences. It reinforces the need to ask young adolescents directly what are their concerns and questions. Most young adolescents revealed deep concerns about certain issues as well as frustrations about which few, if any, adults are aware.

Over 500 students in rural, urban, and suburban school districts participated in our initial survey. The following are representative excerpts of student responses:

> *I wish I knew why some people are popular and others aren't and why when a popular person cracks a joke everyone laughs but when a loser says the same thing, everyone makes fun of them...P.S. I think all programs like Catching Kids Being Great are bull because only the popular preps are caught being good because the teachers only want to find them. Us losers have feelings, too!*

> *I wish I knew why women never go into puberty the same time men do.*

> *I wish I knew how to start a recycling program in the community. I am very concerned about environmental problems.*

*I worry that my parents will get divorced. They always fight and I try to stop them, but they never listen to me.*

*I wish I knew why people don't keep our world clean for theose who will live here in the year 2200.*

*I wonder what I did wrong to deserve my life the way it is now.*

*I worry about my reputation and the earth. Both are in lousy shape.*

*I wish I knew more about religion. I'm Catholic and I'm supposed to believe that God is going to save us all, but then I start thinking about the Buddhists. What if they're right and I am wrong? Or what about the Muslims? What if they're right? And what if there isn't any god or anything like that? What if when we die we just die?*

*I wonder if I'm a virgin or not?*

*The things I worry about is my second child who has Down's Syndrome and my first child who was a drug baby.*

*I wish I knew more about my father. He's just like me, he closes up like a clam. And ever since my mother died, I've needed him more. I try to get closer to him but it's so hard.*

*I wish I knew how to be a better friend. I find myself in many different kinds of cliques and wondering why I can't hold onto one.*

*I worry about dying from AIDS either from a rape or from a careless husband or because everyone in the future has it.*

*I wonder if I'll ever change back to how I was when I was 2 or 3. I liked those years because I didn't care how I acted, looked, or talked.*

*I wish I knew why the world has so many problems and why the different countries just can't get along with each other. I wish I knew why people treat the earth the way they do, spraying aerosols into the atmosphere, ruining the ozone burning trash, filling landfills, using up all our natural resources.*

*I wish I knew why my parents worry soooo much about my grades instead of how I feel.*

*I am a ballet dancer. I have been dancing practically all of my life. I am short, pudgy, and stupid.*

As demonstrated by the concerns above, the middle level curriculum must address and reflect the unique developmental and social needs of young adolescents and their changing society. The world around them poses questions and problems that they need to explore. As the young adolescent works to resolve an issue, defend a position, or solve a problem, the curriculum should integrate the personal, social and global domains.

## What are the outcomes of the curriculum?

What do we expect from such a curriculum? What behaviors do we expect to see in young adolescents and the school community? Drawing from the questions and concerns young adolescents raise, as well as from the questions posed to students by the world in which they live, our curriculum would find students:

— engaging in worthwhile and compelling learning;
— questioning, challenging, applying, and valuing their own ideas and knowledge as well as those of others;
— coming into closer connection with the world at large;
— struggling to construct powerful meanings from their own experiences and the experiences of others;
— more fully integrating self and social interests; and
— striving for self-actualization within a personal and global context.

While these are general descriptions of outcomes, we believe that each school community must engage in dialogue to develop its own outcomes. From this list would come organizational arrangements, institutional arrangements, instructional strategies, and integrated curriculum that provides the means for students' search for self and social meanings. These institutional features, however, are not so heavily prescribed that they dictate what students will be doing next week or next month. Rather, teachers encourage, facilitate, and guide students as they extend their knowledge and skills in their search for understanding.

## *How should middle level curriculum be organized?*

We believe that young adolescents' own experiences, knowledge, and questions constitute valuable bases for developing curriculum. The middle level curriculum is most responsive when the questions, concepts, and ideas upon which it is built are organized cooperatively by teachers and students, and when both are involved in active processing, questioning, analyzing, and reflecting. Such a curriculum blends the usual roles of teacher and student as teachers become more concerned with facilitating learning than with simply disseminating a pre-selected set of facts and requiring recitation.

A curriculum which values young adolescents' search for self and social meanings cannot be comprised of a series of separate subjects or occasional shared topics that cross subject lines. Traditional subject boundaries inhibit the discovery of relationships in the exploration of powerful and relevant meanings. Much of the present effort to develop interdisciplinary curriculum through multi-subject team organizations, though better than the isolated separate subject approach, still assumes a priority of those subjects. Moreover, interdisciplinary team structures that are typically organized around mathematics, language arts, social studies, and science create a hierarchy of knowledge in which concepts from other areas are unwisely eliminated or wrongly devalued. As experienced, life is an integrated whole and the middle level curriculum should model this unity.

The curriculum we envision is not based upon fixed or static knowledge. Rather it is fluid and evolving. "Learning to do" and "learning about" are inevitably related as are curriculum and instruction. They involve exploring, creating, and relating rather than finding the right answer. Exploration involves much more than just a series of courses labeled as "exploratory." Instead it is an underlying premise for the whole middle level curriculum and all of the programs and experiences it includes. This understanding of exploration suggests that all learning is activity-based, contextual, and well-integrated with real life experiences leading to self and social understanding.

In the context of self and social questions, where knowledge from the larger world has explicit importance, we expect that young adolescents will come to learn, apply, and value that knowledge. As we come to value young adolescents' own experiences and questions as essential bases for the curriculum, they are more likely to integrate such knowledge from the larger world with their own experience in terms of genuine learning. Moreover, in posing self and social questions and seeking answers to them, young adolescents will inevitably improve their abilities in areas such as communication, calculation, critical thinking, creativity, citizenship, interpersonal relations, research, and problem solving.

Again, such an authentic approach to learning cannot assign knowledge to discreet subject areas. Rather it must involve unified knowledge that transcends subject area boundaries. This integrated interaction of posing questions and seeking answers will vary in form, process, and content from school to school and community to community. In some cases the questions and concerns may be organized around units or semester/annual themes. In other settings, the format may be organized using problems or concerns. In any event, the curriculum begins with the world of the young adolescent and moves outward to encompass global society. This kind of middle level curriculum can provide the momentum to empower the school community to personally and collectively fulfill their rich potential.

## What activities comprise such a curriculum?

Much of the content contained in traditional subject areas is obsolete in an era of information and knowledge explosion. The very structure of these content areas is questionable in a world where multiplicity is valued and complexity is viewed as natural. Therefore, the inevitability of change must be a significant focus of middle level curriculum. Change cannot be addressed through a passive instructional process. While direct and formal instruction may occasionally have a valid place in the lexicon of classroom activities, other approaches must play a larger role. Activities and experiences for teachers and young adolescents include:

— cooperative planning and organizing;
— seeking out collaborators for learning;
— analyzing one's own needs and interests;
— exploring and linking with parents and the community as exte nsions of the classroom;
— creating technological and artistic forums for sharing knowledge and information;
— articulating and valuing knowledge already possessed; constructing meaningful evaluation for processes and creations, including portfolios and journals;
— posing questions and hypotheses for search and research.

These activities address the social, emotional, and psychological changes that are experienced by young adolescents and which reside with them regardless of where they are during the day. The needs and concerns which emerge from these developmental changes can and should be served in the context of exploring self and social meanings throughout the school.

Resources for such activities must be plentiful and varied. Middle schools must provide access to a variety of resources both human and material, rather than solely relying on textbooks and other commercially prepared materials. The middle level curriculum should invite the collaboration of teachers, students, parents and community. Such collaboration is a rich resource for learning. The Middle Level Curriculum Project views all members of the school community as learners and believes the middle level curriculum is enriched when all learners teach and learn together.

Content specialists who recognize and appreciate the subtleties and detail of particular knowledge areas are a valuable resource to a curriculum designed for and with young adolescents. However, their contributions to the middle level curriculum should not be bound by their discreet area of certification. The experiential activities embodied in a middle level curriculum challenge specialists to explore knowledge in a more broadly defined way. This involves conceptualizing, organizing, applying, and expressing the nuances of a body of knowledge, as perceived through the broader framework that is the search for self and social meaning. This role of specialist also removes the teacher from the isolated classroom setting and offers possibilities as a resource teacher for colleagues as well as students.

## How can this vision of middle level curriculum be implemented?

The Middle Level Curriculum Project recognizes that implementation of this curriculum requires a comprehensive and coordinated effort. The transition of ideas into educational practice demands that educators, as much as students, learn through direct experience and coordinated efforts. The following steps provide a path for the movement of curricular theory into practice:

1. Initiation process
2. Implementation process
3. Continuing the vision

During the initiation process, those who share the responsibility for the school community must reach consensus and develop a vision for a new middle level curriculum. The next step involves moving from the philosophical vision and outcomes to identification of concrete outcomes based on the school community's curriculum vision. Identification and development of the curricular content and process to address and assess the outcomes is the final step of the initiation process.

To implement this curriculum, three areas need to be addressed. The first area to be considered is the school community. Past practices and school traditions handicap the school community from engaging in an effective change process. Long-term staff development to address changing roles is essential for the implementation of a visionary curriculum. In addition, many educators suffer from a loss of self-esteem because of their lack of meaningful involvement and passive participation in decisions that affect them.

Time is another area that affects implementation. The traditional school schedule that divides student and staff time into periods impedes the flexibility that is essential to continue the creation of a living curriculum. The school community must have the opportunity to develop flexible school schedules that allow for change from hour to hour, day to day, or week to week, not just year to year.

Facilities are the third area for consideration in the implementation process. Existing school buildings should no longer determine or limit how curriculum is delivered. Creative changes and new notions of where the curriculum can be explored must be adopted. The community becomes the school building.

While successful implementation is important, it will take cooperative planning and effort to maintain the evolving middle level curriculum. The school must establish a means by which students, staff, parents, and community members provide continuous input and evaluation. This can be accomplished by asking the extent to which the three curriculum source questions are being addressed:

Is our curriculum effectively addressing questions young adolescents have about themselves?

Is our curriculum effectively addressing questions young adolescents have about the world around them?

Is our curriculum effectively addressing question posed to young adolescents by the world in which they live?

Answers to these questions provide the framework to continue the development of effective middle level curriculum, a curriculum that serves self and social meanings.

### What should assessment look like in this curriculum?

The curriculum we envision requires multiple sources for assessment. We are concerned more with young adolescents' abilities to integrate and connect knowledge than we are in their ability to display concrete content information on a paper and pencil test in a competitive situation. We believe that authentic assessment of outcomes proceeds from the young adolescent's search for self and social meanings and the activities which provide the means for that search. Did the search involve group projects, reports, research papers, portfolios, products? Were students involved in community projects and programs? These kinds of activities provide the basis for evaluation. They are broader and require input from more than one source as contrasted to a multiple choice standardized test. In this kind of assessment, students could participate in the development of the assessment plan as a step in their project or research activity design. Authentic assessments which include process as well as content become benchmarks of student progress along the continuum of learning. Grades become irrelevant. When evaluation focuses on the outcomes of the middle level curriculum, assessment not only reveals student learning, but leads to areas for further curriculum development. The report of such outcomes is individualized and meaningful to both young adolescents and the adults who live and work with them. These outcomes may then become incomes—personal dividends for all the learners in the middle level community.

### A call to action

We have described a new vision of curriculum for young adolescents. It reflects a concern for the needs and interests of young adolescents and the world in which they live. It is generated out of an awareness of the need for an initiative which respects both the uniqueness of their personal world and their interdependent relationships within wider social contexts. We have not described a specific curriculum design. That ultimately is the right and responsibility of those who live and work with young adolescents in particular local communities and schools. It is hoped that this statement will initiate dialogue among middle level educators seeking to develop a genuine middle level curriculum.

The vision of middle level curriculum presented here suggests that what students need to know stems from questions they have about themselves and the world around them, and questions posed to them by the world in which they live. It also suggests that a search for answers to these questions cannot be pursued by following traditional subject area lines. Since answers to life's questions do not fall within subject boundaries, course and discipline divisions prevent their realization.

It is hoped that those who read this article will accept the need for experimentation with and fundamental revision of conventional middle level curriculum. However, an understanding and acceptance of the ideas presented in this statement—while extremely important—can only be evaluated with reference to what teachers and administrators actually do about curriculum in their school. Curriculum revision is not a simple process. It is a process which takes place over time. To think differently about curriculum and to act on that thinking provides for an element of risk—a risk not only on the part of teachers, but also on the part of administrators, for it necessitates cultural change. Visionary instructional leaders versus building level managers are key attributes required to facilitate this change process. Administrators need to become involved and familiar with instructional issues, as well as make a commitment to the issue of long-term staff development and its importance in the change process. Translation of philosophical ideas into functional practice will require that teachers—like the students themselves—learn through direct experience. Opportunities to provide these experiences become the responsibility of the change agents within the school. Thinking and believing must be translated into doing for all participants in the school community.

*The **Middle Level Curriculum Project** is a group of educators, including teachers, administrators, state department personnel, and university professors. The group began its work in May, 1990 and developed this paper through several meetings sponsored by the Universities of Wisconsin at Platteville and Green Bay.*

*Members of the project are:*

| | |
|---|---|
| Jerry Adrian | Thomas Lo Guidice |
| John Arnold | Lee McDonough |
| James A. Beane | Thomas Morris |
| Edward Brazee | Mary Lochner-Olson |
| Judith Brough | Gary Peal |
| Gail Burnaford | Judy Peppard |
| John Daly | Ellen Shiflet |
| Janet Hagen | Preston Smeltzer |
| Richard Halle | Robert Skaife |
| David Brauny | James Stoltenberg |
| Jane Howell | Robert Stone |
| Kathy Jochman | Marianne Strozewski |
| Sandra Johannsen | Martin Tadlock |
| David Larkin | Gordon Vars |
| B.J. Lavrakas | Lynn Wallich |
| Brenda Leake | |

# The Cardigan experience —
# An eighth grade integrated curriculum
*Charlene E. Carper*

Almost twenty years ago, a science curriculum philosophy focusing on "the learner learning best by doing" was melded with the middle school movement at McKelvie School in Bedford, New Hampshire, and the seeds of what is now the Cardigan Unit, an integrated curriculum, were sown. The goal of the developers of this unit was to create an exciting, hands-on adventure for eighth grade students in the area of science. Since the concept of interdisciplinary units was an important component of the middle school movement, the teachers began to look for connections with the other content areas. Math was found to be a natural component of the unit with one after another of the remaining content areas finding linkage to this experiential, learning unit. In reviewing the development of the unit, its focus was found to be multi-disciplinary in approach rather than interdisciplinary. It resembled what Beane wrote about in *A Middle School Curriculum: From Rhetoric to Reality* (1990) as a "broad fields approach" (p. 21). It was not until later in the unit's ongoing development that the McKelvie staff began to look at the unit as a curriculum unto itself. At that time, it moved from being a multi-disciplinary unit to becoming an interdisciplinary curriculum.

### *Multidisciplinary to interdisciplinary*

To fully understand the unit and the curriculum theory behind the integration, a brief history of the program is needed. A visionary science curriculum coordinator for the Bedford School District had an opportunity. It was the science curriculum's "turn" for revision. In keeping with the science curriculum philosophy of "learning by doing," the coordinator, in a brainstorming session with other eighth grade teachers, came up with the idea for an environmental unit. The seeds of that idea were taken to the principal and the assistant superintendent of curriculum and instruction, both of whom provided the much needed administrative support. Using summer curriculum time, the unit was developed by the teachers. Knowing the community, the staff recognized the need for measurable goals as well as community understanding and support so that the unit was not seen as a big field trip, but rather as a total learning experience which used a form of field trip as a test.

The teachers recognized early that false connections had little meaning for students. There had to be a use for each of the components of the curriculum. The staff sensed the value of students being able to put to practical use what they were learning in the classroom. Consequently, each year as the curriculum was evaluated, it was assessed for real connections versus contrived ones. Today, students review basic math concepts and skills while working on such activities as pacing, stream flow, mapping and soil analysis. They build vocabulary through an extensive glossary which accompanies the unit. They work on writing skills as they do journal entries and study environmental authors. The whole area of self-reliance, self-esteem, group dynamics, how people get along with one another is cultivated. The physical training or "physical torture" prepares students for the hiking and climbing. Finally, students learn the demands humanity puts on the ecosystems.

In developing the curriculum, it was also realized that there were no textbook or printed materials that would adequately serve the needs of this unit. Teachers took the initiative and developed a manual and all the attendant materials to support and reinforce the skills in the unit. This ownership of the materials has had a tremendous impact on the success of this curriculum. Because curriculum is a living, breathing document, the Cardigan curriculum continually undergoes revision. The manual itself is updated as needed. Changes are made in the content area as well as in the process area. The manual reflects the most current information on how students learn.

The manner of instruction has also changed over the years from being more content specific to being more holistic. The current approach is to utilize large group as well as small group instruction, cooperative learning, and peer tutoring, all in an effort to have students be as successful as possible during the unit. Each new concept is presented in a large group with the expert from the staff presiding. Lecture and demonstration in the large group is followed by small group activities back in the homeroom. All teachers have become teachers of students rather than teachers of content.

While the science curriculum and other content areas were the initial focus, the teachers also recognized the need for the affective component of education. An emphasis on team building, self-esteem, problem solving and decision making became very important components of the unit. Another goal, the building of a strong teacher-student relationship, also became a reality. While this is not a traditional advisor/advisee program, the same results are accomplished. The bonding that takes place and then continues throughout the eighth grade experience is unparalleled. The homeroom/camp groups are the advisory groups. They meet together every day throughout the year, building on the Cardigan Unit. Student/teacher relationships do not end with the 8th grade but continue for years as demonstrated by students coming back once they finish high school and asking to go along as chaperons or runners for the Cardigan Experience.

---

*Practical experiences in town*

Three special activities reinforce the program prior to the final mountain experience. These are designed to provide students with a team building experience, an on-site experience and a test of both academics and peer interactions. The first activity, which takes place during the first full week of school, is held at a local scout camp, Camp Foster. The "Camp Foster Derby" engages the students in a variety of problem solving activities. Each camp group (homeroom) begins the day with a hike to the camp, followed by the opening of a set of sealed instructions. Under the direction of their elected student leader, each group sets out for a designated station. They may arrive at the station like honking, migrating geese or a hissing Shaker, or perhaps they are carrying their leader or whistling a tune. It all depends on their sealed instructions. Once at the station, they will set up a tent, blindfolded, and collect water from a pond with a bucket that is full of holes. During the day, group members will also cross the human/rope bridge and be led blindfolded over the bed of "quicksand." By the time the nine problem solving activities have been completed, the camp group has become a more cohesive unit.

The second activity day comes after several weeks of academics. This activity takes the students and teachers to a local conservation area, Pulpit Rock. The experience at Pulpit Rock is a mirror of the experiences the students will have on the mountain. The area has well-marked trails and various geological formations along with an abundance of flora. Once at this area, the students set-up study sites where they will identify and research the vegetation. These sites are revisited each year with the data being compiled to note any changes. Water testing, the taking of soil samples, the calculation of stream flow, and the recording of observations in journals are all practiced.

Finally, for three days prior to leaving for the mountain, the students participate in PACS—Practical Application of Cardigan Skills. This is an exam modeled after a college biology practical. Students, working in squads of eight or nine members, complete assigned tasks and receive a grade based on the groups' accomplishments. Over the three days, the squads travel to 24 different stations at twenty minute intervals. Some of the stations focus on academics, others on problem solving and group dynamics, and still others on hiking and camping skills. Academic stations include identification of vegetation, computation of the board feet in a tree, traversing a compass course, and describing, in the squad journal, the activity at each station and how it was completed. Problem solving stations include escaping from an "electric fence," getting a tire over a nine foot pole and walking the wire over the "dreaded swamp." Camping skills incorporated in the stations include fire building, both wet and dry, and packing a back pack. The fire starting station helps students realize the importance of what they need to know in order to be responsible not only for themselves in case of emergency, but also for the well-being of the group.

With twenty-four stations to supervise over a three day period, the use of volunteers is crucial. With most of the stations set up on the school acreage (only a few are inside the building), parents and community volunteers numbering 25 to 30 must come prepared for rain or shine. Their assignment is to keep a score card on each squad along with helping the squad when/if things get too difficult.

With all of the academics, problem solving activities, and physical training that goes into this ten week program, the culminating event is the trip to Mt. Cardigan, a four-day, three-night adventure where students use the skills, academic and social, they have learned. For four days and three nights, these students put all of these various components to the test to make the experience on the mountain something that cannot be reproduced in the classroom.

## The experience on Cardigan Mountain

How is what was learned in the classroom played out on the mountain? An account of the trip to the mountain with 220 students plus teachers and chaperons will assist one in answering this question.

All day Monday and Tuesday morning are spent in packing the students' and adults' backpacks with all the gear and food, everything that will be needed for the stay on the mountain. The packs go up separately in a large tractor trailer donated yearly by a community member. Students and teachers ride on school buses with parents and other community chaperons following in their cars. Everyone disembarks at the AMC Lodge. In the early years of the program, the camp groups stayed at the AMC Lodge and went out from there to do the academic work on the mountain and to climb the Hold Trail, the face of the mountain. Today, each of the eight homerooms scatters across the mountain. Each camp group has a predetermined campsite which will be their home for four days.

Once the camp group gets to the campsite, tents must be set up, food tent secured, fire ring constructed, and wood gathered, remembering that only wood found on the ground may be used since this is an exercise in minimal impact camping. Students' knowledge of water testing is used immediately as the stream is the only source of water for the camp. Next, knowledge about a water source and latrine building must be put to use as the latrines are dug. While the adults complete the final set-up, the camp group goes off to one of their two study sites. At the study site, students collect data on the merchantable height of the trees and the regeneration of the forest in that area. These data are sent to the University of New Hampshire which is compiling them to follow changes in the vegetation on Mt. Cardigan and in the Northeast in general. Working in squads on specific parts of the study site, students use their meter strings, their math, and their knowledge of trees in order to collect the data. Once back from the site work, dinner must be made and cleanup completed. Cooperation is the key word.

Sitting around the camp fire at night provides an opportunity to share some thoughts of the day and to plan for the next day's activities, as well as providing some simple good times. This time might be used to read Robert Frost's poem, "The Mountain," and liken it to this mountain, or to talk about his poem, "Mending Walls." There are a lot of stone walls along the trail into the camp sites. The galaxy overhead also prompts comments and questions.

Early to bed, early to rise. Someone has to get the fire going; someone has to make the breakfast. It is all part of teamwork. Once breakfast is finished and cleanup has occurred, the squad responsible for making lunches for the camp group takes over. It will be a full day of hiking the various trails in the area as the students go about completing the manual. The first stop may be Welton Falls. There the student will participate in a stream flow activity where they will time Ping Pong balls floating down the stream to calculate the flow.

After Welton Falls, it is time to attack the Holt Trail. The Holt Trail is "infamous" in McKelvie students' minds for being the most difficult part of the hiking adventure. Not only do they scale the face of Mt.

Cardigan, but the feat also builds a sense of accomplishment and achievement in all students. Each can make it with the help of others—even the adults. Weather observation must be taken and recorded. Once back, everyone has an opportunity to write in their journals. In addition, the weather observation at the camp site must be taken for the day and the camp site must be accurately paced for the map work that must be completed back at school. All of these components of the curriculum must be put into play now—the math, the science, the language arts, and the social studies but students see it simply as the Cardigan experience.

The second night might be the time for the night sensory walk. What are the sights and sounds at night in the forest when one is alone? How do you feel? What do you hear? Each student is left off along the trail, alone, without a flashlight. The task is to sit and listen. Once picked up and back at the camp site, students go to their tents and record their feelings. Later around the camp fire, anyone who wishes to shares what he or she has heard, saw, or felt.

The third day is the time for bushwhacking. The compass work learned and practiced back at McKelvie is used to get the group from the camp site to Grand Junction. The students set the course by averaging their heading. Each student is then paired up with another and takes a turn at leading the group through the forest to the trail. Sometimes the heading is fairly accurate, sometimes not, but in either case, it is a learning experience. Next, the second study site must be completed. The students need all the data in order to be successful in their work as environmental scientists. The final night around the camp fire is a time for special sharing. Skits are performed and games played.

The final morning brings a sense of sadness. Everything must be dismantled. Everything that was taken in, must be taken out. It is a lot harder to get all the items back into the backpacks after they have been taken out and used. Latrines must be closed and all of the surrounding land must look like no human has been there. It truly is amazing that the students have learned so much and can, as a group, leave a spot of nature as it was when they found it. The biggest push is to get back to the AMC Lodge and see the friends that have not been seen for days. Sometimes camp groups pass each other along the trails, but there are groups that one might not see for the whole four days on the mountain. Kids are anxious to see each other and to tell their stories.

Back at school, parents are waiting. The smell of camp fire smoke has permeated everyones' clothing as well as the school buses and the school itself as students unload all the gear. Once again, as when they met their friends at the AMC Lodge, the students are ready to share all of their experiences with their parents. For the reluctant or for the eager, it has been an experience. All that was learned in the classroom was used on the mountain. There was a reason for learning and it was tested.

## *Changing the assessment procedures*

The assessment model for the curriculum has been slow to evolve. While the walls between the content areas have been broken down, the use of traditional reporting remains. In their efforts to address assessment, the staff has redesigned the progress report. The new report shows no delineation of subject areas but rather lists all the activities of the unit, not just the academics. A point value is assigned to each. This new format has been well received by parents who indicate that it provides them with more information than was provided before. The next step is re-designing the traditional report card to reflect the integration rather than the separation.

## *Components for success*

Why is this unit so successful and what has sustained it for all these years? The dedication and commitment of the eighth grade staff is the key. Most of the teachers who were part of the vision twenty years ago are still part of it today. They have spent untold hours in planning, developing, assessing, and redeveloping the many components of the curriculum. As a team, they meet daily to plan the instructional program for their students. They work hours after school, before school and during the summer (without pay) so that the curriculum can incorporate the most current content material, teaching practices and knowledge about learning. Problem solving activities must be continually changed or refined. These new and different activities have kept things alive and have offered staff an opportunity to "do things differently." The curriculum never stops developing. The process is dynamic, changing, and responsive to individual teacher's new ideas and new concerns. It is exhausting in many respects. However, these professionals are open and willing to change and to learn from each other so that the ultimate goal of providing a meaningful education in which each student has the opportunity to be successful can be reached.

Community involvement is also a critical element in the success of this curriculum. As indicated earlier, PACS could not take place without the volunteers, nor would the experience on the mountain be possible. In addition to the physical involvement by the community, the moral support for the curriculum is also outstanding. Parents anticipate their childrens' eighth grade experience and are positive spokespersons for the program. Many parents continue to be active in the experience long after their sons and daughters have left the middle school.

## Intersections of personal and social concerns

It was not until reading Beane's monograph (1990) that anyone of the staff at the McKelvie School analyzed the Cardigan curriculum in terms of intersections. Everyone knew that the unit was a vital, interesting, motivating educational experience for children in which a lot of learning took place in an atmosphere both in and out of the classroom. What they had not realized was that this unit's theme was at that intersection of social and personal concerns about which Beane wrote. For this unit, the social concerns, the environmental crisis, and the personal concerns, finding a place in the group, self-esteem, personal fitness, and independence intersect at the stewardship or interdependence theme. While the staff had never explored this connection before, it does make sense to them now. In exploring the stewardship or interdependence themes, the McKelvie students utilize not only the traditional academic skills but also reflective thinking, problem solving, valuing, self-concept, self-esteem, and social action skills. The integrated curriculum allows the students to put to the test, in a real situation, what they know. The students find value in their learning. The Cardigan curriculum "connects cognition and affect and applies them to compelling themes" (Beane, 1990). Consequently, intersection can also be added to the list of components for success.

The stewardship/interdependence themes do not disappear once the Cardigan experience is complete. Not only has the McKelvie staff reviewed the Cardigan curriculum following their reading of Beane's monograph and meeting with him, but also they reviewed the entire eighth grade curriculum. What they found was that other units which they have created over the years have the same themes. These units include the McKelvie Stock Project, Your Town—Your Choice, and the Consumer Unit. Their continuing goal is to work towards greater integration and refinement of these units along with the development of the new integrated reporting system. The continuing goal is that of integration rather than separation.

### References

Beane, J. A. (1990). *A middle school curriculum: From rhetoric to reality.* Columbus, OH: National Middle School Association.

**Charlene Carper** *is Assistant Principal at McKelvie Middle School, Bedford, New Hampshire.*

# Curriculum for identity:
# A middle level educational obligation
*Conrad F. Toepfer, Jr.*

*C*  *urriculum is the tool, the "stuff" of education. Through the curriculum students learn the skills, the attitudes, and the knowledge they need. Curriculum is a vehicle, a device.*

This cogent description of curriculum by Mamchur (1990) is realistic. Today, as "the stuff of education," curriculum must keep current to meet the dynamics of change inherent in the information age. Curriculum should be expansive, not restrictive. However, both the form and substance of today's middle level curriculum remain remarkably similar to that found in schools in 1960. Also, the United States now seems to be moving toward a national curriculum. Smith, O'Day, and Cohen (1991) observe that effort in itself may only duplicate the singular focus which already exists in contemporary curricula. Piecemeal school reform by a national curriculum and testing program poorly suits our nation's diversifying educational needs. It seems that a national curriculum and testing program will only further tilt the decline of school achievement among impoverished and diverse school-aged youth. That increases the dangers of re-segregating particular groups into a permanent American underclass.

The failures this writer sees resulting from a national skills curriculum will eventually gain our attention. Now or then, systematic, systemic curriculum planning and development will be needed to develop curricular alternatives appropriate for the needs of youth (Beane, Toepfer, & Alessi, 1986). A national middle level skills curriculum cannot meet the widening educational needs of middle school-aged youth from diverse backgrounds. At the same time, individual states need to examine their middle level program standards. If those regulations are largely high school driven, they can thwart schools from developing middle level program identity based upon adolescent developmental characteristics and the learning needs of today's youth.

The orthodoxy of both the elements of middle level curriculum and their structure in schools today is inadequate for solving existing curricular problems. Curricular alternatives are needed that facilitate individual progress toward desired curriculum goals. Middle level curriculum functions have to be reconceptualized in terms of the needs of contemporary and emerging society and be based upon differences in kind and degree of the needs which young adolescents bring to school.

## Middle level curriculum focus

The core of a school's educational identity resides in its curriculum and programs. Middle level educational effectiveness centers in the degree to which curriculum and programs respond to early adolescent characteristics and needs (Toepfer, 1990). Eichhorn (1966) developed terms to describe the tasks young adolescents face during their middle level school years. He defined this epoch as *transescence*. The term deals with the nature of the tasks youngsters need to master in their metamorphosis during that period. Eichhorn defined transescence as:

> ...the stage of development which begins prior to the onset of puberty and extends through the early stages of adolescence. Since puberty does not occur for all precisely at the same chronological age in human development, the transescent designation is based upon the many physical, social, emotional, and intellectual changes that appear prior to the puberty cycle to the time when the body gains a practical degree of stabilization over these complex pubescent changes (p. 3).

The definition of transescence (roots are *trans* from transition and *escence* from adolescence) cogently identifies the focus needed to develop curriculum which addresses the growth, development, and transition tasks experienced during the developmental stage previously called "young adolescence," "early adolescence," or "emerging adolescence." Most adults largely fashion their character, ethics, and attitudes about life and learning during this period of development, building upon their childhood experiences. Few of us substantially change in those dimensions after reaching high school. Therefore, middle level instructional practice should be rooted in differences of kind and degree from things appropriate in either elementary or high school programs.

Elementary and high school curricula have characteristically differed from each other. Should not the substance of middle level curricula then differ from that of both elementary and high schools? Agreement on the answers to the following questions is necessary to define such a differentiated middle level curricular identity. What are the differences in purposes of elementary, middle level, and high schools, from each other? Do the developmental differences of young adolescent learners from elementary and high school learners require unique middle level curricula based upon those developmental differences?

Some middle level educational national spokespersons boldly state that what is taught in the middle level school is not as important as how it is taught. This writer rejects that position completely. If that notion is correct, the case for separate middle level curricular identity is defeated. The educational bases for middle level curriculum still pivots on Tompkins' concern (1960):

> Do early adolescents, 11 to 14, and later adolescents, 15 to 19, generally have systematic differences? If they do, then it is essential that schools serve the educational, social, and emotional needs of youth. If there is no difference (how anyone can credit that viewpoint psychologically is difficult to comprehend), then it really doesn't matter whether we have junior high schools or not (p. 22).

The problems stemming from the lack of local middle level curriculum and program identity have been many. Among the most harmful has been the willingness of school districts to move middle grades students into whatever local school settings temporarily offer the most logistical or economic expedience. Districts would not do that with elementary or high school programs. Toepfer (1989) observed:

> This legacy of reshuffling of form has not given adequate concern to the specific educational substance of early secondary education. Such changes have been largely based upon administrative convenience with minimal curricular reorganization for instructional improvement. As a result, the

clientele in early secondary schools probably has experienced less discrete definition of basic curricular experiences than those at either the elementary or high school levels (p. 10).

Eichhorn (1972) emphasized the importance of defining middle level curriculum upon adolescent needs.

This writer is firmly convinced that research and logic have clearly indicated that there is a developmental level between the childhood years of the elementary school and the adolescent years of high school. In the final analysis, there is only one middle school differentiation. This difference is the developmental uniqueness of student clientele. Possibly the greatest challenge for the future of middle schools is the willingness of those committed to this organization to pioneer creative programs designed specially for the early adolescent learner. While in many cases these programs have yet to emerge, the future worth of this level of schooling demands that they be created (p. 51-52).

Toepfer (1971) recommended steps for defining middle level curriculum in that manner:

1.  Identify and study the characteristics, needs, and developmental profiles of the emerging adolescent population in the local school-community setting.

2.  Develop a curricular rationale which will complement and support those needs within the local setting.

3.  Organize and implement an administrative vehicle to spell out an appropriate design for the community's total elementary, middle, and high school curriculum (p. 3).

In reviewing program progress in exemplary middle level schools, it was noted (Toepfer, 1976) that "systematic curriculum planning on a district-wide basis is the only consistent way to refine the middle level school program and avoid the regression syndrome which lurks around us" (p. 22). Middle level program differentiation needs are more diverse than those at either elementary or high school levels. Thus it becomes essential that middle level curriculum options respond as best as possible to the wide range of developmental and learning needs. Staff must develop curriculum planning processes that can organize middle level curriculum elements into effective programs (Toepfer, 1977a). Toepfer (1977b) also discussed how a middle level school as a multiple school should attempt to develop the widest possible local range of teaching-learning environments. "To accomplish this objective for students and teachers, a middle school must carefully draw upon the existing range of capabilities of its staff to become as eclectic as possible.... Possibility of long term "lock-ins" must be avoided through the dynamics of flexibility" (p. 142).

With a focus on middle level curriculum the staff can identify and define local curriculum organization issues. The following concerns could be helpful in examining those issues.

## Curriculum organization issues

Curriculum goals and standards of performance have no value or influence if they are beyond the learner's capacities. Educational goals and curriculum expectations which are beyond the realities of learner readiness only thwart school responses to learner needs. Because of that, success in learning should not be measured with single performance standards. An appropriate range of performance standards is needed to measure what individual students can and do achieve. High expectations and appropriate standards for learning and achievement must be defined responsively.

Middle level curriculum should deal with intellectual development issues in the entire context of young adolescent development. Cognitive and affective concerns should be interfaced, not separated. Success in dealing with cognitive needs seems to be best realized when instructional programs accommodate learners' affective concerns (Beane, 1990a). Middle school curriculum should not organize learning arrangements upon ascending intelligence alone. Gesell, Ilg, and Ames (1956) pointed out that intellectual development is tempered by the wholeness of one's growth and development:

Indeed, intellectual growth itself has sometimes been considered to be "the" course of development, with mental age as it main measure. The limitations of such an approach are all too often demonstrated in a real-life situation. "Mental age," as the term is generally used, is actually a score obtained on a test; it is a valuable index of brightness. But a normal 10 year-old with a mental age of fourteen does not necessarily act like a 14-year-old; he tends to act more like a "bright" ten-year-old (p. 30).

Middle level curriculum organization has to deal adequately with the learning styles and levels inherent in such broad ranges. Departmentalized instruction separates learning within content areas. It does not facilitate articulation of learning experiences among content areas. Teaming can reduce problems of dealing with departmentally isolated subject information. For that reason middle level programs should carefully assess any advantages claimed for retaining departmentalized instruction. Departmentalization does not provide the capacity for cooperative planning needed to integrate learning in middle level programs. Research (Feldlaufer, Midgley & Eccles, 1987) has shown departmentalization to be the least desirable organizational pattern in middle level programs.

That study also revealed that self-contained classrooms provide more correlation of learning and learning opportunities than departmentalization in grades five through eight. Advantages of self-contained over departmentalized classrooms at the middle level seem clear.  However, no case has been made for the advantages of self-contained classrooms over teamed approaches.

This writer believes that middle level schools should be "teaming schools" (1988). The teaming of teachers to plan and develop programs for those whom they commonly teach can extend interdisciplinary learning arrangements. Joint planning can define a solid foundation for real classroom "team," rather than "turn" teaching. In that regard, core curriculum approaches which enable individual teachers to integrate multiple disciplines for students should also be considered (Vars, 1987). Cooperative study among staff is needed to develop their ownership of the program.

Teamed learning in middle level schools needs broader application than it typically is given (Merenbloom, 1986). If teaming is important for organizing instruction in academic areas, it should be equally important for all areas. Experiences in art, music, health, physical education, and the like can be powerful sources of intellectual growth. Adolescent intellectual development is facilitated through the interrelationship of all curriculum areas in the school. Attempts to integrate learning in middle level programs are frustrated by the separate subject organization of middle level curriculum.

An insidious hierarchy is established by designating specific areas and courses "academic" and others "non-academic." This is counterproductive. It hinders articulation among subject areas and can lead to divisive arguments over the relative importance of "essential" versus "frill" areas. Instructional practice must not be prejudicial against students with high abilities in so-called "non-academic" content areas.

A student may acquire basic information in a mathematics or science class. However, that student's conceptualization of that information can develop from learning experiences in other content areas.

Experiential and "hands-on" activities in "non-academic" areas, such as industrial arts or home economics, often develops a student's understanding of a learning experience initiated in an academic class. Attention to the following guidelines can improve middle level curriculum integration (Toepfer, 1988):

> 1. Make certain that efforts to integrate learning are present in all areas in the middle level school's program.

> 2. Identify opportunities to integrate learning within each subject area.

> 3. Identify approaches especially appropriate for integrating learning among subject areas.

> 4. Develop teaching strategies particularly suited for integrating learning among subject areas.

> 5. Identify how extra class activities can be related to interdisciplinary program activities.

Young adolescents learn best when they can see the importance of the facts, skills, and information from classroom lessons in their young lives. The success of interdisciplinary planning, teaching, and learning is best reflected in the accomplishments of students. The desire to learn is enhanced by success in classroom performance. The exuberance some young adolescents display about learning is needed by all. Middle level curriculum organization should seek to broaden that joy in learning. Beane (1990c) assessed the separate subject approach and pointed out two realities of teaming.

> 1. The subject approach presents numerous problems to schools in general and the middle school in particular...it is alien to life itself (p. 29).

> 2. Interdisciplinary teaming does not necessarily lead to interdisciplinary curriculum organization (p. 21).

> 3. When interdisciplinary teaching does take place it is usually a simple correlation of subject areas (p. 21).

While it cannot eradicate separate subject teaching, interdisciplinary planning can lead to the articulation of learning across middle level curriculum areas. For that reason, interdisciplinary organization remains the best option for pursuing the goal of integrated learning in middle level school programs. Integrated learning goals break from the instructional emphasis in schools organized as "junior editions" of programs designed to meet high school needs. To identify the best alternatives to deliver interdisciplinary learning activities, both instructional grouping and scheduling need to become staff decision-making variables.

Integrated learning procedures should influence how middle level schools organize the "what," or substance, of the curriculum. While interdisciplinary planning and teaching do not automatically eliminate the separate subject curriculum organization, it can articulate learning across all areas of the school program. It also can lead to recognition of the need for curriculum organization that facilitates integrated learning. Success in middle level school interdisciplinary teaching parallels that found in cooperative student learning activities. Cooperative, interactive teaching and learning are powerful means for delivering middle level curriculum. Their invitational postures reinforce student confidence that they can succeed in achieving curriculum goals.

Beane (1990b) noted that "the persistent organization around a collection of academic and separate special courses is not developmentally appropriate" (p. 2). It is the curriculum which organizational and methodological efforts then organize and implement in local school programs. What is the nature of curriculum in effective middle level schools? Aside from middle level school exploratory programs, the curriculum does not have significant differences of kind from high school curriculum areas. This should be more than mere degrees of difference from greater difficulty and more advanced levels of study found in high school curriculum.

However, more often than not, middle level curriculum decisions focus primarily upon organizational features, the "how to" concerns, and frequently are made apart from the substance of the curriculum itself. In view of that, Beane (1990b) raised the following concern:

> What should be the planned curriculum of the
> middle school? The importance of the "curriculum"
> question cannot be overestimated since it opens up
> the way to several key factors that are partially
> addressed by structural reform. For example, if the
> middle school is to be based upon the characteristics
> of early adolescence, then the curriculum ought to

be redesigned along developmentally appropriate
lines rather than simply a slightly revised version of
the traditional high school curriculum (p. 1).

Yet the need to develop a middle level curricular identity separate
from elementary and high school persists. Beane (1990b) further suggested that staff be reorganized to accomplish this.

This description of a desirable curriculum also
suggests that teachers be repositioned in relation to
the themes rather than separate subjects. A small
group of teachers might stay with a particular group
of early adolescents for all three or four years of the
middle school and work through a series of units
with them. Some teachers might work with particular units with different groups of students in a self-
contained setting. Again such matters must be
decided locally and would likely differ from school
to school (p. 5).

## *Middle level curriculum for identity development*

Reality-based learning requires that curriculum be delivered in the
most appropriate community and school settings. However, the hope
once envisioned for learning becoming an interactive school-community experience continues to erode. Concerns about safety, insurance
liabilities, and transportation costs have combined to make middle
level curriculum an increasingly school-bound phenomenon. Yet, the
form of schooling must respond to how learning effectiveness can be
increased. Beane (1990c) has suggested the following:

The centerpiece of the curriculum would consist
of thematic units whose organizing centers are
drawn from the intersecting concerns of early
adolescents and issues in the larger world (p. 45).

The middle school ought to be a general education school with a coherent, unified, and complete
curriculum (p. 47).

Middle level education's failure to base learning on the daily needs
of young adolescents in their school-communities makes curriculum
increasingly unrealistic to youth. Many middle school students fail to

see how the curriculum could help them deal with the real needs and interests in their lives. Furthermore, existing artificiality in curriculum certainly contributes to emotional decisions to drop out upon reaching legal school leaving age. While learning is probably as natural for humans as walking, contemporary curriculum, as it is planned and delivered, fails to take "learners where they are." To facilitate and nurture personal learning interests, middle level curriculum must forsake its forced choice posture and provide realistic options for learning. The following "curriculum for identity" rationale frames such an approach.

The theory and practice of identity development (Erickson, 1968) states that individuals need to gain experiences which develop personal and social bonding. The teaming of students and teachers to deliver curriculum areas has proven an effective means for social bonding among students in middle level schools (Arhar, 1990). Identity development requires opportunities to pursue things youth see as important to them and which they believe they can accomplish. This offers an exciting frame for organizing curriculum.

In past times, circumstances in family and home combined with community institutions and agencies to better facilitate youth identity needs. However, changing structures in contemporary families continue to erode the contact hours between youth and adults outside of school (Johnston, 1990). As a result, the opportunity for youth to interact positively with adults outside of school continues to decline.

Because of those societal changes, school now offers the best possibilities of assisting increasing numbers of students to deal with developing identity needs. This is particularly important at the middle level. The Carnegie Council on Adolescent Development (1989) states that for many, the age 10 to 15 year period is "the last best chance to avoid a diminished future" (p. 8). Their report, *Turning Points*, further sees middle level schools "as potentially society's most powerful force to recapture millions of youth adrift" (p. 8). Appropriately organized, middle level curriculum can assist the developmental need of young adolescents to discover who and what they are, and formulate who and what they may and can become.

Unfortunately, middle level curriculum goals have provided minimal attention to those concerns. As a result, students seem to be lowering their value for school and what it offers. They also appear to be turning to less positive arenas to pursue identity development needs. Therefore, it is suggested that identity development must become a major middle level education curriculum goal. Middle level curriculum has to meet the persisting need of young adolescents to develop ownership and define direction in considering serious issues in the contemporary world. To do that, curriculum must organize learning activities that involve students in learning about aspects of real life issues at developmentally appropriate levels. Within such a curriculum structure, young adolescents' altruism and concern can focus their learning upon local implications of those issues in their school-community. Their progressing identity development can facilitate powerfully internalized learning of skills, concepts, and information in the curriculum.

The unit teaching approach to planning and organizing instruction (Nerbovig, 1972) is essential in implementing such an initiative. If they are needed, in-service education and staff development activities should provide teachers and other curriculum planners with skills for organizing local middle level curriculum in such a fashion (Toepfer, 1972).

This critical procedure identifies tasks and sequences necessary to move forward in both planning and implementing the innovation. The development of this actual curriculum plan should identify a time schedule for designing and implementing the innovation as well as the kinds of staff experiences necessary to prepare the staff to begin the program (p. 2).

Middle level curricula should include processes, skills, concepts, and information which can be organized around local social needs and problems requiring study and action. Possible concerns might be day care needs, care of the elderly, care for the handicapped, care for the environment, recreation, transportation, and communication problems. Students would study and work on appropriate aspects of those concerns under supervision of school personnel and other adults. Curriculum processes, skills, concepts, and information needed to work within locally defined middle level curriculum units of study have to be interfaced with community service projects and topics based upon local problems and needs.

Possible unit topics would deal with local environmental problems, providing services needed by the elderly, meeting day care and babysitting needs, recycling and the costs of trash and garbage disposal, local employment needs, local transportation needs, services for special needs people in the community, and more specific localized concerns. Information gathered in studying such topics should focus on developing action agendas. To the greatest possible degree, the search for tentative solutions should provide students with experiences that apply and examine proposed solutions in community settings.

Settings for these experiences could be through service in day care or with younger students in school settings, volunteer service with the elderly, handicapped, and others, using school technology and home economics program resources to work on rehabilitating local recreation facilities, participating in appropriate environmental clean-up or recycling activities, cooperating with local governmental and community agencies on telephone or personal surveys; performing appropriate information gathering activities with local newspapers, radio, and television agencies, and studying traffic frequency patterns to determine local transportation problems and needs.

Under guidance of teachers, students can observe, participate in planning, and work on aspects of projects. They can give feedback and evaluate what was accomplished through their learning and involvement in these projects. The satisfaction of being involved and working on real-life issues which impact their lives helps develop a sense of belonging in their community. This facilitates growth of participatory skills and can develop a personal sense of social responsibility.

Exploration should be embedded in all curriculum activities in this approach. That will help students bridge the gap between learning in school and personal concerns about community needs. It facilitates their becoming involved in overcoming community problems that impact their lives. This use of processes, skills, concepts and information to explore personally focused needs and interests leads to powerful learning. Those experiences can increase the numbers of students completing school as well as helping them shape their post-secondary school learning goals. Carry-over of participatory citizenship skills into adulthood increases the potential for dealing more responsibly with local community and broader societal conditions.

Projects and student roles in those projects must be planned carefully. Lengthy and sometimes seemingly impossible tasks can be organized into short-range activities appropriate to student developmental capacities. That helps assure completion, satisfaction, and growth among participants. Evaluation of student performance in those activities will identify individual readiness for moving on to further projects and tasks. Elective courses organized as internships or contract learning arrangements in specific areas of concern can provide follow-up or advance opportunities for students with continuing interests. Cooperative learning arrangements, peer mentoring, teaching, and counseling are effective in this approach. The carry-over of skills gained will enhance their continued learning and personal development.

Three concerns must be addressed in pursuing such approaches. First, artificial divisions among middle level curriculum areas have to be eliminated. Second, teachers from varying content background areas have to be repositioned in enclaves to facilitate study around theme areas as necessary. Third, middle level schools need to be organized so that groups of students and teachers can work together beyond a single school year.

This could be facilitated by organizing curriculum around a progressing series of themes and issues which reflect developmental ranges of student identity needs (Beane, 1990c). The teaching and learning of important processes, skills, concepts, and information would be organized within that rubric. This "curriculum for identity" approach could provide the kind of experiences the Carnegie Council on Adolescent Development (1989) envisioned in recommending that community service projects be organized in middle level schools.

## *Conclusion*

Those involved in middle level curriculum planning and development activities need to wrestle with two serious conclusions made by Beane (1990c).

> Curriculum change is the weak link in the chain
> of concepts that constitutes the middle school (p. 19).

> As more and more middle level school educators work out the organizational reforms and think about early adolescents, they will eventually see the organizational "restructuring" is an incomplete version of reform (p. 64).

This writer strongly agrees that efforts to improve middle level curriculum must avoid pitfalls inherent in the currently popular notion of educational "restructuring." In itself, restructuring may only rearrange the sequence of existing curriculum or program elements. Needs for vitality require that middle level curriculum be much more than "old wine in new bottles." Existing middle level curriculum and program elements are not adequate for the challenges currently facing school and society.

The first task is to "revision" or reconceptualize middle level curriculum to identify program elements adequate to the wholeness of learner needs (Toepfer, 1990). That will also help validate which existing middle level curriculum elements are still appropriate for pursuing current needs. Additional elements must then be developed to replace those which are put aside. Restructuring then can improve the sequence of middle level curriculum elements. The need for middle level curriculum to meet the duality of appropriate expectations and responsive options for students persists (Council on Middle Level Education, 1989):

> Instead of trying to force the masses of early adolescents to higher-level thinking, ready or not, perhaps we should help each student become the best thinker she or he can be at the rate and pace that her or his capacities and developmental readiness will allow. Such an approach will help ensure a

better attitude toward learning and prepare youth for a long-term learning effort that extends far beyond the middle grades (p. 42).

The "stuff of middle level curriculum" must lead to school programs based upon what individual learners can do, instead of what they cannot do. The goal is to send the largest possible number of students to the high school with realistic chances for continued success in living and learning. To accomplish that, middle level curriculum must provide opportunities for students to learn as fast as they can, or as slow as they must. In turn, high schools have the responsibility for developing programs which allow students to continue their progress at paces that do not violate the integrity of their individual readiness. That involves improving the articulation of middle level school's curriculum with those of the district's elementary and high schools (Toepfer, 1986). NASSP's Council on Middle Level Education (1984) recommended creating transition teams to plan that articulation from one school level to the next. A middle level-high school transition team would bring together representative teachers from the last middle level and the first high school grade, some parents, and the principals of both schools. Agreeing upon realistic expectations for entering high school students is central in improving curriculum and program articulation between both school levels. Finally, student ownership in and enthusiasm about what is learned in school is essential. Without that ownership, youth in this critical epoch may get "all dressed up but have nowhere to go." As stated earlier most persons largely fashion their character, ethics, and attitudes about life and learning during this period of development. Because of that, identity development must become a prime middle level curriculum priority.

### References

Arhar, J. (1990). *The effects of interdisciplinary teaming on social bonding of middle level students.* Unpublished doctoral dissertation. University of Cincinnati.

Beane, J. A. (1990a). *Affect in the curriculum: Toward democracy, dignity and diversity.* New York: Teachers College Press.

Beane, J. A. (1990b). Rethinking the middle school curriculum. *Middle School Journal, 21(5),1-5.*

Beane, J. A. (1990c). *A middle school curriculum: From rhetoric to reality.* Columbus, OH: National Middle School Association.

Beane, J. A., Toepfer, C., Jr., & Alessi, S., Jr. *(1986). Curriculum planning and development.* Boston: Allyn and Bacon.

Carnegie Council on Adolescent Development. (1989). *Turning points: Preparing American youth for the 21st century.* Washington, DC: Carnegie Corporation.

Council on Middle Level Education. (1984). An *agenda for excellence at the middle level.* Reston, VA: National Association for Secondary School Principals.

Council on Middle Level Education. (1989). *Middle level education's responsibility for intellectual development.* Reston, VA: National Association of Secondary School Principals.

Eichhorn, D. *(1966). The middle school.* Columbus, OH: National Middle School Association.

Eichhorn, D. (1972). The emerging adolescent school of the future— now. In J.G. Saylor (Ed.), *The school of the future—now.* Alexandria, VA: Association for Supervision and Curriculum Development.

Erikson, E. *(1968). Identity: Youth and crisis.* New York: Norton.

Feldlaufer, H., Midgley, C., & Eccles, J. (1987). *Student, teacher, and observer perceptions of the classroom environment before and after the transition to junior high school.* Ann Arbor, MI: University of Michigan.

Gesell, A., Ilg, F., & Ames, L. (1956). *Youth: The years from ten to sixteen.* New York: Harper & Row.

Johnston, J. H. (1990). *The new American family and the school.* Columbus, OH: National Middle School Association.

Mamchur, C. (1990). But...the curriculum. *Phi Delta Kappan, 71,* 634-638.

Merenbloom, E. Y. (1986). *The team process in the middle school: A handbook for teachers* (2nd ed.). Columbus, OH: National Middle School Association.

Nerbovig, M. (1972). *Unit planning: A model for curriculum development.* Worthington, OH: A. Jones.

Smith, M., O'Day, J., & Cohen, D. (1991). A national curriculum in the United States? *Educational Leadership, 49*(1), 74-81.

Toepfer, C., Jr. (1969). Curricular imperatives for the middle school. *The Quarterly, 20*(3), 9-12.

Toepfer, C., Jr. (1971). Stone walls do not a prison make nor iron bars a cage: Schools for emerging adolescents. *Association for Supervision and Curriculum Development News Exchange, 8*(5), 3-5.

Toepfer, C., Jr. (1972). Guidelines for effective curriculum planning in the middle school. *Dissemination Services on the Middle Grades.* 7(4), 1-4.

Toepfer, C., Jr. (1976). Challenge to middle school education: Preventing regression to the mean. *Middle School Journal, 7*(3), 3, 18, 19, 22.

Toepfer, C., Jr. (1977a). Planning...the mortar that binds the middle school program. *Dissemination Services on the Middle Grades.* 7(8), 1-4.

Toepfer, C., Jr. (1977b). The middle school as a multiple school: A means for survival. In P.George (Ed.), *The middle school:A look ahead* (pp. 139-147). Columbus, OH: National Middle School Association.

Toepfer, C., Jr. (1986). Middle level transition and articulation issues. *Middle School Journal, 18*(1), 9-11.

Toepfer, C., Jr. (1988). Recognizing the capacities of teaming in middle level schools. *Dissemination Services on the Middle Grades. 19*(9), 1-4.

Toepfer, C., Jr. (1990). Revisioning middle level education: A prelude to restructuring schools. *Educational Horizons, 68*(2), 95-99.

Tompkins, E. (1960). What's new and interesting at the National Association of Secondary School Principals? *National Association of Secondary School Principals Bulletin, 44*(2), 44-55.

Vars, G. (1987). *Interdisciplinary teaching in the middle grades: Why and how.* Columbus, OH: National Middle School Association.

*Conrad F. Toepfer, Jr. teaches at the State University of New York at Buffalo.*

# Middle level curriculum: Making sense

*Edward N. Brazee*
*Joseph Capelluti*

*W*hen we encounter life situations or problems
we do not ask, which part is science, which is
mathematics which is history, and so on ?" Rather
we use whatever information or skills the situation itself calls
for, and we integrate these in problem solving. Certainly such
information and skills may often be found within subject
matter areas, but in real life the problem itself is at the center
and the information and the skills are defined around the
problem. In other words, the subject approach is alien to life
itself. Put simply, it is "bad learning theory."

—James A. Beane, *A Middle School Curriculum:*
*From Rhetoric to Reality*

The curriculum issue is much more complex than answering the
question, "What should we teach?" It is more involved than a team
deciding to use an interdisciplinary unit by setting aside the "regular
curriculum" before school vacations or at the end of the school year.

Middle level curricula consists of courses, activities, and expectations; many exist, not for their inherent worth, but because they always
have been there! Most curriculum for middle level schools is not based
on what we know about young adolescents, principles of learning, the
nature of various disciplines, or other important curriculum considerations. The "why fix it if it ain't broke" scenario applies to middle level
curriculum but only if the *it* (the curriculum) works correctly in the first
place and that has not always been the case.

143

For the middle level school to deal with curriculum as a legitimate part of total school development, those involved must understand the powerful impact of tradition and the assumptions which limit thinking about curriculum. These assumptions are visible in common practices and expectations relative to curriculum and its ultimate support or non-support in middle level schools throughout the country.

**Assumption #1.**     There is a curriculum which is *the* standard against which all others should be measured. "If our school would use the right curriculum, our problems would be solved." Curriculum in this case is seen as static, not everchanging to meet the needs of students, community, and teachers. It is also seen as originating from outside the local district, often by experts.

**Assumption #2.**     Not all areas of the curriculum have equal importance or value. Core, academic, or basics (usually language arts, social studies, science, and mathematics) are generally considered more important than most other areas (home economics, foreign language, art, industrial technology, music and others) . And yet it is those other areas that often supply a learning spark which the core subjects do not.

**Assumption #3.**     Curriculum is a set of narrowly defined courses. In actuality, curriculum is all courses, learnings, activities, which collectively make up the school day. Curriculum is planned and unplanned experiences which provide opportunities for learning. Extra-curricular or co-curricular activities are misnamed. They are a part of *the* curriculum of schools. Those involved in curriculum work have a larger vision of what school can be, a vision larger than assignments, homework, and textbooks, a vision that curriculum is more than the sum of its parts.

**Assumption #4** .    "The 'old style' curriculum was good enough for me, it should be good enough for my child." Very few people would accept medical care they received during their youth as good enough for them now. Very few would hire a lawyer whose practice had not been updated since 1945, but curiously many will not support a curriculum which is different from the one they experienced as students. Stated simply, the curriculum of most middle level schools prepares students for life in the United States 40 years ago, not for today.

**Assumption #5.**     Curriculum is too important to leave to teachers. Those most closely responsible for curriculum development in middle level schools are teachers. We need to allow teachers to use the knowledge and skills they have acquired to develop the most appropriate curriculum for their students.

Unfortunately, these assumptions have limited thinking about the possibilities for curriculum development in middle level schools and until recently, relatively few people have asked serious questions about middle level curriculum development. Fortunately, the work of Beane, Stevenson, Arnold, Toepfer, and others has stimulated thought and action in this critical area.

A crucial question for us is how do we then change our paradigms about curriculum development?

### A new paradigm—Beane's model

Beane (1990) provides us with a new view when he encourages us to critically examine the historical barriers to changing the curriculum. He talks about the obstacles of tradition found in the separate subject and separate program approach. He speaks of the vested interests of subject specialists and groups such as central office curriculum staff, university academics, professional associations, and subject matter teachers. He also raises the issues related to centralized mandates and teacher autonomy in the classroom. And finally, he asks us to look at the expectations of those parents who argue for the classical humanist curriculum. Clearly we must begin with the fundamental question: *Is curriculum based on what was important to know in the past, now appropriate for the 21st century?* The first step in revising the curriculum may be to redefine the kind of individual the curriculum is designed to produce.

Hoffmann (1991) of Champion International Corporation lends some insight to this question when he talks about what Champion looks for when they have new employees. Hoffman comments that Champion seeks to hire individuals who can:

1. communicate effectively—read, write, speak, and listen effectively;
2. work in a group structure as a contributing member of a team;
3. presently use technology or be able to be trained;
4. solve problems and demonstrate critical thinking skills.

The logical question would be: "Does our present curriculum as intended or experienced produce individuals who could be employed by Champion?" The obvious answer is *no*. If we believe the curriculum needs revision and we find merit in Beane's proposals, how do teachers get there? Cognizant that formidable barriers and strong assumptions exist, the authors propose an intermediary stage.

## A proposal—transitional model of curriculum development

We propose a transition model which assists teachers in moving from the traditional curriculum and ways of teaching it to the Beane model. Like Beane, we believe the curriculum should focus on learning opportunities for students based on current adolescent issues as well as larger issues in society that they will face as adults (Beane, 1990).

The curriculum would be based on Beane's work; the learning would be meaningful because it: (a) is relevant to the students at the time they are learning it, (b) deals with issues that are real in today's world, (c) involves the student as an active not a passive learner, and (d) requires that skills and knowledge are not learned in isolation from practice.

Our model assumes that teams have limited experience in interdisciplinary unit development and the subsequent process of teaching such a unit. Where Beane calls for individual subject matter teachers to begin to work together in ways where they are no longer bound by subjects, we suggest that teachers need assistance in that process as they begin to combine elements of traditional and newer models of curriculum into interdisciplinary units and eventually fully integrated programs. Beane's vision of curriculum topics emanating from the "intersection of personal and social concerns" is exactly the type of *new* curriculum which teachers intuitively know is needed. However, as teachers move from traditional, subject matter based curriculum to an integrated curriculum, they need specific help in getting there.

Although many interdisciplinary models exist, the models themselves do not provide guidance for individual teachers who wish to write units and carry them out. Interdisciplinary units should be flexible, easily-adapted resource plans, thus we advocate the interdisciplinary curriculum resource unit, not rigid lesson plans. Unique to our model, we believe, is that assistance for teaching the unit is included within the resource unit itself.

Components of our model described below give teams opportunities to plan flexible interdisciplinary curriculum resource units:

### 1.   Title/theme
Topics are based upon personal concerns of young adolescents and the common issues they currently face and will face in society. All units emphasize the concepts of democracy, human dignity, and cultural diversity. (For examples of such curriculum themes, see Beane, 1990, p.41.)

2. **Short description**

   An abstract of the unit is presented in narrative ("snapshot") form. Information is provided which allows readers to understand what curriculum is being addressed and what the learning experience will look like.

3. **Describe the problem focus**

   Success in the adult world requires the ability to effectively identify and solve problems. All units should be experiences in inquiry. The problem focus should be clearly stated so that it is understood by students and teachers.

4. **List student generated questions and their influence on the unit**

   The experiences of students and their current areas of interest and inquiry serve as a primary focus in unit development. Student questions should be listed with major inquiry questions highlighted about the area to be studied. This is a critical part of unit development and occurs at the beginning.

5. **Goals, major objectives**

   These are listed in terms of student outcomes and curriculum compatibility. Each objective should relate to the problem focus and student generated questions. Goals and major objectives need to be individualized and adapted to meet the needs of the student and resources of the team.

6. **Relationship to the existing curriculum**

   Reference should be made to the skills, knowledge, and content the unit is attempting to address. In addition, specific mention should be noted as to which of the "approved" curriculum is covered, for example math, science, art, health, and others.

7. **Activities**

   A detailed description of the activities must be provided. The activities should be described and categorized according to type: initial, on-going, culminating, and evaluative. Although it is important to be succinct and clear when describing all activities, particular attention should be given to evaluative activities. It is in this domain that we assess the impact of the unit with regard to student learning and the success of the unit development process.

8.  **Action-plan and time-line**

    This serves as the blueprint for the unit. Carefully constructed it serves as the lesson plan for teachers and students. It should describe in detail the activities, when and where they will occur, deadlines, responsibilities, and other information crucial to the plan. It might be helpful for one short and one long scenario to be written for each unit.

9.  **Annotated list of resources and materials**

    A simple listing of the resources to be used is essential. Attention should be given to what is available in the community. It is here that teachers can expand their notion of the classroom to include community resources.

10. **Responsibilities of team and individuals**

    This is a list of what needs to be done and who is responsible for doing it. This would include responsibilities of students and teachers. It is helpful to include a time line and a mechanism for monitoring.

11. **Reflections, notes**

    While not a part of unit development, all teachers should keep a separate journal where they record thoughts comments, and suggestions for future reference. It need not be lengthy or complex but could be of considerable value during assessment and in future unit development.

## Planning for assessment

A new curriculum demands that diversified and imaginative forms of assessment be developed. Whereas our definition of an educated person has broadened and changed so must our assessment strategies go beyond the narrow confines of simple cognitive recall. We must look to assessment strategies such as observational measures, performance assessments, and portfolios. Wolf (1987), commenting on reflection as a naturally occurring form of assessment states:

> No part of artistic learning--neither production, perception, nor reflection--moves ahead smoothly or automatically. Certainly students mature or practice or bump into moments of insight. And teachers teach. But at least as powerful are the times when students and teachers step back from performances

or paintings or poems in order to evaluate what is
being learned.

Evaluation needs to take many forms. It has the potential to alter
and increase the quality of student learning if we can look beyond our
simplistic historical frameworks. The effectiveness of a new curriculum
can not be measured by old yardsticks. We need to be creative, diversified, and authentic in our approach. Excellent examples of these
alternate measures are being tried in middle level schools throughout
the country.

### Redefining the team

For this model to work, there are some organizational "givens" and
the functions, goals, and purposes of the core team must be redefined.
Since the new curriculum intentionally extends beyond the core team
so should membership in that team be enlarged. The new team delivering the experienced curriculum should include other staff in the
building and district, workers in the community, and parents. If we
demand that skills and knowledge not be learned in isolation from
practice, then it follows that the definition of the classroom be revised
to include the total resources for the community.

Although many schools brag about their interdisciplinary teams, in
actuality, far too many teams are nothing more than interdisciplinary
departments with subjects as the primary focus. In these "teams in
name only" quite often there is minimal attempt at integrating curriculum. Most often that is a once-a-year interdisciplinary unit where each
subject teacher in the team teaches something related to the theme of the
unit. In a unit on survival, the math teacher teaches map scale reading,
the social studies teacher teaches about great survivors of the past, the
language arts teacher teaches several novels and/or short stories about
survival and the home economics teacher has kids make beef jerky for
a survival food!

Far too often, interdisciplinary units are seen as *curriculum way-
stations*—a nice place to visit, but not a place to call home. Interdisciplinary units are viewed outside the real curriculum—fun, exhausting,
and active—but not the *real* curriculum.

As successful as these units often are (students generally like them
because they give a break from the usual routine), they usually serve to
reinforce the notion to teachers that interdisciplinary curriculum is too
difficult and requires too much planning, and besides we neglected the
important stuff while we did the unit!

## Change—just do it!

The barrier to changing the curriculum may not be the curriculum. The real obstacle may be the people who are responsible for implementing the curriculum. Lounsbury (1988), with tongue in cheek, believes that when you attempt to alter the curriculum, your first call should not be to the curriculum director, but rather to a psychiatrist, because the beginning stages of any change, let alone one so personal as the curriculum, involve anxiety and uncertainty.

Teachers, at times, tend to be cautious about change because the "new thing" may require them to alter their established beliefs, behaviors, objectives and may require new skills to be learned. However, Block (1985) and Sergiovanni (1986) state that teacher attitudes and beliefs must be considered in any attempts to bring about changes and new practices. Unless a teacher believes that what is being proposed is better than current practices and worth the additional effort, the curriculum will not improve appreciably.

It would follow then that for any meaningful change to occur in the delivery of curriculum to students, a reexamination of the kinds of curriculum would be valuable. In most districts there are four types of curriculum:

1. The intentional—the ideal
2. The approved—the officially adopted version
3. The assumed—what people believe is being taught
4. The experienced—what students encounter

Real barriers exist at each of these curriculum levels but what matters to the student is what is experienced.

We need to look beyond the belief that problems of the future can be solved with solutions that worked in the past. Our present and future issues are not the same as yesterday's and what worked then will not work now. We must look beyond the territorial academic and professional self-interests and move dramatically in a new direction. Barker (1988) argues that when paradigms shift everyone or everything goes back to zero. The paradigm of what an educated person is has shifted; now it is time for middle level school curriculum to do the same.

Success at learning the old curriculum is no longer a guarantee of achievement in the adult world. Changing the curriculum is no longer a question of should we--it is a complex matter of when and how.

Barriers do indeed exist and they are formidable. Educators at times resist change because it requires giving up something that is known and tried, practices that at times may have proven successful (Capelluti & Eberson, 1990). Change can therefore create a feeling of loss, a fear of losing something already possessed.

It is abundantly clear that significant curriculum change is very hard to come by and very difficult to make stick. How will we avoid the new curriculum becoming simply an additional appendage to the existing curriculum like so many earlier efforts?

At a recent staff development session designed to elicit teachers' involvement in developing and implementing Beane's proposals, a teacher commented: "You don't have to convince us that Beane's ideas make sense. We know that our most successful teaching and learning moments have come when the conditions he describes take place. Let's just get on with it."

Why will it stick this time? Because if you know anything about young adolescents and their future needs "it just makes sense."

## References

Barker, J. (1988). *Discovering the future.* (Videotape).

Beane, J. A. (1990). *A middle school curriculum: From rhetoric to reality.* Columbus, OH: National Middle School Association (p. 29).

Block, S. (1985). *Belief systems and instructional improvements: A lesson in mastery learning.* Paper presented at the annual meeting of American Educational Research Association, Chicago, IL.

Capelluti, J., & Eberson, J. (Eds.). (1990). *Change in education: Strategies for improving middle level schools.* Rowley, MA: New England League of Middle Schools.

Hoffman. (1991). Speech at New England League of Middle Schools, Hyannis, MA.

Lounsbury, J. H. (1984). *Middle school education: As I see it.* Columbus, OH: National Middle School Association.

Sergiovanni, T. (1986). Understanding reflective practice. *Journal of Curriculum and Supervision, 1,* 353-359.

Wolf, D. (1987). *Portfolio.* The Arts Research Project.

*Edward N. Brazee teaches at the University of Maine, Orono.*
*Joseph Capelluti teaches at the University of Southern Maine, Gorham.*

# The core curriculum in the middle school: Retrospect and prospect

*William G. Wraga*

T he middle school curriculum of the future should be informed by the educational record of the past. At midcentury, the core curriculum movement was transforming junior high schools across the United States. The term core curriculum has several meanings. Currently, in common usage it refers either to a series of required courses or to an agreed upon set of learning objectives. Historically, however, core curriculum referred to a problem focused and interdisciplinary curricular organization. What are the origins of the core curriculum? What are some specific characteristics of the core curriculum? How viable is the core curriculum concept for the middle school of the 1990s and beyond?

## *History of the core curriculum concept*

Although antecedents to the core curriculum can be found in John Dewey's work at the University of Chicago's Laboratory School around the turn of the century, and at the Lincoln School of Teachers College, Columbia University during the 1920s, the Eight-Year Study (1932-1940) is credited with developing the core approach into a formalized curriculum arrangement (Dewey, 1956; Cremin, 1964; Tanner & Tanner, 1990; Wright, 1952). The popularity of the core curriculum during the 1940s and 1950s was documented in three publications of the United States Office of Education prepared by Grace S. Wright (1950, 1952, 1958). In short, core curriculum programs first appeared in the Federal survey of offerings and enrollments during the 1948-49 school year, peaked in popularity during the period spanning the 1956-57 and 1960-61 surveys, and declined thereafter (Wright, 1958,1965; National Center for Educational Statistics, 1975, 1984).

This decline was probably due in part to the dominance of the discipline-centered national reforms of the late 1950s and early 1960s, to the retrenchment and back to basics of the 1970s, and to the return of the disciplinary priority of the 1980s. This impact of wider sociopolitical forces on educational trends, combined with implementation challenges, discussed below, seem to have created a climate inhospitable to the core curriculum. While it has become rare to find a description of a middle school core curriculum program per se in the mainstream professional literature, interest in interdisciplinary middle school programs remains relatively strong (e.g., "Interdisciplinary Instruction," 1987; Alexander, 1988; Quatronne, 1989; Maeroff, 1990).

## Characteristics of a core curriculum

The core curriculum has been called by any of a variety of names, including general education, unified studies, common learnings, and integrated program. Yet Wright (1950) found that, despite the variety of names, "two major ideas common to the current concept of core" were "that they provide experiences needed by all youth and that the experiences cut across subject lines" (p. 1).

Wright (1958) identified four types of interdisciplinary programs that were typically taught in a block-time class arrangement: Type A, Separate or Correlated Subjects; Type B, Unified Studies or Subject-Centered Core Programs; and Types C and D, Experience-Centered Core Programs. These four types were based on the work of Harold Alberty at Ohio State University. Table 1 offers an overview of these four types of core programs. Wright found that Types A and B accounted for approximately 82% of the existing core courses in the United States during the 1956-57 school year. Types C and D were referred to as *true core*. Wright (1952) explained *true core* courses in the following way:

> Block classes which are true core recognize the importance to youth of acquiring skill in democratic living through actually practicing it in the classroom. Core issues may be topics to find out about; ideally they are problems to be solved. Problems grow out of the personal, social, or civic needs of youth. Problem-solving techniques are used. Working in groups and in committees is common practice.

Activities are so varied that each member of a class, whatever his level of ability, will be able to participate and to feel that he is making a contribution (p. 6).

TABLE 1

## Types of Interdisciplinary and Core Programs

| | |
|---|---|
| **Type A** | Each subject retains its identity in the block-time class, that is, separate subjects are taught (1) with consciously planned correlation, (2) with no planned correlation. |
| **Type B** | Subjects included in the block-time class are unified or fused around a central theme or units of work problems stemming from one or more of the subject fields in the block-time class. |
| **Type C** | Predetermined problems are based upon the personal-social needs of adolescents—both needs that adolescents themselves have identified and needs as society sees them—determine the scope of the core program. Subject matter is brought in as needed in working on the problems. Pupils may or may not have a choice from among several of these problem areas; they will, however, have some responsibility for suggesting and choosing activities in developing units of study. |
| **Type D** | The scope of the core program is not predetermined. Pupils and teacher are free to select the problems upon which they wish to work. Subject matter content is brought in as needed to develop or help solve the problems. |

From Wright, G.S. (1958). *Block-time classes and the core program in the junior high school* (pp. 9-10). Bulletin 1958, No. 6, Office of Education. Washington, DC: U.S. Government Printing Office.

The concept of the true core is illustrated in Figure 1. The problems identified for the core program at Fairmount Heights High School during the 1956-57 school year are outlined in Table 2, as an example of a core program from mid-century.

FIGURE 1

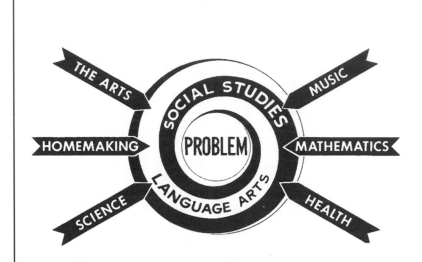

**The problem-focused, interdisciplinary, "true core."**

From Wright, G.S. (1958). *Block-time classes and the core program in the junior high school* (pp. 16). Bulletin 1958, No. 6, Office of Education. Washington, DC: U.S. Government Printing Office.

In summary then, the characteristics of a core curriculum depend on the particular type of core program implemented. In correlated and unified interdisciplinary programs, subjects retain their identity and either share a topic or theme (Type A) or are fused, that is, combined into a single class (Type B) . True core programs focus on personal-social problems of youth, and apply information and skills from all areas of the curriculum. In a *structured* core program (Type C), teachers predetermine the problems for study; in an *unstructured* core program (Type D), teachers and students collaboratively identify and define problem areas for study.

Wright's distinction between Types A and B (in which subjects are correlated and fused, respectively) and Types C and D (which apply knowledge and abilities to a consideration of personal-social problems, and which she, therefore, called true core) is crucial. Educational scholars such as Tanner and Tanner (1980) and Beane (1990s) have demonstrated that the rationale underpinning the discipline centered curriculum is both antiquated and educationally questionable (but politically potent). Tanner and Tanner (1980) indicated that the disci-plinary curriculum was originally designed to facilitate the search for new knowledge on the university level. In the schools the discipline-centered curriculum typically exalts the acquisition of specialized knowledge at the expense of the application of knowledge to addressing complex societal problems and issues. "This does not mean that disciplinary knowledge is not valuable," Tanner and Tanner (1980) cautioned, "but rather that it has severe limitations in broaching problems on the human condition." They concluded, "Such problems require a wider synthesis and application of knowledge" (pp. 522-523). Beane argued this case particularly with respect to the middle school curriculum that purports to serve the personal-social needs of young adolescents. Beane (1990s) put the issue this way: "Certainly...[Important] information and skills may often be found within subject matter areas, but in real life the problem itself is at the center and the information and the skills are defined around the problem. In other words, the subject approach is alien to life itself. Put simply, it is 'bad learning theory'" (p. 29). For these reasons, the term *core curriculum* herein will refer exclusively to true core programs that apply knowledge and abilities to a consideration of personal-social problems and issues free of any concern for the pretense of subject divisions.

TABLE 2

**Outline of Problems for Core Program
at Fairmount Heights High School, 1956-57**

**Seventh Grade**
  *Problems of:*
        School Living
        Personal and Community Health with Emphasis on
            Personal Health
        Intercultural Relations
        Economic Relations

**Eighth Grade**
  *Problems of:*
        School Living
        Self-Understanding
        World Peace
        Conservation of Natural Resources
        Home and Family Living

**Ninth Grade**
  *Problems of:*
        School Living
        Finding Values by Which We Live
        Democratic Government
           (Processes and Development)
        Communication in a Contemporary World
        Vocations and Employment

From Wright, G.S. (1958). *Block-time classes and the core program in the junior high school* (pp. 17). Bulletin 1958, No. 6, Office of Education. Washington, DC: U.S. Government Printing Office.

## Core curriculum for the 1990s

A simple comparison of Wright's 1952 description of true core programs above to recent developments in educational research and practice clearly suggests that the true core remains a viable component for the middle school curriculum of the 1990s. Further, the true core approach is particularly suited to accommodating the developmental characteristics of young adolescents and to tackling the issues they face at present and in the future.

At mid-century, core programs emphasized education for citizenship in a democracy; in the early 1990s there has been a resurgence of interest in citizenship education (Boyer, 1990; Wraga, 1991). At mid-century, core programs stressed the application of knowledge and skills to resolving personal social problems; during the late 1980s a number of subject area reports called for the application of subject matter to "real-life" problems (e.g., American Association for the Advancement of Science, 1989; Commission on Standards for School Mathematics, 1989). At mid-century, core programs sought to engage students in collaborative resolution of problems through group and committee work; in 1992, research and experience have made cooperative learning strategies and techniques powerful alternatives to conventional individualistic and competitive classroom organizations (Johnson et al., 1984; Slavin, 1991). Finally, at mid-century, core programs aimed to serve a heterogeneous student population; in 1992, the case for heterogeneous grouping has never been stronger (Oakes, 1985; Slavin, 1990).

A problem-focused, interdisciplinary core curriculum program can effectively address developmental characteristics associated with early adolescence. In an overview of early adolescent development, Hillman (1991) described the age as "characterized by rapid physical growth, concerns about body image, movement from concrete to more abstract ways of thinking and intense conformity to and acceptance by peers" (p. 4). In a true core program, for example, both the acceleration and varying rates of physical change, rather than being neglected or treated clinically in a conventional subject-centered curriculum, could be examined in their biological and social contexts in a unit on Personal and Community Health (Table 2). A study of biological and physiological changes and their causes could be integrated with a study of early adolescence in other cultures and with a consideration of literature about the experiences of agemates. Students could then collaboratively generate ways of coping with the varying rates of maturation. An interdisciplinary study of a personal-social issue like this would lend intense personal meaning to what was previously fragmented and remote information. Accompanying an increased facility with abstract thinking, young adolescents become able to use multiple problem solving strategies and to think hypothetically, among other things (Hillman, 1991). A problem-focused true core program would provide fruitful opportunities for applying and developing these emerging abilities. Similarly, collaborative group work would offer students opportunities to develop important cooperative and social skills that would be of value far beyond the young adolescent years.

Beane (1990) identified the "emergence of issues centering around self-identity," "a compelling desire to earn a place in the peer group," and "the exploration of moral/value themes" as prominent developmental characteristics of the age group (pp. 109-110). Again, a core curriculum program that engages students in a cooperative collaborative investigation of personal-social issues can make an important contribution to meeting these developmental needs both by addressing these issues directly and by engaging students in close working relationships with their peers. Beane also pointed out that "these personal/social issues are the most powerful factors in the lives of young adolescents— much more so, for example, than the academics and skills that fill most of the school agenda" (p. 110). The interdisciplinary core curriculum program enables students to develop important academic and skill-based competencies while examining personal-social issues.

Perhaps most importantly, young adolescents continue to face an array of puzzling issues and problems that are best addressed in a focused, highly structured, and interdisciplinary fashion. Developmental concerns include wrestling with an emerging self identity and assimilating oneself into the peer group. Societal problems and issues that impinge on middle level schooling, often in direct ways, include dilemmas of drug abuse, divorce, media manipulation and exploitation of the young, and the AIDS epidemic. There is little evidence to suggest that this reality will change significantly in the near future. Indeed, many of the problems addressed in 1956-57 by the core program at Fairmount High School (Table 2) remain pressing concerns for young adolescents in 1992. The public schools serve a vital role as neutral ground upon which citizens-to-be can examine societal issues—controversial or not—in a reflective, non-threatening manner.

What can the core curriculum contribute to students' success at dealing with future economic and social concerns? A core curriculum experience can help students develop abilities necessary for productive employment in the future world of work, if employment forecasts are a reliable indication of things to come (Bailey, 1991). Harvard economist Robert B. Reich's (1989, see also Reich, 1991, chapters 18 & 19) thumbnail sketch of the qualifications essential to jobs of the future bears remarkable resemblance to what a student would expect to do in a true core program:

The intellectual equipment needed for the job of
the future is an ability to define problems, quickly
assimilate relevant data, conceptualize and reorganize the information, make deductive and inductive
leaps with it, ask hard questions about it, discuss
findings with colleagues, work collaboratively to
find solutions, and then convince others (p. 31).

The pertinence of the core curriculum to enabling students to cope
with future concerns is revealed by comparing the problems listed for
a core program in 1956-57 (Table 2) with the principal socioeconomic
trends forecasted by futurists (Benjamin, 1989; Shane, 1990): national
and global interdependence; increase in pace and complexity of change;
rapid growth and restructuring of knowledge; shift of information- and
service-based economy; necessity of frequent job change; environmental problems; and expansion of minority populations. Clearly, a confi-
dent grasp of these complex concerns requires the application and
synthesis of knowledge best provided through a problem-focused,
interdisciplinary true core program. Core programs can engage students collaboratively in direct examination of these trends and associated problems, as well as develop the cognitive and affective dispositions and competencies necessary to solve future problems that even
futurists are unable to anticipate. In short, it would seem imperative
that the problem-focused true core program serve as a vital, unifying
component of the middle school curriculum of the 1990s and beyond.

## Contemporary opportunities for the core curriculum

In addition to the characteristics of the core curriculum and their
contemporary—and future—counterparts discussed above, several
other educational developments provide favorable conditions for implementing core programs. Agreement seems to have emerged, for example, about the imperative for interdisciplinary studies in the schools.
Recent subject area reports, such as those cited above, have advocated
greater correlation among school subjects. The American Association
for the Advancement of Science's report *Science for All Americans* (1989)
maintained that in order to approach mass scientific literacy among the
next generation of citizens, schools must consider measures that would
"weaken or eliminate rigid subject-matter boundaries" (p. 5). Similarly,
the National Council of Teachers of Mathematics' (NCTM) notable
*Curriculum and Evaluation Standards for School Mathematics* (1989) in-
sisted that the school "curriculum should include deliberate attempts,
through specific instructional activities, to connect ideas and proce-

dures both among different mathematical topics and with other content areas" (p. 11).

Prominent educators in the areas of science, social studies, and curriculum development have generated useful strategies and approaches that can facilitate the implementation of interdisciplinary and core programs, as well. In the field of social education, for example, Engle and Ochoa (1988) recommended that each year one social problem be studied in depth for an extended period of time in social studies classes, but ideally as a school-wide project involving all subject areas, as well as resources from the local community. In the field of science education, Yager (1987) described the Science-Technology-Society (STS) focus as "science that starts with problem identification, proceeds to problem resolution, and involves the student in decision-making" (p. 19). For Yager, problem- and issue-focused STS education "has implications for all subject areas" (p. 20). Yager (1988) identified eight characteristics of an STS program:

1. a focus on social problems and issues;
2. practice with decision making strategies;
3. concern for career awareness;
4. local and community relevance;
5. application and science content;
6. focus on cooperative work and real problems;
7. emphasis upon multiple dimensions of science; and
8. evaluation based on ability to get and use information (pp. 187-188).

In the curriculum field, Jacobs (1989a, 1989b) developed a continuum of six options for content organization that moves from discipline based, parallel disciplines, and multidisciplinary options, to interdisciplinary units/courses, the integrated day, and a completely integrated program. These options resemble the four types employed by Wright. Jacobs offered a variety of suggestions and examples of interdisciplinary programs that have been implemented successfully in schools. These, and other (e.g., "Integrating the Curriculum," 1989, 1991) recent conceptions of interdisciplinary studies point to the educative value of integrated curriculum and can serve as useful resources in developing a true core program in the middle school.

In fact, consensus seems to exist about the appropriateness of interdisciplinary studies at the middle level. In its recommendations for grades 5-8, the NCTM (1989) asserted that "mathematics teachers must seek and gain the active participation of teachers of other disciplines in exploring mathematical ideas through problems that arise in their classes" (p. 84). Likewise, the National Council for the Social Studies

(1991) identified interdisciplinary instruction as "especially appropriate for middle level social studies" (p. 290). Indeed, both the report of
the Carnegie Council on Adolescent Development (1989), *Turning
Points Preparing American Youth for the 21st Century* and the State of
California's report *Caught in the Middle* (1987), recommended the correlation of learnings among the subjects, as well as, minimally, the fusion
of learnings from social studies and English into a humanities course.
Although both reports used the term "core" to designate common,
required learnings, both reports stopped well short of even mentioning
a core curriculum in the sense of Wright's true core program, advocated
here. Furthermore, according to McEwin (1990), a recent national study
of middle level education revealed an "encouraging" trend toward
increased use of "the interdisciplinary team organization plan and
flexible scheduling" (p. 102). In another survey, Epstein and Mac Iver
(1990a) found that, "Regardless of grade span,..., principals who have
well-organized programs for interdisciplinary teams of teachers (i.e.,
with adequate common time that is used for team planning and
activities) report stronger middle grades programs overall" (p. 90).
Most importantly, the prevalence of teams establishes an essential
condition necessary for implementing an interdisciplinary core program.

## Implementing a core curriculum program

How can middle level educators implement effective core curriculum programs? As noted above, the team concept offers a special
opportunity for developing interdisciplinary studies since common
planning time is already built into the schedules of teachers from
various subject areas. Fundamental, common team planning time in
and of itself obviously does not guarantee the emergence of interdisciplinary and core programs. Purposeful planning and organizing are
required.

Before undertaking a campaign to implement core curriculum
programs, middle level educators should anticipate obstacles they will
likely encounter along the way. The encroachment of departmentalization on the middle school curriculum, accompanied by the disappear-
ance of self-contained classrooms, must be approached with sensitivity.
Due in part to the discipline-centered nature of their higher education
experience, teachers tend to grow comfortable with the identity and
routine offered by their respective subject specialties. This mindset is
difficult to overcome, and probably is addressed best by appealing to
teachers' professional judgement through building a persuasive case
for the educative value of a core program. Significantly, Epstein and

Mac Iver (1990b) also report that, "Schools committed to departmental organization are not less likely than others to be committed to interdisciplinary teaming, indicating that a departmental emphasis and interdisciplinary teams can coexist" (p. 37). It is likely that an interdisciplinary, problem focused core program and a departmentalized, discipline centered program, *offered in concert,* will increase the purposefulness and meaning of each other.

Middle schools dominated by a subject-centered curriculum organization, but with the team concept in place, could ease into interdisciplinary planning and teaching by conducting one or two correlated units per year. In this way teachers accustomed to the privacy and isolation of departmentalization would not be overwhelmed by the time-consuming demands of collaborative planning. The four types of interdisciplinary organizations identified by Wright (Table 1) could serve as stepping stones toward an increasingly interdisciplinary core program. That is, planning could begin with correlated topics, then move to fused units, and eventually advance to true core arrangements organized around personal-social problems and issues in which subject divisions would vanish (Table 2). This process would likely happen over a three to five year time span.

In addition to problems posed by the pervasiveness of both a disciplinary mindset and departmental organization, inadequate planning time, insufficient materials, and ineffective leadership can impede efforts to establish interdisciplinary and core programs (see Wright, 1952; Vars, 1969; Remy, 1990). Team planning for interdisciplinary and core programs requires ample common planning time. Some combination of common planning periods, after school meetings, summer curriculum workshops, and even released time will be needed for effective planning. This time should also be devoted to acquiring or creating specialized instructional materials tailored for interdisciplinary and core studies. A curriculum resource center and/or a well-stocked library/media center will prove indispensable in this regard. Finally, a high profile commitment on the part of all involved—including teachers, supervisors, principals, and parents—will foster the cohesion and perseverance needed to undertake such a demanding endeavor successfully.

### Curriculum development tasks

The actual planning and organizing of an interdisciplinary or core curriculum can proceed according to a standard curriculum development process. Tanner and Tanner (1980, p. 85) offer the following set of interrelated steps for developing curriculum:

1. Diagnosis of needs
2. Formulation of objectives
3. Selection of content
4. Organization of content
5. Selection of learning experiences
6. Organization of learning experiences
7. Determination of what to evaluate and ways and means of doing it

The importance of thorough, thoughtful planning to the success of a core curriculum program cannot be overemphasized, considering the non-traditional forms of content organization that will result.

During the last decade, educational reforms have placed special emphasis on accountability and assessment. While popular reforms usually conceive of assessment in terms of standardized achievement tests, educators concurrently have called for a reassessment of this traditional form of assessing student learning. New approaches, which have been called "authentic" or "performance" assessment, have moved beyond paper and pencil tests to a consideration of actual student products in determining the integrity of both student learning and program efficacy (Shepard, 1989; Wiggins, 1989a, 1989b; Stiggins, 1988; Archbald & Newmann, 1988). Given the wider range of learnings that a true core program seeks to promote, particularly as the core curriculum blurs the distinctions among subject areas, traditional forms of achievement assessments such as paper and pencil tests are inadequate. It is important, therefore, to employ a rich variety of evaluation procedures appropriate to a wide range of cognitive and affective learnings when developing and evaluating a core curriculum.

Indeed, progressive educators developing core curriculum programs at mid-century advocated ways and means of evaluation that went beyond not only traditional testing, but even beyond many of the recent proposals for performance or authentic assessment. Significantly, the concept of the core curriculum, the interrelated tasks for curriculum development listed above, and wider evaluation procedures all grew out of the work of the Eight Year Study. Evaluation in the Eight Year Study was based on the assumption "that the methods of evaluation are not limited to the giving of paper and pencil tests; any device which provides valid evidence regarding the progress of students toward educational objectives is appropriate" (Smith, Tyler et al., 1942, p.13). The wider range of objectives sought in the Eight Year Study called for "a much wider repertoire of appraisal techniques" that included "observational records, anecdotal records, questionnaires, interviews, check lists, records of activities, products made, and the like" (p. 14).

Likewise, in their 1951 text on *Developing the Core Curriculum,* Faunce and Bossing recognized the variety of evaluation techniques required by the wider range of learnings in the core curriculum, and recommended the following: "common devices" such as intelligence tests, aptitude tests, achievement tests, health records, grades, participation in school activities, employment records; anecdotal records; "actual dated samples of student's written work" including autobiographies prepared at various points of a student's career; sociograms; peer judgements; interviews; interest inventories; questionnaires; attendance records; and participation in extra-curricular activities. The similarity of recently developed authentic assessments to the evaluation procedures prescribed for core curriculum programs at midcentury and the belated but increasing recognition of the validity of using a wide range of evaluation procedures further point to the appropriateness of the true core to the middle school curriculum of the 1990s and beyond.

## Resources

In the process of developing core curriculum units and projects, middle level educators would do well to consult myriad examples available in the literature from midcentury to the present. An essential resource for this is the still active National Association for Core Curriculum (NACC) at Kent State University, founded in 1953 (NACC, 1985; Vars, 1987a). The bulletins prepared by Grace S. Wright for the United States Office of Education, especially the 1952 and 1958 volumes, are also informative resources for developing core curriculum programs. In addition to the works just mentioned and those cited earlier, a rich literature about the core curriculum exists (e.g., Aikin, 1942; Giles et al., 1942; Educational Policies Commission, 1952; Lurry & Alberty, 1957; Vars, 1969, 1987b; Beane, 1975, 1990b; Wright, 1954).

## Conclusion

The pertinence of the core curriculum concept from midcentury to the middle school of the 1990s and beyond is striking. The renewed interest in the imperative of education for democratic citizenship and new awareness of the educative power of cooperative learning, heterogeneous grouping, and the application of subject knowledge to real life problems and issues, as well as proposals for authentic assessments, seem to corroborate the work of core curriculum pioneers from the 1930s, 1940s, and 1950s. These developments, together with the array of contemporary issues that face today's young adolescents, the developmental appropriateness of the core approach, and the opportunities the true core offers for addressing future concerns and acquiring abilities vital to coping with life in the next century, make the 1990s a propitious time for middle level educators to revitalize the core curriculum.

## References

Aikin, W.M. (1942). *The story of the eight-year study.* NY: Harper.

Alexander, W.M. (1988). Schools in the middle: Rhetoric and reality. *Social Education, 52*, 107-109.

American Association for the Advancement of Science. (1989). *Project 2061: Science for all Americans.* Washington, DC: American Association for the Advancement of Science.

Archbald, D.A., & Newmann, F.M. (1988). *Beyond standardized testing.* Reston, VA: National Association for Secondary School Principals.

Bailey, T. (1991). Jobs of the future and the education they will require: Evidence from occupational forecasts. *Educational Researcher, 20*(2), 11-20.

Beane, J.A. (1975). The case for core in the middle school. *Middle School Journal, 6*, 33-34, 38.

Beane, J.A. (1990a). Affective dimensions of effective middle schools. *Educational Horizons, 68*, 109-112.

Beane, J.A. (1990b). *A middle school curriculum: From rhetoric to reality.* Columbus, OH: National Middle School Association.

Benjamin, S. (1989). An ideascape for education: What futurists recommend. *Educational Leadership, 47*(1), 8-14.

Boyer, E.L. (1990). Civic education for responsible citizens. *Educational Leadership, 48*(3), 4-6.

California State Department of Education. (1987). *Caught in the middle.* Sacramento, CA: Author.

Carnegie Council on Adolescent Development. (1989). *Turning points: Preparing American youth for the 21st Century.* Washington, DC: Carnegie Corporation.

Commission on Standards for School Mathematics. (1989). *Curriculum and evaluation standards for school mathematics.* Reston, VA: National Council of Teachers of Mathematics.

Cremin, L. (1961). *The transformation of the school.* NY: Vintage.

Dewey, J. (1956). *The child and the curriculum/The school and society.* Chicago, IL: University of Chicago Press.(Originally published in 1902 and 1900, respectively.)

Educational Policies Commission. (1952). *Education for ALL American youth—A further look.* Washington, DC: National Education Association.

Engle, S. H., & Ochoa, A. S. (1988). *Education for democratic citizenship.* New York: Teachers College Press.

Epstein, J. L., & Mac Iver, D. J. (1990a). The middle grades: Is grade span the most important issue? *Educational Horizons, 68,* 88-94.

Epstein, J. L., & Mac Iver, D.J. (1990b). National practices and trends in the middle grades. *Middle School Journal, 22*(2), 36-40.

Faunce, R. C., & Bossing, N. L. (1951). *Developing the core curriculum.* New York: Prentice-Hall.

Giles, H. H., McCutchen, S. P., & Zechiel, A. N. (1942). *Exploring the curriculum.* New York: Harper.

Hillman, S. B. (1991). What developmental psychology has to say about early adolescence. *Middle School Journal, 23*(1), 3-8.

Integrating the curriculum. (1989). (Theme issue). *Educational Horizons, 68,* 6-56.

Integrating the curriculum. (1991). (Theme issue). *Educational Leadership, 49*(2), 4-75.

Interdisciplinary instruction. (1987). (Feature Section.). *Middle School Journal, 18* (4), 3-16.

Jacobs, H. H. (Ed.). (1989a). *Interdisciplinary curriculum: Design and implementation.* Alexandria, VA: Association for Supervision and Curriculum Development.

Jacobs, H. H. (I989b) . Interdisciplinary curriculum options: A case for multiple configurations. *Educational Horizons, 68,* 25-27, 35.

Johnson, D. W., et al. (1984). *Circles of learning.* Washington, DC: Association for Supervision and Curriculum Development.

Lurry, L. L., & Alberty, E. J. (1957). *Developing a high school core program.* New York: MacMillan.

Maeroff, G. I. (1990). Getting to know a good middle school: Shoreham-Wading River. *Kappan, 71,* 504-511.

McEwin, C. K. (1990). How fares middle level education? *Educational Horizons, 68,* 100-104.

National Association for Core Curriculum. (1985). *Core today! Rationale and implications.* (3rd ed.). Kent, OH: Author.

National Center for Educational Statistics. (1975). *Summary of offerings and enrollments in public secondary schools, 1972-73.* Washington, DC: U.S. Government Printing Office.

National Center for Educational Statistics. (1984). A *trend study of high school offerings and enrollments, 1972-73 and 1981-82.* Washington, DC: U.S. Government Printing Office.

National Council for the Social Studies. (1991). Social studies in the middle school. *Social Education, 55,* 287-293.

Oakes, J. (1985). *Keeping track: How schools structure inequality.* New Haven, CT: Yale University Press.

Quatronne, D. F. (1989). A case study in curriculum innovation: Developing an interdisciplinary curriculum. *Educational Horizons, 68,* 28-35.

Reich, R. B. (1989, April). The future of work. *Harper's,* pp. 26-31.

Reich, R. B. (1991). *The work of nations: Preparing ourselves for 21st century capitalism.* New York: Knopf.

Remy, R. C. (1990). The need for science/technology/society in the social studies. *Social Education, 54,* 203-206.

Shane, H. G. (1990). Improving education for the twenty-first century. *Educational Horizons, 69,* 10-15.

Shepard, L. A. (1989). Why we need better assessments. *Educational Leadership, 46*(7), 4-9.

Slavin, R. (1990). Achievement effects of ability grouping in secondary schools: A best-evidence synthesis. *Review of Educational Research, 60,* 471-500.

Slavin, R. (1991). Synthesis of research on cooperative learning. *Educational Leadership, 48,* 71-82.

Smith, E. R., & Tyler, R. W., et al. (1942). *Appraising and recording student progress.* New York: Harper.

Stiggins, R. J. ( 1988). Revitalizing classroom assessment: The highest instructional priority. *Kappan, 69,* 363-368.

Tanner, D., & Tanner, L. (1980). *Curriculum development:Theory into practice.* (2nd Ed.). New York: MacMillan.

Tanner, D., & Tanner, L. (1990). *History of the school curriculum.* New York: MacMillan.

Vars, G. F. (Ed.). (1969). *Common learnings: Core and interdisciplinary team approaches.* Scranton, PA: International Textbook.

Vars, G. F. (1987a). Association for Core Curriculum is alive and well. [Letter to the editor.] *Educational Leadership, 44*(7), 95.

Vars, G. F. (1987b). *Interdisciplinary teaching in the middle grades: Why and how.* Columbus, OH: National Middle School Association.

Wiggins, G. (1989a). Teaching to the (authentic) test. *Educational Leadership, 46*(7), 4-17.

Wiggins, G. (1989b). A true test: Toward more authentic and equitable assessment. *Kappan, 70,* 703-717.

Wraga, W. G. (1991). The return of citizenship education. *The Clearing House, 64,* 401-402.

Wright, G. S.(1950). *Core curriculum in public high schools:An inquiry into practices,* 1949. Bulletin 1950, No. 5, Office of Educational. Washington, DC: U.S. Government Printing Office.

Wright, G. S. (1952). *Core curriculum development: Problems and practices .* Bulletin 1952, No. 5, Office of Education. Washington, DC: U.S. Government Printing Office.

Wright, G. S. (1954). *1953-54 references on the core in secondary schools.* Circular No. 323, Supplement No. 2. Washington, DC: Office of Education.

Wright, G. S. (1958). *Block-time classes and the core program in the junior high school.* Bulletin 1958, No. 6, Office of Education. Washington, DC: U.S. Government Printing Office.

Wright, G. S. (1965). *Subject offerings and enrollments in public secondary schools.* U.S. Department of Health, Education and Welfare: Office of Education. Washington, DC: U.S. Government Printing Office.

Yager, R. E. (1987). Problem solving: The STS advantage. *Curriculum Review, 26*(3), 19-21.

Yager, R. E. (1988). A new focus for school science: S/T/S. *School Science and Mathematics, 88*,181-190.

**William G. Wraga** *is District Supervisor, K-12, for Social Studies at Bernards Township Public Schools, Basking Ridge, New Jersey.*

# What is your dance?
*Greg Hart*

W hen James Beane (1990) asks in his book, *A Middle School Curriculum: From Rhetoric to Reality*, "What ought to be the curriculum of the middle school?" he is, I believe, asking us to go beyond the usual framework for this question. The usual framework in curriculum simply compares teaching techniques and promotes one over others based on outcomes or bias. But whether basal reading, individualized, or whole group literary experiences are best is a small question compared to Beane's. Whether new math or old or some other math system is best is also a small question. Beane's question is an opportunity to examine all that we do in schools and to critically ask ourselves, "How should we best educate our middle schooler?" This is a question gnawing at American education. To date, it has been poorly answered.

## Colby could dance

Middle schoolers should be seen as initiates into the world of adulthood. They thirst by their nature for adult guidance into that world of the larger society. They are emerging from a concrete, cared-for world of the self to the larger world of the society. Their emergence should be no accidental floundering of adolescence but the purposeful and celebrated blossoming of a new member of society tended by adult guardians.

The unique opportunity of this stage in a person's growth was not overlooked by the ancients. Entry into adulthood was guided by ritual and ceremony for most tribal societies. Even then, the age of entry was middle school age. Today the catechism in many churches is offered to the middle school aged Christian. The bar mitzvah is administered to the middle school aged Jew. Perhaps these are vestigial remains of a more tribal time, but they are maintained because people realize the power of the ceremony continues to work in the life of the church.

In our complex, multi-layered society today the rites of passage have been lost or diluted or misconstrued. The passage today is marked by the keys to the car, a PG-13 movie or being able to stay up past 9:00—hardly a significant welcome to the adult world. More importantly though, these passages are not guided by tradition and ceremony which would promote the larger adult agenda. Taking the written test for the temporary driver's permit may be traditional, but its significance is minimal. Society would be better served with a ceremony to establish sober driving.

A 13 year old Tulalip Indian boy in my class, Colby, was invited to dance. At first glance this seemed like just one more occasion where the bureaucracy was working to assure the academic failure of a Native American student, pulled out for this, pulled out for that, and failing in everything. Yet I sent Colby to dance. Would a list of 20 spelling words better connect him to his world? Would the ability to dismember an improper fraction give him a sense of direction and purpose? No, Colby should dance. He should dance the way his people have always danced. When Colby later talked about his lessons he smiled with pride and a fierce sense of purpose came through his eyes. "I have learned some dances, but I am not ready for many of them." He knows he will need a guide. The success of his culture depends upon adults like Janice Smith who will show him how to dance and will introduce him to his culture's dancers.

Colby's dance caused me to ask about my other students, "What is your dance?" Is your dance a completed homework assignment, legibly written, turned in on time, and accurately computed? Is your dance a memorized list of spelling words regurgitated on the Friday post-test? Is your dance to quietly sit while some adult drones on about the facts which will appear on your next test? Is your dance to cheerlead? Is your dance to play football, to toss the perfect spiral, finger tips scratching the air to make the impossible catch? I look out on my class and muse, "What is your dance?"

In its simplest form the middle school curriculum should guide the student from the egocentric self of childhood to the others-centered self of adulthood. The curriculum is not a laundry list of facts and knowledge to be gained but rather a collection of opportunities and celebrations to which the student is invited. The middle school curriculum abounds with opportunities to discover the power of the group, from team sports to action committees. There must be time in the middle school curriculum to talk, to socialize, to bask in the thrill of and pleasure of socialness. Few of us who still have friends made in middle school would trivialize this function of the curriculum. The curriculum should encourage students to believe in their potential. The curriculum must offer hope, inspiration, discovery, and joy to our children. Whatever theory guides our education, all curricula eventually have to answer the question, "What do the children do each day?" Here is the middle school I envision.

## A middle school vision

Our goal during the three years would be to bring each student to at least a sixth grade competency level in the course of their middle school career. To ensure an adequately trained citizenry students would be required to pass a test of basic competency during their middle school tenure. This would help structure remedial efforts. But once having passed the test, students and the curriculum would be free to develop other goals dependent upon student and teacher interests, upon events and serendipitous circumstance. These explorations are central to the curriculum, not a diversion subtracting valuable time from the acquisition of knowledge bits. Further acquisition of prescribed knowledge could wait until high school. This is not to say that students will not be learning anything. Chances are many will go far beyond the bounds of the present curriculum prescriptions. We will leave to the high schools sequential knowledge development using strict organization and departmentalization.

Competency testing is only one aspect of knowing our students. Assessment of students must look beyond competency to talents. Focusing on a student's paper and pencil 3 R competency may be an impediment to recognizing a student's talent. It will be the special responsibility of teachers to encourage students, their parents, and peers to promote individual talents. We must be prepared to look broadly at our students. Some will excel in sport, some in academics, some in relationships, some in patience and wisdom, some in art, music, or poetry, some in sensitivity and caring. We must seek out these talents, and we must be sure that students find affirmation and support to develop what they find. How many students think they are worthless because they do not get good grades in school? We can no longer afford, as a society, to throw away the talent of our youth because their talents are not in the 3 Rs.

## Sixth grade

The sixth grade curriculum will include several major projects. Students will each produce a major, written work on their family history. Biography, interviews, and prose will blend to produce the work. Additionally, students will develop basic computer and video literacy. Our future citizens must sense control over these technologies, not control by them.

Sixth grade classrooms will be run on a democratic model. It will be a shock to displace the present autocracy with a model used by the larger society, but it is time. Citizens today are too cynical toward our democratic institutions. We must persuade our students that a democracy is worth sacrifice. It is worth our time and even frustration. It is more than a cherished institution, it is a sustainer of our freedom, and it is our responsibility to guard the institution with our vote.

The classroom democracy will extend well beyond a show of hands for who wants an ice cream party or a pizza party. Democracy might take the form of a caucus system. It might take the form of a corporate democracy with CEO and a board of directors. Depending on the interest and sophistication of the students, other elements of a democracy might be incorporated in the class like a judiciary. The development of the democracy will be a major project for the class. Is our governmental system worth a major commitment by our curriculum? Could it be that the sound bite campaigns we presently experience are as much the responsibility of schools as TV?

Sixth grades will clean and maintain their own classrooms. It is time we teach our citizens that when you make a mess you clean it up. We presently have a whole citizenry who think cleanup is someone else's job. From CEOs who allow their companies to foul our air to homeowners spraying weed killer on their dandelions our attitude is that someone else will clean up our mess. It is time we teach our future CEOs, secretaries, laborers, and pilots that we clean up our own messes.

Every sixth grader will participate in a major outdoor education experience. Learning that you can live away from your parents without a TV is a valuable experience. Living with others and local ecology would be the focus of this experience.

Every sixth grader will participate in vigorous daily exercise. A student committee would set the daily routine. It may involve walking, yoga, marshal arts, fly casting, active games, or even walking to school for a week.

## Seventh grade

Seventh grade marks a move toward independence and leadership. Seventh graders are responsible more for others and are encouraged to be involved in more group activities. Seventh graders will be given assessment tests in the three Rs to check progress and to assure appropriate individual instruction.

Seventh graders will expand on the participatory democracy experienced in sixth grade. They will begin to run the morning meetings that they only sat through as a sixth grader. They will be members of school meetings. In school meetings student representatives and faculty meet to discuss and consider the life of the school.

Seventh graders are fascinated by the customs of others. They will develop a major writing project which compares their local history and customs with other cultures, both contemporary and ancient.

Seventh graders are creative. They constantly find ways to express themselves. Therefore, seventh graders will use the computer and video camera in their school projects. It is our responsibility to have sufficient technology available for their creative expression.

Seventh graders will be involved in activities which expand or extend their areas of talent. A student might write for the local paper, become involved in an ecology issue, work a political campaign, perform in music or drama or art or do anything which brings their talent to the life of the larger society where they can find acceptance and encouragement for their contribution. The student should be exploring individual and group opportunities to develop further their areas of talent.

Seventh graders will begin to explore the group dynamic through activity-based counseling or some similar outdoor experience. This is a gold mine of group process and an opportunity for students to see how they are both a part of and empowered by groups. To complement the ABC (activity based counseling) training, seventh graders will participate in some kind of organized team sport. We may have to include math teams and chess, but we will get them all involved. Seventh graders will be more involved in the daily running of the school. They will be responsible for hall and office cleanup. They will care for the grounds and flower beds. They will see that a daily bulletin of notices and events is printed and circulated.

Seventh graders, too, will participate in daily exercise. We must instill in our students that the purpose of sport and exercise is health and vigor. The purpose is not to make stars of a handful and let others be couch potatoes. Consequently, it is critical to maintain a daily regimen with great diversity in activities, games, and sports that we introduce and promote.

## Eighth grade

The eighth grade is a time of celebration and organizational responsibility. Eighth graders will celebrate themselves with the preparation of their graduation portfolio. This will display their academic acumen, and it will include a significant communication experience such as a math theorem and proof, a computer program, dance, video, poetry, prose, or performance. Teachers will take pains to insure that the portfolios are an impressive display of talent and brilliance. The support and acclaim our students gain by this effort will be a sign of their acceptance into the larger community. The eighth grade will be marked by many such rites of passage: the trek, elected office, committee chairs. The important distinction between present recognitions like the traditional teas or performances is that the portfolio review and presentation will have deep, personal significance. It will, after all, represent the culmination of three years' work.

Eighth graders will celebrate their commitment to the group by their involvement in larger school activities and community activities. Eighth graders will maintain and develop their group involvement begun in seventh grade sports by participating in a smorgasbord of activities such as student newspaper, student government, business affairs, food service, supervisory committee for grounds, behavior activities, sports, intramurals, school calendar, or student court.

Community activities will entail work, time, and caring shared with others. Nursing home contacts, animal shelter volunteer, injured animal rescue, repair and painting of housing for the needy, teaching younger kids to read, or cleaning up a park. Records of these experiences should be significant parts of the graduation portfolio.

Eighth graders will be responsible for student council leadership, and they will be the committee chairs of the school oversight committees. The multitude of committees and group experiences will offer the democratic training which we hope will make intelligent, caring, voting members of our future society. It is important that the school authorities give over significant power and responsibility to the students. This is not an exercise in make-believe politics. This is the real thing. It must be, for no age is more sensitive to sham and hypocrisy.

Eighth graders will continue their exploration of themselves and group roles through advanced activity-based counseling which will culminate in an eighth grade trek. This is a self-powered journey climbing up mountains, paddling down waterways, or peddling our roadways. In groups of six to ten, the eighth graders will initiate, plan, pay for, and carry off their trek. The trek will be an element of their portfolio. The trek will be a significant sign of their self-reliance and accomplishment. Importantly, it will assure that our students sense their potential. They will discover that without a car or jet they can travel greater distances. The power of this discovery will move them to hopefulness and confidence, and in a larger sense the trek is a metaphor for their school experience. They leave the comfort and protection of their school society, discover their emerging power and ability, only to return prepared to participate in the larger society. We will welcome them back!

In order to accomplish this school transformation we will need to step off the 44 minute, 7 teachers a day treadmill. One teacher will suffice for each class of 15-20 students. No building administrators, no custodians, no special education, no counselors, no PE teachers, no special music teachers, no teacher planning time will be needed in these groups of 100 to 150 students.

## *The day*

An average day might look like the following. Though we should note that unlike the present bell schedule, which ratchets us through the day, this schedule could be amended at any morning meeting for the day or week. It will be an exercise in democracy just to set the daily schedule.

8:00 - 8:30
Walk to school, jog to school, bike to school.

8:30 - 9:00
Morning meeting—This is a group building time. Its theme should be that we care about one another. If someone is absent a student will call to see how things are going and to let them know we miss them. We will just check up on one another. During morning meetings we will talk about current events, worries or concerns of the group. We will discuss procedural difficulties of committees or groups. This is a time to set up direction for the day. To that end, each morning meeting will conclude with the setting of the daily schedule. By the eighth grade the morning meeting will be run by a student committee.

9:00 - 10:30
Project time—The first half of this time will be devoted to committee work and group activities. Students may be working to solve a student council problem or planning their eighth grade trek. They will use this time to get together with others across the school. Just before individual quiet time we will have a refueling break. The last half of this time is for quiet, individual work. Some will be working on assignments, projects, or studying.

10:30 - 10:45

Exercise break—Whether calisthenics, yoga, marshall arts, or fly casting, this is a student committee choice. The only requirement is that students are physically moving—and having fun.

10:45 - 11:30

Reading/writing instruction time—This is a teacher organized and controlled time. Because of the small number of students, instruction will be individualized. Students will be working along a spectrum from contest essays to remedial skills, from college reading to phonics.

11:30 - 12:15

Lunch and intramurals—Intramurals are student organized and led.

12:15 - 1:00

Crafts/story—Crafts will involve some small motor therapy. Students might knit, weave, spin, whittle, carve, string beads, or weave baskets. It should be small, engrossing, and calming in its repetitiveness. The result of our work should be a product significant as a gift or useful to the producer. The last half of the time will be reserved for an oral story. Even eighth graders can appreciate a good story, well read. By eighth grade the students will be doing many of the readings.

1 :00 - 1 :45

Math/science instruction—Teacher controlled, individual and group instruction. Elements of the traditional curriculum that relate to class projects can be taught. A pre-planned curriculum will also be available.

1 :45 - 2:00

Exercise break

2:00 - 2:45

Break-out sessions—This is a time for school-wide committees to meet or work. The court, student council, peer counseling, bulletin committee, and others would be able to meet. This is a time for school-wide contact. Happening, as it does, at the end of the day provides all classes with the maximum possibility to adjust their daily schedule. Only during the last hour do other teachers and students depend on the presence of all students. Fridays are set aside for all class activities. There will be no break-out sessions then.

2:45 - 3:00
Debrief—We evaluate the day and organize for tomorrow.

3:00 - 3:30
Walk, jog, peddle home.

---

## Conclusion

Is this a curriculum for every middle school? I think not. Should it be in most middle schools? I do not know. I do know I would like to teach in this kind of school, and I know many teachers and students who would thrive with this breath of freedom.

I do not think there is anything magical in this formula which will save American education. There is nothing here that has not always been here. There is the vigor and intelligence of our children, and there is the need for our teachers to inspire and shape the student's world view.

What is important about the curriculum I have outlined and what is important about Beane's question, "What ought to be the curriculum of the middle school?" is that in America we can dream a new solution or a hundred new solutions and if all is well with American education those dreams can be implemented.

Is there not something primal about the whole enterprise of education? We perform its rites almost instinctively. In that sense it is like a great dance in which we are all caught. Students, teachers, and administrators dancing: dancing to music unheard, dancing to musicians unseen and dancing to choreographers unknown. We must ask of ourselves "What is our dance?"

### References

Beane, J. A. (1990). *A middle school curriculum:From rhetoric to reality.* Columbus, OH: National Middle School Association.

*Greg Hart teaches at Whatcom Middle School, Bellingham, Washington.*

# Sexuality education
# in the middle school curriculum

*Cheryl Budlong*
*Mary Franken*

S exuality education is an important issue for middle school educators. The recent Carnegie report, *Turning Points: Preparing American Youth for the 21st Century* (1989), views sexuality as being related to broader health issues affecting students' beliefs, learning, and life decisions. In a typical classroom of 24 young adolescent students (age 11-14), four boys and two girls are already sexually active. Before these students reach 18, two girls will become pregnant, one having an abortion. Seventeen of the 24 will be sexually active. In addition to taking risks of being pregnant or contracting a sexually transmitted disease including AIDS, students may have limited their educational and life options.

Helping adolescents develop positive sexual attitudes, acquire appropriate sexual information, and make healthy life style choices is a challenge for middle school educators. Now, more than ever, young people need assistance in coping with personal, family, and societal changes. While developing sexually at varying rates, adolescents are reaching puberty at a younger age, resulting in increased early sexual exploration and activity (Van Hoose & Strahan, 1988). Myriad family changes affect adolescents. Increases in the numbers of dual-worker families, single-parent families, and blended families have resulted in adolescents often receiving less parental supervision as well as confusing role models. They live in a society bombarded with sexual stimulation and exploitation in all forms of advertising and media—television, music, and print material.

## Sexual development of adolescents

The period of adolescence is marked with the onset of sexual development. There is much variation as to when these changes begin and how rapidly they take place. Girls develop earlier than boys during this time period, and both boys and girls are maturing earlier than they did in previous generations. About half of the girls will have begun to menstruate by age 12 years, 8 months, which means that they have begun their childbearing years during middle school. The ability to father a child is also possible for middle school boys since the average age for the growth of the penis is 12 years, 3 months (Van Hoose & Strahan, 1988). It is important to note that these ages are central tendencies in a wide age range. Young adolescents need to know basic facts about the ranges for the events of puberty and facts about sexual development. Educators at the middle level are in a logical position to provide both information and the reassurance that differing developmental rates are normal.

Young people may struggle as they form their sex role identities. Same-sex friendships are the dominant pattern during this period of development. However, society imposes many pressures on young adolescents to become involved with members of the opposite sex in a sexually precocious manner. Media sources—television, movies, music—convey many misconceptions to young adolescents about their sexuality. They also hold the unfounded belief that almost all teenagers are having sex.

## Sexual activity in adolescents

Young adolescent sexual activity is a concern to middle level educators because it affects the future educational, economic, social, and health consequences of these young people. An adolescent is considered sexually active when he or she experiences sexual intercourse at least once (Hayes, 1987). Hayes reported 1983 data which indicated the sexual activity rates by age at initiation, gender, and race and ethnicity for various groups. Of particular interest to middle school teachers was the finding that 28.7% of boys and 12.6% of girls were sexually active by age 15. In addition, consistently higher percentages of the black populations, 59.6% of boys and 20.1% of girls, were sexually active. These facts substantiate the need to encourage adolescents to abstain from intimate sexual behavior and to personally recognize the value of waiting—to believe delaying sexual activity and parenthood is in their best interest. In helping them cope with their developing sexuality, they need to understand their sexual feelings as normal and that there are ways they can express their sexuality without having intercourse. Sensitive adults can assist adolescents learn about appropriate touch, which may be missing in their lives. Teens can realize that kissing and petting do not have to lead to intercourse, that masturbation is normal, and that they can appropriately communicate their changing maturity through dress and appearance and through verbal and written expression. Adolescents' rights to information and support are summarized in Figure 1 (Franken & Budlong, 1988).

FIGURE 1

## Rights of Adolescents

*Adolescents have a right to:*

- Talk with their parents or teachers about their values and decisions.
- Clear and accurate information about reproduction and ways to prevent pregnancy, including sexual abstinence and responsible use of contraceptives.
- Preventive programs which promote responsible sexual behavior.
- Clear and accurate information about all sexually transmitted diseases including prevention, identification, treatment, and responsibility of informing sexual partners.
- Educational programs which help define the consequences of sexual behavior in relation to life options.
- Programs which help them understand negative social and emotional impact in their lives when sexual relationships are started too young.
- Programs which enhance their self-esteem and their concept of themselves as responsible people who can make independent decisions.
- Programs which will teach communication, assertiveness, and interpersonal skills.
- Programs which promote the concept of wellness and the importance of health care of all types, including proper nutrition, exercise, and prevention of substance abuse.
- Dropout prevention services for teen parents to remove barriers to finishing school.

From Franken, M., & Budlong, C. (1988). *Adolescent pregnancy: Facts and consequences.* Cedar Falls, IA: University of Northern Iowa.

## Rationale for a comprehensive sexuality curriculum

Educators have the responsibility to develop and implement a comprehensive sexuality education curriculum in the middle school. The mission of a comprehensive sexuality curriculum is to encourage children and youth to make healthy sexual and relationship decisions that enhance the well-being of the individual, the family, and society. Ideally, the outcome will be adolescents who are well informed, who understand themselves and others, and who can make wise and responsible sexual decisions.

With these purposes in mind, several assumptions must be clear:

1.  Sexuality is a more encompassing term than *sex*, involving many aspects of a person. Because sexuality includes much more than a physical act or *plumbing*, the curriculum must be comprehensive as well.

2.  Sexuality concepts can be integrated into subject areas across the curricula and are not designed to be a separate course at the middle level. For example, self-esteem and responsible decision making may be the topic of an introspective writing activity as a language arts assignment. It will also be a central component of a health education program.

3.  Healthy life styles must be modeled, promoted, and reinforced.

4.  A collaborative effort among families, schools, and community is necessary to promote the positive growth and development of all adolescents.

Ideally, because it emphasizes self-esteem and responsible decision making, a comprehensive sexuality curriculum should help prevent or reduce the occurrence of all high-risk behaviors, which include sexual behaviors, and consequently improve adolescents' health and future life options.

## Support for sexuality education in the schools

Sexuality education has earned wide support among the American people, with more than 85 percent of adults favoring such instruction (Louis Harris & Associates, 1988). One reason Americans support sexuality education is that they think it can be effective in decreasing the negative consequences of early sexual activity (Alan Guttmacher Institute, 1989). They believe that students who take sexuality education courses are less likely to become (or to get someone) pregnant, are more likely to practice birth control if they do have sex, and are less likely to acquire a sexually transmitted disease (Quinley, 1986). American teachers tend to support sexuality education in the middle school. Of the teachers surveyed in a 1989 Gallup poll, 55% responded that sexuality education should be taught in grades 4 through 8 (Elam, 1989).

The Alan Guttmacher Institute (1989) conducted three major nationwide surveys of public school teachers, state education agencies, and large school districts (representing about 29% of all public school students). Five key findings emerged from the surveys:

1. The vast majority of sex education instructors are teaching their students about abstinence, birth control methods, use of condoms, transmission of sexually transmitted diseases (STDs) including acquired immune deficiency syndrome (AIDS), and sexual decision-making.

2. Almost all teachers not only think it important that sex education be taught but also think that some topics—such as birth control, AIDS, STDs, sexual decision-making, abstinence, and homosexuality—be taught earlier than they are.

3. Eight out of ten sex education teachers say they need more assistance in teaching about prevention of pregnancy and STDs.

4. The biggest problem sex education teachers believe they face is pressure from parents, the community, or school administrators, especially when they teach topics such as homosexuality, condom use, abortion, and "safer sex" practices.

5. State education agencies and large school districts generally place greater emphasis on education about STDs and AIDS than they do on instruction about prevention of unwanted pregnancies or on sex education generally.

States' policies on sexuality education vary from requiring it, encouraging it, to not having any position at all. Flax (1989) found that approximately 80% of the states either require or encourage a sexuality curriculum, with about one third having a requirement. Findings confirm the perception that both the AIDS crisis and increasing evidence of earlier sexual activity among adolescents have caused the development and implementation of sexuality education curricula by states and school districts during the past three years. The report also indicates the need for helping teachers prepare for teaching sexuality education because many have gaps in their own knowledge (Flax, 1989).

## Content of a comprehensive sexuality curriculum

Most schools, rather than completely adopting published materials, prefer to develop, modify, and adapt a curriculum which meets the needs of students in their community. Many states have developed curriculum guides to address the issues of early sexual activity, adolescent pregnancy, and STDs. For example, in 1988 the Iowa legislature mandated a K-12 Human Growth and Development curriculum that provides all students with information and instruction in essential living skills, including sexuality education (Iowa Department of Education, 1989). Each Iowa school district has the responsibility for including the following topics in their curriculum:

- self-esteem, responsible decision-making, and personal responsibility and goal setting
- interpersonal relationships
- discouragement of premarital adolescent sexual activity
- family life and parenting skills
- human sexuality, reproduction, contraception, and family planning, prenatal development including awareness of mental retardation and its prevention, childbirth, adoption
- available prenatal and postnatal support, and male and female responsibility
- sex stereotypes
- behaviors to prevent sexual abuse or sexual harassment
- sexually transmitted diseases, including AIDS, and their causes and prevention
- suicide prevention
- stress management

These eleven topics can readily be infused into a middle school curriculum. The Iowa guide (1989) illustrates how sexuality content can be incorporated into language arts, science, mathematics, social studies, home economics, health, and art classes. Content and activities should be selected consistent with the developmental maturity and needs of students. Repetition of content at various age levels with varied activities will insure that students receive sexuality information that is appropriate to their developmental stages. Evaluation techniques should measure student learnings—knowledge, attitudes, and skills—using a variety of assessment strategies (Budlong & Franken, 1991).

*Developing a personal philosophy*

Teachers are the key to successful implementation of a sexuality curriculum (Budlong & Franken, 1991). However, not everyone has the qualities of an effective sexuality educator. Because of lack of knowledge, stereotypic attitudes, or low comfort level with the topics involved in the curriculum, some educators should not be involved in directly delivering this curriculum. Many others, however, can acquire the information and confidence they lack.

Teachers are an important influence on student development. They are the role models, sources of information, and providers of guidance and support that affect student values, decision making, and behavior patterns. They have the opportunities for enhancing self-esteem and for encouraging formulation of life goals. For a number of students, teachers are a greater source of interest and attention than their families. Years later many students remember the concerned, caring teachers who were significant in their lives.

FIGURE 2

---

**Sexuality Education Activities**

*For use with individuals:*
- Self assessments
- Questionnaires
- Individual interviews
- Journal writing and/or focus writing
- Sentence completion
- Drawings
- Rank order activities, including Q-sorts (card sorts)
- Computer simulations
- Written responses to "Dear Abby" letters
- Tests and quizzes
- Individual research

*For use with groups:*
- Trigger films and other audio visual materials
- Resource speakers
- Case study vignettes
- Group discussions—dyads, triads, small groups
- Task groups
- Question box
- Role playing
- Modeling
- Fish bowl
- Continuum or forced choice
- Games
- Simulations
- Debriefing of all activities

Before an educator can plan and implement a comprehensive sexuality curriculum, it is important to articulate a personal philosophy that focuses on the knowledge, attitudes, and skills students need to make effective personal decisions about sexual behaviors. A philosophy that reflects sensitivity to diversity, a non-judgmental attitude, and open communication will encourage students to develop a positive self- image and make responsible sexual decisions.

## Teaching strategies

Selection of appropriate instructional strategies is characteristic of effective teachers. The age, composition, expectations, and needs of a group served must be considered when choosing methods, materials, and activities. Using a variety of educational techniques makes curriculum topics more interesting and personally applicable to students. Interactive activities—such as case study analyses, role playing, and simulations—provide opportunities for higher order and critical thinking skills, such as analysis, synthesis, and evaluation.

Assessment of personal teaching styles and strengths will help educators to be more aware of their skills and limitations as group facilitators. Experience as a facilitator is helpful to sexuality educators. Working together in multidisciplinary teaching teams is another effective way to present activities and to infuse sexuality topics into several content areas. When choosing an appropriate teaching technique or strategy, Helmich and Loreen-Martin (1979) suggest consideration of the following:

- comfort, confidence, and competence as a facilitator with the technique

- suitability of the technique to the content or desired outcome

- projected effect of the technique on the group as a whole, on individual members of the group, and on the community to which the individual is to return

- age appropriateness of content and process for the group.

Figure 2 identifies a variety of classroom activities which may be used or adapted in presenting sexuality content (Budlong & Franken, 1991).

An excellent array of instructional activities is only effective in a classroom environment that promotes respect, acceptance, and trust. The middle school teacher sets the stage by modeling these qualities and expecting students to develop them as well. Because sexuality is a sensitive topic, an open, honest, and confidential environment allows students to ask questions and participate in discussions without embarrassment. The Community of Caring (1988) has been a leader in efforts to help school personnel implement programs which stress caring, educational environments which give attention to the total school and community milieu. This is particularly critical in the middle school years, when teachers have the opportunity to strengthen students' self-esteem, expect school success, promote equity in gender roles, and encourage respect for diversity.

### *Implementing a sexuality curriculum*

Initiating a sexuality education curriculum requires cooperative planning. Following are several guidelines to assist in this process:

1.  Involve a team of teachers, administrators, and parents in developing the curriculum, selecting materials, and interpreting the curriculum to the community.

2.  Form an advisory committee that includes parents, teachers, school administrators, pupils, health care professionals, members of the clergy, members of the business community, and other residents of the school district deemed appropriate.

3.  Initiate a curriculum mapping process. Identify what topics that are already being taught and in what content areas. This process may also pinpoint topics that are not being adequately covered.

4.  Infuse sexuality topics into several curricular areas.

5.  Work in teams. Seek preparation and training to enhance content background, teaching skills, and personal comfort level with the topics.

6.  Consider what students want and need to know. Remember that peers are an important source of information for their friends.

7.  Review a variety of curriculum materials. Modify or adapt published materials to fit individual classroom needs.

Middle school educators have the challenge to provide sexuality education and to develop a school climate which fosters self-esteem and responsible decision making. Through this curriculum, they have the opportunity to increase their students' life options and decrease their at- risk behaviors.

Middle school students live in a world bombarded by sexual stimuli and the temptations of early sexual intercourse. Unless these students receive accurate information, develop healthy sexual attitudes, and exhibit responsible sexual behaviors, the predictions for an increase in AIDS in the adolescent population and continued high pregnancy and abortion rates will accelerate the health risks of middle school students.

## References

Alan Guttmacher Institute. (1989). *Risk and responsibility: Teaching sex education in America's schools today*. New York: Author.

Budlong, C., & Franken, M. (1991). *EMPOWER: A self-guided study for teachers of sexuality education*. Manuscript submitted for publication.

Carnegie Council on Adolescent Development. (1989). *Turning points: Preparing American youth for the 21st century*. Washington, DC: Carnegie Corporation.

Community of Caring. (1988). *Growing up caring: A guide for teachers, staff, and parents in a community of caring school*. Washington, DC: Author.

Elam, S. (1989). The second Gallup Phi Delta Kappa poll of teachers' attitudes toward the public school. *Kappan, 70*, 785-798.

Flax, E. (1989). Study finds fast growth in sex education, but sentiment for classes in lower grades. *Education Week, 1*(19).

Franken, M., & Budlong, C. (1988). *Adolescent pregnancy: Facts and consequences*. Cedar Falls, IA: University of Northern Iowa.

Louis Harris and Associates. (1988). *Public attitudes toward teenage pregnancy, sex education, and birth control*. New York: Author.

Hayes, C. (Ed.). (1987). *Risking the future: Adolescent sexuality, pregnancy, and childbearing*. Washington, DC: National Academy Press.

Helmich, J., & Loreen-Martin, J. (1979). *Sexuality education and training: Theory, techniques, and resources*. Seattle, WA: Planned Parenthood of Seattle/King County.

Iowa Department of Education. (1989). *Human growth and development:A guide to curriculum development*. DesMoines, IA: Author.

Planned Parenthood Federation of America. (1986). *Caring for children*. New York: Author.

Quinley, H. of Yankelovich Clancy Shulman. Memorandum to all data users regarding Time/Yankelovich Clancy Shulman Poll Findings on Sex Education, Nov. 17,1986.

Van Hoose, J., & Strahan, D. (1988). *Young adolescent development and school practices: Promoting harmony.* Columbus, OH: National Middle School Association.

**Cheryl Budlong** *teaches at Wartburg College, Waverly, Iowa.*
**Mary Franken** *teaches at the University of Northern Iowa, Cedar Falls.*

# Turning the floor over:
# Reflections on *A Middle School Curriculum*

*James A. Beane*

There is a conversation heating up around the country and it is one that holds enormous promise for young adolescents and their schools. The conversation is about a topic that the popular reform movement in middle level education has left alone for too long, namely the middle school curriculum.

Three years ago I wrote a small book, *A Middle School Curriculum: From Rhetoric to Reality* (Beane, 1990), that has been part of the middle level curriculum conversation. In it, I posed the question, "What should be the middle school curriculum?" By that question, and the proposal that followed, I meant to address the curriculum as a broadly conceived whole rather than the usual issue of what ought to be done in one or another subject area or program. The purpose of this paper is to extend the ideas in that book and describe some of the important themes that have emerged in the conversation.

I proposed that the rhetoric of the middle school philosophy be extended into the area of curriculum. To me this meant that if we claim to be after schools that are responsive to what young adolescents are about, then the curriculum ought to grow out of the concerns of young adolescents and the larger world in which they live. That argument clearly suggests that the subject area curriculum, so long a characteristic of middle level education is not a satisfactory way to work with young adolescents. Since the compelling and significant concerns these young people (and we) have transcend subject boundaries, the separate subject approach to organizing knowledge and skill turns out to be an artifice of real life. Moreover, the interdisciplinary efforts that have surfaced in middle schools, though certainly an improvement over the usual curriculum organization, have almost always retained the place and space of the traditional subjects.

Following this line of reasoning, I proposed that we abandon the separate subject approach and instead organize the middle school curriculum around thematic units whose topics might be found where widely shared concerns of young adolescents intersect with significant issues in the larger world. The idea of using such personal/social sources is not anti-intellectual as it does not walk away from knowledge and skill, but rather repositions them in the context of engaging themes where they might be brought to life and more thoroughly learned.

Such a framework, then, could offer a kind of parallel structure in which the general idea of this kind of curriculum would persist across middle schools while the actual themes and their implementation would be worked out collaboratively by young adolescents and their teachers in local schools. In this sense, my proposal was not another top-down, imposed "curriculum" but a context for curriculum conversation and planning. More importantly, a thematic curriculum would bring young adolescents into closer connection with the larger world, encourage a sense of personal and collective efficacy, and offer a relevant context for the knowledge and skill that both they and we desire.

## Turning the floor over

In my work, I raised the question, "What ought to be the curriculum of the middle school?" Less explicit in my answer was another question which is perhaps more suitable for the problem at hand and the conversation now emerging: "*Whose* curriculum ought to be the middle school curriculum?" The meaning of this second question is revealed in a remark made by Mikel (1990) upon hearing about the ideas now afloat. He said that what we are doing is "a leap of faith—to turn the floor over to the traditionally disempowered." In other words, what Mikel had seen was that finally, as our rhetoric had seemed to promise, we would be willing to turn to young adolescents themselves to form the curriculum. Whose curriculum? Theirs! And ours too, though not by pre-planned imposition, but by virtue of the fact that we live and work with them and, as adults, have an obligation to help them confront their questions and concerns at this time in their lives.

By now, most of us know thousands of success stories that can be told out of the middle school movement. However, we must sooner or later admit that even the best of these are almost all cases of young adolescents finding more success and enjoyment through adaptations we have made to traditional school structures and programs. We are nicer, we encourage cooperative work, and we plan more exciting activities. This is all for the better, but not for the best. The fact is that the curriculum of most middle schools still belongs to the adults and to the subject area organization of knowledge and skill that they represent.

If we truly mean to have a school that is responsive to young adolescents, then we must ask, "Where are their voices in this effort?" The fact that we know the litany of so-called characteristics of early adolescence is wonderful, but those are simply abstract conceptions of real human beings. They may help us to understand the young people we see every day, but such abstractions are not a substitute for *really* knowing them. Thus, to plan a curriculum apart from them by predicting what they like, or want, or need is not a sufficient version of a genuine middle school curriculum. Why should we speak for them when they can speak for themselves? To be really responsive to young adolescents we must invite them to participate in curriculum planning, to say what questions they have and what concerns them.

I suspect that a large part of the issue here can be found in the fact that we often *appear* to be listening to young adolescents. We have gone from a position where their voices were completely silent to one where we presumably hear them through knowledge of young adolescent characteristics. But, again, these group conceptions are not authentic voices. And I wonder, too, if some of those characterizations reveal another clue to our resistance. When we say that young adolescents are "brain dead " or "hormones with feet," we confuse their observed behavior with a deeper reality that is behind it. Why is it so hard for us to understand that behavior is mostly culturally induced and in this case, often by the alienating curriculum that so many young people face every day?

One way to understand this idea is to look at the work coming out of the Middle Level Curriculum Project (1991). One task undertaken by the Project was a survey of young adolescents in various school settings. The young people were asked to respond to a number of questions regarding what they wonder about and what they want to know. Among the responses were a large number that had to do with concerns about prejudice, environmental problems, fairness and justice, war and peace, cultural differences, poverty and hunger, personal values, family relations, and prospects for the future.

Clearly these are not the whimsical and superficial concerns that we might expect if the "hormones with feet" stereotype were really accurate. The fact is that young adolescents are real people living real lives in a real world. That world is not apart from them. They live in it and they are concerned about it. Why do we refuse to acknowledge and act on this? And why can't we see that the questions and concerns of young adolescents offer a powerful and significant source for themes around which to organize the middle school curriculum?

## Interdisciplinary vs. integrative curriculum

One of the hallmarks of the middle school movement has been the widespread establishment of interdisciplinary teams. Presumably this arrangement promotes two possibilities. One is to decrease anonymity and inconsistencies young people often experience in school through collaborative, interdisciplinary discussion among their teachers. The other is to create connections among subject areas and thus bring a degree of unity to learning experiences. While some stunning examples of the latter have emerged, interdisciplinary teaming has most often had more to do with teaming than with interdisciplinary curriculum.

Moreover, the usual arrangement, in which a team consists of the "big four" subjects (language arts, mathematics, social studies, and science), has perpetuated the hierarchical status differentiation between these and other subjects like art, music, home economics, industrial arts, and so on. In too many places, these subjects may reasonably be described as the place the kids go while the real teachers plan. The designation of the big four as *academic* and the others as *exploratory* demeans the latter and ignores the idea that all experiences at the middle level ought to involve exploration. It is sad to remember that the status distinctions among subjects was originally a product of the university-driven, classical curriculum intended for the high school (Kliebard, 1986)—the very one the middle level movement claimed to escape when it dropped the "junior" high school philosophy.

However, the problem with the usual interdisciplinary approach is really deeper than this. Most teams I have met with take on collaborative planning by selecting a theme and then asking how each subject area might fit into it. Depending upon the theme, the fit of each one is more or less difficult and often artificially stretched as team members strain to make connections. And almost always, the subsequent teaching is done through the usual round of subject classes. In short, what we claim is interdisciplinary is really multidisciplinary in that it retains the identity and priority of separate subjects.

The same criticism can be leveled at the recently surfaced idea of curriculum integration, which for the most part is simply used interchangeably with interdisciplinary. Here, however, the criticism may justifiably be made in even harsher terms, while simultaneously shedding light on the current curriculum conversation. The notion of curriculum integration has two concepts behind it. The first is that learning is wasteful and ineffective when it lacks unity and coherence in relation to some large question or issue, something like trying to piece together a jigsaw puzzle without knowing what picture the pieces make. In knowledge, as in the jigsaw puzzle, the pieces have no meaning independent of the whole picture of which they are a part.

The second, and perhaps more important idea, has to do with who does the integrating. Authentic and powerful learning occurs when interactions with our environment are integrated into our scheme of meanings (Hopkins, 1937; Kelley, 1947). Integration, then, is something we do ourselves; it is not done for us by others. In other words, the large picture we are constructing is shaped by the problems and issues we see and the questions we have about them. When new experiences promise to help us answer those questions, they are inviting and engaging. When they do not, we place less importance on them and often try to avoid them altogether.

Understanding integration in this way reveals the path to a powerful middle school curriculum and to understanding the emerging conversation about it. If we want genuine learning, we must begin with the questions and concerns of young adolescents and help them to find answers and meanings that they may integrate into their understanding of themselves and their world. In short, we must ask, "What sort of curriculum is most likely to be 'integrative' for young adolescents." The answer to this question not only takes us past the separate subject curriculum, but beyond our present interdisciplinary efforts as well.

## *Life in the integrative classroom*

Perhaps this whole idea of an integrative curriculum might be clearer if we were to imagine what classroom life might be like in it. The picture I will sketch out and comment upon here is drawn partly from what the theory suggests and partly from my recent experience with a few eighth grade teachers when we tried out an integrative, thematic unit.

We began by asking the students to identify questions and concerns they had about themselves and their world (immediate to global). Having done this individually, they then met in small groups to find shared questions and concerns, to cluster similar questions from the personal and larger world lists, and to name themes that characterized those clusters. We then asked the whole group to select one theme, to identify activities they might do to answer the questions and concerns within it, and to name any knowledge or skills they thought they might need to carry out the activities. Throughout this planning process, the young people were the primary source for ideas; the teachers played a facilitative role in helping to clarify questions and ideas.

As the thematic unit unfolded, the teachers continued in the facilitative role, asking and clarifying questions, but also became more instrumental in helping to organize activities, find resources, and develop needed skills. They also met regularly to discuss how the unit was going, what responsibilities they would each assume in upcoming activities, and what suggestions they might make to help students in their work. An important and frequent topic in those teacher discussions centered on how to maintain the facilitative role in guiding student work without assuming control over it. An indication of how these discussions went is revealed by noting that in the end the students did a self-evaluation of their work, including naming the grade they thought should be attached to it.

This brief vignette provides an opening to imagine what classroom life might be like in an integrative curriculum. The most noticeable aspect is the redefinition of roles assumed by teachers and students. Since the questions and concerns of the young people served as a primary source for the curriculum, their voices became more powerful than they had previously been. They articulated the questions around which the curriculum would be organized and, therefore, were genuine decision-makers. But more than that, these young adolescents also identified the central theme for our unit and the activities they felt might help them to answer the questions related to that theme.

Meanwhile, the teachers facilitated the work of the young people by asking for clarification of questions and guiding planning activities. Once the activities were identified, the teachers played a more visible, but not more controlling, role by helping to organize the activities, guiding the search for resources, teaching skills that were needed, raising more questions, and generally watching over the flow and direction of the unit. Since the teachers did not know the answers to the questions raised in the unit, they became learners alongside the young people.

Again, it is important to understand here that knowledge and skill were not treated lightly. In fact, the array of both used in the unit was remarkable. They were not, however, pre-defined and introduced according to some scope and sequence plan. Rather they emerged and were addressed as questions and activities called for them. A crucial role for the teachers here was to continuously watch for such openings and to bring important knowledge and skill to light as they were pertinent to the task at hand.

From this description it is clear that the teachers' role was quite different from that in the traditional subject-centered classroom. Yet it would be a serious mistake to say that the teachers' knowledge or work was devalued or demeaned. Quite to the contrary, the teachers became more important than they might otherwise have been. Let's face it, facilitating young adolescents' search for answers to compelling self and social questions is a more significant and difficult activity than simply disseminating information and then checking to see if it is learned.

The teacher in an integrative curriculum, then, is an adult who is interested in helping young people to construct meanings around self and social questions. This means that the teacher helps pose questions, identify possible ways to answer them, and reflect upon experiences and interactions. The teacher does not have the answers, but can help to create ways of finding out. Nor, incidentally, do the young people have the answers. This is neither a didactic, imposed approach in which knowledge comes from the teacher nor is it a Socratic one in which the teacher supposedly draws out knowledge that is ostensibly inside the student. Instead it is an approach in which adults and young people raise questions and construct possible meanings around them; reflective questioning is a way of life for the teacher, not just a technique. The teacher is a whole, deeply human person defined more broadly than by a particular subject area on a teaching certificate. The teacher, too, is curious about her/him self and the larger world and is a learner alongside the young. This teacher does not give up power, but instead becomes more powerful just as the students do. It is in this blending of roles that an authentic learning community is created in the middle school.

Inside the integrative curriculum we can also expect to find other characteristics. People are engaged in small group and individual work as well as whole group activities. While the latter may not be used as frequently as they are now, participating as a member of the whole group is important in developing a sense of belonging and collective efficacy. Moreover, the work of the group is most often active and interactive, rather than passive, with a premium placed on discussion, debate, projects, and so on. And the classroom walls, like the boundaries of subject areas, begin to dissolve as the real life nature of the curriculum leads beyond the school and into the community where information gathering, intergenerational interaction, and service projects are expanded and extended.

Since the integrative curriculum involves searching for answers and constructing meanings, assessment and evaluation also take on a new look. Young adolescents and adults are more interested in those meanings and how they are formed than in right or wrong answers in relation to some abstract and imposed body of facts. For this reason, portfolios, journals, project displays, and reflective self-evaluation become increasingly important.

Having sketched out this brief picture, I also want to acknowledge that it is an idealized one. As we learned in the day to day life of the unit described above, the integrative approach, even as it literally evolves from young adolescents' own concerns, does not automatically or completely engage every young person. Everyone has good and not so good days; after all, school is not the only thing in the lives of young people. Moreover, by the time they are in the middle school, many have already experienced some years of a fragmented curriculum; a few we worked with even asked, "When will we get back to real school stuff?" In this sense, the integrative curriculum is just as much of a "leap" for some young people as it is for many adults.

The point of those statements is that while we can expect things will go well in an integrative curriculum, we cannot expect they will always go smoothly. After all, school is about real people living real lives. On the other hand, our experience and reports from other schools indicate that young adolescents are, on the whole, much more engaged in this kind of curriculum approach than they are in a subject-centered one.

## Developing an integrative curriculum

The basic premise of a subject-centered curriculum is that there is a body of knowledge(s) that resides out in the world and our job is to transfer that knowledge into the minds of young people. Thus, planning for a separate subject curriculum involves three main questions: What knowledge should students acquire? How can we get them to acquire it? And, how can we find out if they have acquired it? Understanding this helps us to understand how many of the regularities of schools came to be like they are: textbooks that contain desired information, tests to measure acquisition of the information, specialized certification in particular areas, central office and state department personnel to manage and monitor particular areas of information, and so on. Beyond this we can also see why certain kinds of questions have recently been raised: Who gets to define what is "desired" information? Who benefits from young people acquiring this information? Why do some young people find this information so much easier to acquire than do others?

These assumptions of and questions about the separate subject curriculum, of course, lead back into the criticism of that approach I outlined earlier in this paper and elsewhere (Beane, 1990). However, they also suggest that the integrative curriculum not only involves a different theory, but a different view of curriculum planning.

Curriculum planning in an integrative context begins with collaborative discussion about young peoples' questions and concerns and identification of the themes they suggest. Once a theme and the related questions are clear, curriculum planning turns to identifying activities the group might use to answer the questions. It is after these "what" and "how" concerns are addressed that questions about knowledge, skill, and resources are appropriate.

In doing this kind of curriculum planning, we depart from the usual separate subject planning that begins with what the teacher knows or what content the textbook contains. Moreover, we also depart from multi-disciplinary planning that begins with a theme drawn from one or two subjects and asks what those and others can contribute. Instead, like real life, we begin with a problem or puzzling situation and imagine ways we could address it.

I have frequently been asked whether I would settle for teachers identifying a theme and then asking young people what questions they have about it. Supposedly this might be a way for some people to begin to see how cooperatively planned, thematic units might look and feel. It seems to me that this kind of compromise ought to be made only under two conditions. The first is explicit recognition that this is a step along the way toward fully engaging young people from the very start of our curriculum planning. The second is that those using this approach would be very careful about selecting a theme. Anyone who has done the kind of work I am proposing knows that the themes that emerge from collaborative planning are almost always of the affective sort—involving significant self and social questions—and that they are identified quite independent of subject area boundaries. When educators name themes there is too often a serious temptation to name one that fits nicely with and is, therefore, assigned to one or two subject areas, much like the present versions of interdisciplinary teaching.

Even when doing integrative planning, there are several criteria that we ought to attach to a theme in saying that it is worth the commitment of our school time, resources, and energy. Among these are that a theme should:

- explicitly involve questions from the young adolescents who will carry out the unit,

- involve a concern that is widely shared by young adolescents, involve larger world concerns that are of clear social significance,

- potentially engage a wide range of knowledge and resources, pose opportunities for in-depth work,

- present possibilities for a wide range of activities, and

- present possibilities for action, including outside the school.

While such criteria might sound strict, it seems to me that they are necessary if the curriculum is to be of significance, not only with regard to self and social issues, but also in terms of the knowledge and skill that it brings to the foreground. Since the criteria clearly would require that young people affirm the theme and identify questions within it I would think that teachers might just as well make the leap into the integrative planning I previously described. After all, I have not asked teachers to give up what they know or want, only to bring it into closer connection with the concerns of young adolescents.

A final point about curriculum planning is also important in light of questions people have raised about the integrative curriculum. As much as many of us have tried to reassure educators that the knowledge they have traditionally valued will be repositioned rather than lost, it would be unwise to say that all such information will actually survive curriculum reform. It is time to face the fact that some of what we teach or are required to teach to young adolescents is not really defensible in the context of the middle school's general education mission. The obsession with subject area interests and the mimicry of the university model has brought the middle level curriculum to increasingly obscure and trivial levels of knowledge and skill.

As we pursue an integrative curriculum we will need to unearth the classic curriculum question of what knowledge is of most worth and place it alongside the newer question of what knowledge is of worth to young adolescents. In responding to these questions we must set aside answers having to do with preparation for the next grade or high school or college or occupations or examinations, and turn instead to the original claim of the middle school movement that middle schools are for young adolescents.

## There is a stream

The idea of an integrative curriculum developed around questions and concerns of young people is hardly new. It is part of a stream of work that has continued over many decades and of which the current conversation is the latest contribution. While commitment to it is a leap of faith for educators accustomed to the separate subject approach, the leap is not a blind one. This is especially true for middle level educators since early proponents of this curriculum organization frequently turned their attention to junior high schools and recorded astonishing accounts of theory, practice, and research in its support.

Nearly twenty-five years ago, a group of us who studied with Conrad Toepfer were introduced to that literature. We read works like *Integration: Its Meaning and Application* (Hopkins, 1937), *The Story of the Eight Year Study* (Aiken, 1942), *Developing the Core Curriculum* (Faunce & Bossing, 1951), *The General Education Class in the Secondary School* (Hock & Hill, 1960), *Modern Education for the Junior High School Years*

(Van Til, Vars, & Lounsbury, 1961), and others, in addition to many from the general curriculum field in which the problem-centered and emerging needs approaches had gained a foothold.

Many of these works are now hidden on the dusty shelves of university and central office libraries. But they need to be discovered again and studied carefully so that our present work is informed by its past and not of the ahistorical kind that so frequently characterizes educational reform. The search for such sources may well surprise some people. For example, members of the Middle Level Curriculum Project turned up a 1950s vintage copy of the Wisconsin state guide for developing the junior high school curriculum that had a haunting similarity to the very issues with which that group has been struggling.

In studying this history we may also come to understand how the current conversation is part of a historic struggle in the curriculum field. Several years ago I wrote a paper entitled, "Dance to the Music of Time: The Future of Middle Level Education" (Beane, 1987). In it I tried to say that if middle level educators looked outside their own movement, they would see that they were in the midst of a new episode in a long-standing tug-of-war. On the one side were those who view knowledge as a fixed and static set of information to be learned by young people as a rite of passage into a narrowly defined academic world. On the other side were those who situate young people themselves at the center of the curriculum and advocate an education based upon their interests, concerns, and evolving experiences.

Proponents of the first view can certainly be found in middle schools but the issue I raised had more to do with a conflict between forces outside the middle school movement and the rhetoric within it. Now, as the 1990s unfold, we are hearing more and more about national standardized tests and a national curriculum. To imagine that these would be developed along lines other than the typical subject and skill boundaries is terribly naive. After all, those responsible for the national movement are the same people who brought us the academic belt-tightening of the 1980s. Moreover, a national curriculum would take us even further from the local schools where particular young adolescents and their teachers ought to be creating the curriculum.

So it is that the current middle level curriculum conversation is more complicated than we might think. Unless the steamroller for a national curriculum is stopped by some unexpected set of events, the middle school movement likely faces tougher times than it ever has before. The flexibility and creativity we have built may simply crumble under the weight of more stringent and complicating requirements unless we are prepared to articulate a clear and coherent concept of the middle level curriculum. Moreover, it is very likely that the progressive work at that level over the past thirty years will compel us to assume a leadership role in collaboration with educators at other levels who are truly concerned about the young people with whom they work.

I sincerely hope that all middle level educators will join the curriculum conversation that I have spoken to here. Many already have and certainly many more will. As we discover the authentic voices of young adolescents and shift our attention to them, it is just possible that in our time we will do something of lasting and significant importance for middle level education. We will finally answer the question, "What ought to be the middle school curriculum?"

## References

Aiken, W. (1941). *The story of the eight year study*. New York: Harper & Row.

Beane, J. A. (1987). Dance to the music of time: The future of middle level education. *Schools in the Middle*, 1-8

Beane, J. A. (1990). *A middle school curriculum: From rhetoric to reality.* Columbus, OH: National Middle School Association.

Faunce, R., & Bossing, N. (1951). *Developing the core curriculum.*New York: Prentice-Hall.

Hock, L., & Hill, T. (1960). *The general education class in the secondary school*. New York: Holt-Rinehart.

Hopkins, L. T. (1937). *Integration: Its meaning and application*. New York: D. Appleton-Century.

Kelley, E. (1947). *Education for what is real*. New York: Harper and Row.

Kliebard, H. (1986). *The struggle for the American curriculum: 1893-1958*. Boston and London: Routledge and Kegan Paul.

Middle Level Curriculum Project (1991). Middle level curriculum: The search for self and social meaning. *Middle School Journal*, 22(2), 29-35.

Mikel, E. (1990). Personal conversation.

Van Til, W., Vars, G., & Lounsbury, J. (1961). *Modern education for the junior high school years*. Indianapolis, IN: Bobbs-Merrill.

*James A. Beane teaches for National-Louis University and is headquartered in Madison, WI.*

# A Continuing Conversation

*Lessons learned from the whole language movement:*
*Parallels to curricular reform*

*Pentimento, Judi! Pentimento:*
*A reply from Jim Beane*

# Lessons learned from the whole language movement: Parallels to curricular reform

*Judith L. Irvin*

Over the years, I have attended meetings with John Lounsbury in which he has drawn an historical parallel to some current middle school event; I nodded respectfully. In May of 1991, National Middle School Association sponsored a Curriculum Institute held in Minneapolis and during a question and answer session, I found myself on my feet offering participants my own historical perspective on this "middle school movement;" I glanced over and John Lounsbury was nodding respectfully. I find it strange that I'm old enough to provide an historical perspective, but I am.

After a day of discussing the rationale for implementing a middle school curriculum that is more relevant to the lives of young adolescents and organizes knowledge in a more integrated way, some questions naturally arose:

*How can we make sure students are taught the necessary skills?*

*Isn't there some content that is essential for kids to know?*

*Teaching themes sounds great, but who coordinates all this?*

*What about the less able teacher...I'm not sure I trust her to decide what is appropriate to teach students?*

*Tests! What do we do about standardized tests?*

*Where is the structure...the plan?*

What brought me to my feet during that question and answer period was the feeling of *déjà vu*. I've heard these questions before because I was fortunate enough to live through the early days of the whole language movement. I remember TAWL (Teachers Applying

Whole Language) support meetings at the annual International Reading Association Conferences. When the questions of skills, structure, and tests arose, the answer was often "don't worry about it." I remember Ken and Yetta Goodman, Jerry Harste, Carolyn Burke and others refusing to define whole language because it would then become too restrictive. I also remember a lot of frustration—teachers who were sold on the philosophy but did not know what to *do* that would be so different. Reading educators were telling teachers what not to do, but few positive examples existed. Teachers were hesitant to give up their phonics worksheets and skill-driven basals before they knew that solid instruction would replace the old way.

Whole language was defined a teacher at a time. The TAWL meetings consisted of teachers sharing what worked, the kids that now loved to read, and how much fun teaching had become. These first adventuresome teachers were saying "It is OK to let go, it will be all right." Many university professors worked along side of teachers constructing literature-based reading programs and exploring the reading/writing connections that naturally exist using literature.

The whole language movement, along with two decades of field-based research, have led most educators to come to new understandings of the learning process. Authentic testing, process writing, strategic learning, reading/writing connections, and the popularization of cooperative learning are all outgrowths of this grassroots movement in education. While, in retrospect, I can appreciate these educational innovations as evidence of real progress, I remember some difficult days. In the early 80s, I was Director of a University Reading Clinic and I spent much of my time in inservice sessions espousing the virtues of a whole language orientation. My viewpoint sobered over the years, though, when I witnessed some students who, under whole language instruction, were not learning to read. These students felt good about themselves, loved literature, memorized stories well, were wonderful conversationalists, and couldn't read on their own. The problem was that some teachers had not discovered how to teach skills *through* whole language. These teachers abandoned the teaching of skills for the sake of whole language not realizing that the two are not incompatible. The key was teaching skills in a meaningful context rather than in isolation. This pendulum swing may not have been beneficial for students whose teachers embraced whole language with reckless abandon, but I believe that educators now hold a more balanced view of teaching reading. Perhaps middle level educators can learn from the growing pains of the whole language movement.

## *A Chronicle of an Attempt at Relevance and Integration*

When I returned from the Minneapolis Institute, I began teaching sixth grade. I volunteered to finish the year teaching along with a sixth grade social studies teacher to try out some strategies and demonstrate some cooperative learning methodologies. I was assigned pages 376-399 on South Asia. As I perused this material, I discovered that I (with a Master's Degree in social studies education) couldn't answer most of the questions at the end of the chapter. That is, I could not name the three rivers that drain the Deccan Plateau in India, I had never heard of (or remembered hearing of) the Green Revolution, I couldn't name any city in the Himalayan Mountains, and I didn't know the main exports in the rain forests of Burma.

After hearing recommendations (in Minneapolis) from The Middle School Curriculum Project, I decided to base my instruction of South Asia on three questions:

1.  questions young adolescents have about themselves,
2.  questions young adolescents have about the world around them, and
3.  questions that are posed to them by the world in which they live.

I decided to use the suggested stems to get the answers to these questions:

> I am...
> I wish I knew why...
> I wish I knew how...
> I wish I knew more about...
> I wish I knew when...

What are things you wonder about yourself? What are things you daydream about? What are things you worry about? Ten years from now, what do you see yourself doing? I like classes that... I don't like classes that...

Predictable answers to questions were that these young adolescents wondered about themselves (are my thighs too fat?), their ability (can I run fast enough to play soccer?), other's perception of them (does Johnny like me?), and some were interesting musings (I wonder how they get the stripes in the Aqua Fresh). Unpredictable answers included young adolescent's worrying about their parents dying, divorcing, or getting sick. The question for me became — how to tie this information to the study of South Asia? I was determined not to get too fancy: I wanted to take what the teacher had to teach and make it more meaningful to students.

After we completed a KWL strategy lesson with all of the proper previewing of the chapter, I asked students to formulate what they wanted to know about South Asia. I awaited this moment—went to the chalkboard to write questions motivated from the personal and social concerns of students (James Beane would be so proud). Guess what they wanted to know—the landforms, the products of India, which is the tallest mountain, and the government and culture of the people. I was crestfallen and wanted to say "get real," but why should I expect differently? These are kids finishing their 7th year of subject matter. A few interesting questions arose—why does Bangladesh flood so much, what was the war about in Afghanistan, and why would India assassinate their leader. So, we took their questions and shaped them—they did a cooperative learning jigsaw—forming expert groups to read the book and answering their questions—and then they taught their material back in their base groups. Expert groups then made up questions for the test and taught in their base groups again. Their test questions were better than their original questions, I saw hope.  They took the test individually. Their final activity was to choose a country in South Asia and answer the *I am... I worry about...* stems from the viewpoint of a 12 year old boy or girl from that country. These led to interesting discussion.

I agree with Beane that the curriculum needs to begin with the personal and social concerns of students. This unit was my attempt to move an inch in that direction, to play with it a bit, and not deviate so far that it scared teachers or left them without support. What I accomplished was to tickle the imagination just a bit — to open the door to questioning the subject matter now held so sacred. As I presented these activities to the whole faculty—one teacher raised her hand and said, "Are you giving me permission to stop teaching the parts of speech?" I don't know the answer to that question yet, but I think it provides for a *very* healthy discussion.

*Déjà vu* again. "Can kids learn to use the dictionary without completing a separate skills sheet on guide words?" "Can kids read before they know the difference between a diphthong and a digraph?" "Can vocabulary be taught in any other way besides looking up the definitions of eight words and writing them in a sentence?" Whole language has brought us a long way and whole language was defined a teacher at a time.

I would be thrilled if, starting in August, every middle school in the nation taught students content using themes developed from their personal and social concerns; but, if I'm old enough to provide an historical perspective, I'm wise enough to understand that won't happen. I think, just like with whole language, an integrated, relevant curriculum will be defined a teacher at a time. Hopefully, university faculty will help form that definition, within the classroom, along side of teachers. Deviating just an inch away from the rigid compartmentalization of subject matter will help all of us answer questions like *what we do about assessment, how we make sure students learn skills,* and *who coordinates all of this stuff.* Along with these personal experimentations, I hope that some teachers are brave enough to reorganize their whole curriculum and use flexible blocks of time to organize knowledge in themes. We can learn from these positive examples.

In the field of reading education, it is "in" to be reflective, process oriented, authentic, strategic, and metacognitive. I hope that in ten years, the culture of middle level schools will have changed so dramatically that it is "in" to be integrated, process oriented, and relevant. This curriculum will be defined a teacher at a time; it is time for a true transformation and it is time to invade the classroom.

*Judith L. Irvin teaches at Florida State University, Tallahassee.*

# Pentimento, Judi! Pentimento
# A reply from Jim Beane*

*James A. Beane*

As Herbert Kliebard reminds us in *The Struggle for the American Curriculum: 1893-1958*, virtually all approaches to and versions of the curriculum have lived side-by-side throughout the twentieth century. Their co-existence, of course, has not been so peaceful and, while one or another may periodically be in ascendance, the others are nonetheless there if only we look carefully enough. In this sense, what feels like *déjà vu* might more aptly be called *pentimento*.

It is not uncommon for artists to paint over another painting. Perhaps it is one of their own that they no longer value or one by someone else they do not admire. Or, maybe, it is that they cannot afford to buy a fresh canvas of their own. Often, as time goes by, the gloss and texture of the new painting wears thin and the old begins to show through. A child may appear where a tree has been or a shimmering lake may replace a street scene. Whatever the case, the effect is *pentimento*, the surfacing of the old as the gloss of the new wears thin. You see, the old painting was always there; it was only hidden by what had been done over it.

If you have this feeling with regard to our present middle school curriculum conversations, imagine how John Lounsbury himself must feel; after all, he was around in the salad days of the earlier junior high school "problem-centered core" movement. Or, how about his colleague and co-author Gordon Vars who has single-handedly kept the

---

*Editor's note: This piece was a personal letter written by Beane to Irvin.

213

National Association for Core Curriculum alive all these years? And imagine Grace Wright who advocated and kept track of trends in the "core" curriculum from her position in the U.S. Office of Education in the 1950s? William Van Til is still with us and so is Alice Miel. And can we forget Ralph Tyler who was instrumental in the Eight Year Study in the 1930s or our younger friend Connie Toepfer who caught the tail end of the progressive movement in his early days of junior high school teaching? How about the many teachers who show up at conferences with stories of their "core" teaching in the 1950s and even those who more recently got the idea that interdisciplinary teaming was supposed to have at least as much to do with curriculum as with teaming?

The work we are now engaged in and which you tried out is part of a large theory of curriculum and teaching and knowledge and learning and it does not belong only to middle school types. It says that knowledge is unitary, that its purpose is deeply human, that it is constructed by people, and that young people have the right to use knowledge in their search for self and social meaning. As you know, this view is quite different from the narrow and restricting one held by subject specialists that has plagued us and the young for so long.

Fortunately, many educators sooner or later come to understand the difference between these two views and give themselves over to the one that is more lifelike and more helpful to young people. They travel many paths to this point. Connie Toepfer was my teacher and early on he suggested I look into this area. You have come the route of the whole language approach. Tom Dickinson talks about his roots in the problems approach to social studies. Non-westerners speak from the concept of unity and wholeness in their cultures. Some people hear about it from colleagues and friends while others are so deeply committed to young people that it intuitively seems the right thing to do. This is what is so difficult to deal with in our current work there is no one path, only the one the people themselves construct and want to act upon. There is no cookbook, no recipe, no ready-made curriculum, no sure-fire staff development program.

From this you might correctly guess that I really like what you have to say. Like you, I recognize the whole language approach as one path some people might travel. I envy the courage its early advocates had in refusing to give into the call for a cookbook and their implicit trust in professional educators. And, I conjure up visions of the whole language movement coming up through the grades and converging with our own work at the middle level. At this intersection we will undoubtedly find the largest prospects for the theory we share and, I hope, the common language of possibility.

In the end, though, I admit I ought to pay attention to your *déjà vu* even if I do like the *pentimento* analogy better. After all, the latter is a story of competing theories at "the top" of the historical curriculum debate while your feeling describes a sense of the real world where that debate has to do with the everyday lives of teachers and kids. If *déjà vu* means roughly the feeling of having been "here" before, then I wonder most about what happened in between. If "here" made sense to us then, why did we let go of it? Why did we let other "artists" paint over our picture? Did we value it as little as they did? And if my *pentimento* analogy refers to those at "the top," could it be that our own picture was just one we drew at someone else's direction?

This is why our middle level curriculum work, like the early days of whole language, can only be a vision of possibility, a broadly sketched philosophy. If it will ever come to anything, then it must be built school by school and teacher by teacher—your own brief experiment as an example—and we must live with the diversity of practical possibilities so long as the philosophy holds sway. I'm glad you see a comparison with the whole language approach. Maybe we will be as lucky as its early advocates have come to be.

*James A. Beane teaches for National-Louis University and is headquartered in Madison, WI.*